Storytelling on the Northern Irish Border

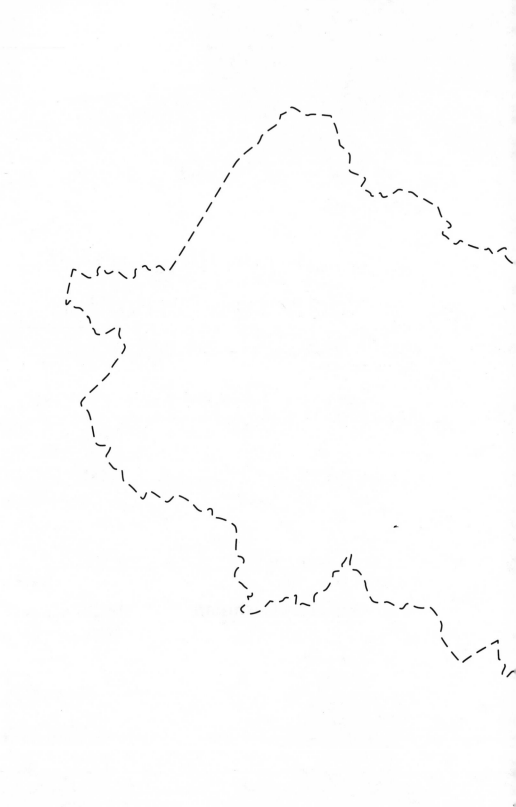

Storytelling
on the Northern
Irish Border

Characters and Community

Ray Cashman

Indiana University Press
Bloomington & Indianapolis

This book is a publication of

Indiana University Press
601 North Morton Street
Bloomington, IN 47404-3797 USA

iupress.indiana.edu

Telephone orders   800-842-6796
Fax orders   812-855-7931
Orders by e-mail   iuporder@indiana.edu

First paperback edition 2011
© 2008 by Ray Cashman
All rights reserved

∞The paper used in this publication meets the minimum requirements of American National Standard for Information Sciences—Permanence of Paper for Printed
Library Materials, ANSI Z39.48-1992.

Manufactured in the United States of America
        Library of Congress Cataloging-in-Publication Data

Cashman, Ray.
    Storytelling on the northern Irish border : characters and community / Ray Cashman.
        p. cm.
    Includes bibliographical references and index.
    ISBN 978-0-253-35252-1 (cloth : alk. paper) 1. Storytelling—Northern Ireland
—Castlederg. 2. Aghyaran (Castlederg, Northern Ireland)—Folklore. I. Title.
    GR148.A45C37 2008
    398.2094164—dc22
                            2008015964

ISBN 978-0-253-22374-6 (pbk.)

1 2 3 4 5 16 15 14 13 12 11

For my mother and in memory of my father

Contents

Preface: The Road to Ballymongan

As a folklorist I consider the stories that people tell each other to be elo-quent of culture, a window into the shared beliefs, values, and worldview of a given group. Moreover, oral narratives—from personal experience nar-ratives to myths, from anecdotes to legends, from jokes to tall tales—per-form important social work in human interaction. The following chapters delve into details, identify patterns, and present a case study of how stories enable people to do important, recurring things with language—entertain, persuade, evaluate one's self and one's social environment, establish and revise identity, imagine and enact community.

My first task, however, is to explain why I chose to study these issues in one particular place in Ireland. Answering "Why Ireland?" is relatively easy. Previous research and fieldwork in Counties Cork, Kerry, and Gal-way had convinced me that Ireland's long association with folklore—tra-ditional, vernacular expressive and material culture—is well-deserved and not simply the concoction of a long line of romantic nationalists bearing witness to a distinct Irish culture to bolster the cause for an Ireland inde-pendent of Britain. Of course, folklore studies—no less than much of Irish folklore—continue to be politically inflected, but I am persuaded that in Ireland people of diverse backgrounds have long privileged and cultivated verbal art in particular—written and oral. Here is a place and society that promises rich materials for study.

Answering the question of how I came to settle in Aghyaran (roughly pronounced "Aw-hee-ARN"), a mixed Catholic-Protestant[1] community in Northern Ireland on the border with the Republic of Ireland, requires a little more effort, and it was a question people there never failed to ask. As one young man asked me early on, "What, have you shot someone? Are you on the run? What could bring you to such a backwards place?" A little taken aback, I began an overly defensive and ultimately futile characterization of his home place as no less a part of this era, no less connected to the rest of the world, than any other part of Ireland. Something along the lines of, "Why, here we are in the townland of Ballymongan, near the village of Killeter, not far from the town of Castlederg, about thirty miles from County Tyrone's commercial and administrative hub in Omagh, suspended between Derry and Belfast, at the heart of an emerging cultural and economic corridor between Ireland and Britain, part and parcel of the new Europe and a global economy. . . ." (Oh, the foot bone's connected to the *leg* bone, the leg bone's connected to the *knee* bone, the knee bone's connected to the *thigh* bone, the thigh bone's. . . .) Neither of us was satisfied.

Although few people were as incredulous as he, many asked me this question—why here?—several times in many ways. My answers varied with my audience and rarely felt complete. One honest, unspoken answer was that I could have conducted fieldwork just about anywhere in Ireland (or elsewhere) and found something worthwhile to report, but people were awfully good to me in Aghyaran. I also came to the field with both conscious convictions and previously unexamined inclinations that guided initial choices.

Grounded in fieldwork, generalizing from particulars, folklore studies is uniquely situated to offer an entry into vernacular Irish life. After a few years' experience in the Republic, however, I found my folkloric interests shifting north of the border that splits the island. Folklore need not be a matter of life and death or even politically charged for it to be worthy of study. Yet north of the border many people invest so much energy into public, identity-touting expressive forms—parades, murals, song—that some are willing to commit violence defending or imposing the positions communicated. Here is a case study in the politics of culture, featuring folklore, where the stakes are high.

Deciding to conduct fieldwork for this study in Tyrone, the largest of the six counties of Northern Ireland, was admittedly somewhat arbitrary. There was a written record that attracted me. Michael J. Murphy's accounts of collecting folklore in Tyrone's Sperrin Mountains for the Irish Folklore Commission fired my imagination, and I admire and enjoy the fiction of Tyrone writers William Carleton, Benedict Kiely, and Flann O'Brien, though for different reasons with each one. In addition, judging from government records and sociological research, demographics and community relations in Tyrone seemed relatively balanced, at least on paper. I was not interested in my presence potentially aggravating an already tense situation in one of the more traditional flash points for political violence, and most of Tyrone seemed less fraught than, for instance, south Armagh, and more mixed in population than, for instance, the north coast of Antrim.

My interest in conducting fieldwork in a rural area of Tyrone was not motivated by an outdated romantic conviction that true folklore can be found only in agrarian settings. Whether viewed as cultural forms enacting tradition or as shared modes of aesthetically marked communication, folklore abounds in cities as elsewhere, and investigating the urban experience is of course relevant in our increasingly urbanized world. I remain unconvinced, however, by reactionary calls in anthropological circles to privilege urban Ireland as somehow more relevant for study and less encumbered with previous scholarly ideological baggage.[2] In part, I was conditioned by Estyn Evans's and others' characterization of the Northern Irish countryside as a place often more socially integrated than the cities, a place where Catholics and Protestants may develop more complicated notions of "us" and "them" through interaction, and a place where neighborliness and shared regional culture have at least the potential to undermine sectarian division. Belfast, for instance, certainly would have been foreign enough for me to perceive readily the contrasts with my own experience, but I admit that having been raised in a city, I wanted to know something entirely different, something about country life. Reports of mumming thriving in west Tyrone also caught my attention. If in Tyrone an ancient form of folk drama found a place in the lives of television viewers and Internet surfers, I reckoned that here was a place that would hold my interest.

Having narrowed the field to Tyrone was enough, and I began fieldwork content—well, OK, mostly content—to be guided by events and strangers, whether agents of providence or of chance. What I have to offer first, then, is a personal account of how and why I came to settle in Aghyaran, conducting fieldwork there from August of 1998 to August of 1999 and during shorter stays in 2000, 2002, 2003, 2006, and 2007. Along the way my methodology for beginning fieldwork will become clear, as will many of my predispositions.

I am far from the most interesting character in this study, which will focus on the actions and words of others. My excuse for beginning in personal narrative is, in part, a felt need to answer more fully the question, "why here?" I have also benefited from contemporary calls for reflexivity in ethnographic practice. On the one hand, I am loath to carry self-revelatory personal narrative as a rhetorical strategy or authorial voice to the point of self-absorption, allowing little room for others to have a voice. On the other hand, self-revelation has a place insofar as it allows, to some extent, readers to judge for themselves the influence of my own subjectivity in what I write about that of others. For this reason, I will occasionally revert to personal narrative as it seems appropriate throughout this book. As a whole, what I have to offer is observation and interpretation, but it is only one perspective and far from the last word.

During the dark, icy January of 1998, my wife, Lorraine, and I wandered the hills of Tyrone, scouting possible fieldwork sites from our base in the central market town of Omagh. It was an anxious visit that did not yield a clear location for settling. As I prepared to return alone in August of 1998—Lorraine would join me later—the people of Northern Ireland were enjoying the strongest, broadest paramilitary ceasefire yet and a fledgling peace process spurred by the majority of political parties signing the Good Friday Agreement. Tragically, this significant progress was threatened by an atrocity committed in the very heart of Tyrone. On Saturday, August 15, 1998, at 3:10 PM dissident republicans detonated a 500-pound car bomb in Market Street, Omagh, wounding approximately 220 people and killing 29, including an expectant mother of twins. It was the most devastating single incident in the three decades of political violence known as the Troubles.

My flight left for Ireland the day after the bomb, and I stayed in Belfast with friends who, like me, had dared to hope in the wake of Good Friday and were taken aback that such an attack should happen now. Talking, grieving, we tried to digest every scrap of information available from newspapers and television, gradually confronting the poverty of language to convey certain experiences. Three days later, I took a bus to Omagh, as originally planned, but I felt that my obligation was to remain mute. To do otherwise—to ask intrusive questions as some sort of amateur journalist—would have been ghoulish. And to be honest, once I arrived all I could manage was observing and bearing witness.

In one respect, the official and civilian response in Omagh was almost familiar, having long been aestheticized and fetishized by movies, newscasts, and novels. This response, however, was no less stunning in its immediacy—a script enacted but live and inescapable, without the remove of the screen or printed page. Along Strule Bridge and near the point of detonation those coming to pay respects shuffled slowly and silently through mist, avoiding eye contact, wooden. They laid countless flower bouquets, dashes of pastel and shiny plastic spilling over slick footpaths. The surrounding streets were dominated by an influx of armed police and soldiers, personnel carriers, and military helicopters—the full Ulster package. As an outsider unaccustomed to such things, I perceived this wider scene as an impressionistic smear of steel-plate grays and camouflage greens with the occasional flash of wet gun metal, the otherwise silent soundscape punctuated by axles whirring under heavy armor, overhead rotors thumping, airborne engines whining. Inside—whether pub, café, or hostel—I remember only cigarette smoke and nonstop radio and television coverage.

The bombing of Omagh was not like that of Enniskillen in 1987, in the dreary middle of the Troubles with no end in sight.[3] Now people were in a post-ceasefire, post-Agreement mind-set. No excuses would be made in public about legitimate targets and regrettable collateral damage. All sides condemned this as the outright murder of a representative cross-section of an innocent market town. The dissidents themselves—the Real IRA, a hard-line offshoot of the majority Provisional IRA—apologized for the loss of life while blaming authorities for garbling their warning about the location of the bomb. "United in grief" and "From this evil something good can come" became the talking points for politicians, and it would take a full week for the reality of continuing tensions to show through the cracks of this hopeful rhetoric.

From the time I learned of the bomb until the Saturday one-week memorial service at Omagh courthouse, I did not give a single thought to being a folklorist or finding a place to settle. Toward the end of that silent, emotional week, however, I felt a pressing need for human contact, and folklore collecting of a sort simply fell in my lap. I was staying at a hostel two miles out of town, and I started to walk back into Omagh but stopped to chat with a middle-aged man rewiring the brake lights on his sheep trailer. By that point, both of us had stranger-friendly, prepared comments to exchange on the bomb, and we quickly forced our conversation toward the record wet summer and the crisis in agricultural prices. After he asked what I did, he waved over his father, who was walking by. His father asked me what sort of folklore was I interested in and, perhaps impatient with my rambling answer, launched into an impromptu lecture on different variet- ies and definitions of folklore. The older man, it seems, is used to folklor- ists of some description or another popping by, and perhaps he expects us with more regularity than we as a breed can muster. Assuming I had a tape recorder, he simply told me to bring it to his home the next evening. Who was I to say no?

My host filled a couple of tapes with reminiscences, recitations, and local legends. It felt awkward simply to mine my subject for the sorts of texts that many folklorists, seeing themselves as salvage ethnographers, have traditionally collected as if these texts were rare butterflies or ancient potshards. However, this was the model he was used to. My asking for and his providing examples of folklore was the pattern for sociability that made most sense to him when searching for a way to interact with an outsider who owns a tape recorder and calls himself a folklorist. I was reminded of storyteller Pat Dirane almost immediately launching into a folktale upon meeting John Millington Synge in the often-visited, often-studied Aran Islands. Regardless of the difference between our conceptions of folklor- istic fieldwork, I greatly appreciated my host's company and hospitality. He thanked me for my time while I tried to out-thank him for his, and then he sent me back into the hills, bidding me to visit his friends at various cultural centers.

As I resumed my wandering I found that my rhythm was off, my energy high but nervous. I have to admit that after the week in Omagh, I found it hard to concentrate. I was prone to snap judgments based on superficial observations. Furthermore I found myself impatient with all the generic heritage prepackaged for tourist consumption. For me, the presence of a burgeoning heritage industry does not render a place "inauthentic" or even unpleasant, just familiar. Cultural tourism and heritage discourse reveal much about contemporary society in a growing number of places (see Kirshenblatt-Gimblett 1995 and 1998). Such analysis is worth undertak- ing, though not to the exclusion of studying other cultural environments and other responses to modernity. I maintain that my hope was not to find somewhere "backwards" or "authentic," just somewhere less familiar. I continued my wandering.

I drove toward the western Derg Valley through the broad, fertile lands of Newtownstewart and Ardstraw. Evidence of the seventeenth-century

Plantation of English and Scottish settlers was clear in the place-names, the architecture and town planning, the wealthy consolidated and modernized farms, the freshly painted Orange Halls, the Union Jacks and emblems of the Red Hand of Ulster. The curbstone colors, graffiti, and surnames on shops and pubs further marked this as a mostly Protestant area.

Then I arrived in Castlederg, a clearly mixed town like Omagh. Unlike Omagh, Castlederg seemed to be a more segregated town, a miniature of Belfast or Derry, with only 2,800 people and even fewer resources to contest. The housing estates have color-coded themselves—green, white, and gold, or red, white, and blue. There seemed to be two real estate agents, two butchers, two chemists, two discount stores, two shoe shops—all where only one of each might suffice if a significant number of people did not mind patronizing the "other side of the house." Castlederg had been repeatedly bombed by republicans from the 1970s until recently, and as one young, somewhat sardonic Royal Ulster Constabulary[4] officer told me, this is the most frequently bombed town in western Europe since World War II. The police station, once designed to fit snugly and modestly into the top of the town, has bulged out into the street with new layers of protection added after sniper and bomb attacks. Various European Union programs have provided funds to give the town center a face-lift, some rather odd public sculpture, and a largely unused tourist center. The logic must be that prettiness and accessibility will pave the way for capitalism, and capitalism will conquer sectarianism. Could happen, at a price.

Having formed an admittedly superficial and uncharitable impression of Castlederg—an impression I would later reconsider and soften—I headed south through Killen to the Blacktown and Scraghey area. Along the way, hills rose to obscure the horizon with each dip in the now-winding road. The houses were neither lime-washed nor thatched, but they had been until recently, when grants became readily available for corrugated metal or ceramic tile roofs and pebble-dashed walls. There were few signs of tillage. In between fields now grazed, but previously in potato ridges, red and white tractors with strange roller attachments scooped up and bound cut grass in airtight plastic bails—silage, essentially pickled grass, for winter fodder.

Often the car is simply too fast to be a good tool for fieldwork. Driving along I began to chide myself for not stopping and talking to more people. About the moment my inner dialogue reached a crescendo, I registered something in my peripheral vision that forced my hands to swerve the rental car off the road and forced my feet to bring it to a screeching, ungraceful halt. I had caught sight of a scene that in retrospect might best be described as quaint, well suited for a postcard. A man on a ladder was repainting "Blacktown Arms" in big block letters on the gable of an attractive pub. The sun had just peeked out from behind the clouds. I am perhaps overly defensive when faced with popular equations of folklore with quaintness, so my involuntarily halting the car in response to this scene gave me pause.

I had made a spectacle of myself, so there was nothing left to do but get out, introduce myself, and see what would happen. Uncharacteristically, I did not say anything more convoluted than "Hello, my name is Ray Cashman. I'm a folklorist from America, and I wonder if you know anybody who could tell me something about the history of this area." The man looked a bit confused for a moment. I could almost see his mental wheels turning: "This may be a mad man. However, he's polite. He's not trying to sell me anything. So far, he seems harmless. . . ." After a little hesitation he recommended John Mongan to me and gave me directions to his "wee museum," past Killeter village, in Ballymongan townland. He also mentioned a Fr. Brendan McGinn who had started *Aghyaran,* a parish historical magazine, some years ago.

We continued our chat, discussing the weather, the unusually saturated state of the land, and the many differences between here and Texas. "What part of the States are you from?" is the inevitable question, and my being from Texas, with the sheer recognition power of its name, has always proved a great benefit. People already have an image, a stereotype, even a cycle of jokes about Texans and Texas. Mentioning my then state of residence, Indiana, regularly produced only a blank stare, polite nodding, and the need for a new topic of conversation. Poor Indiana. I did what I could to make it sound more exotic, but cowboys and ranches the size of Co. Louth simply inspire more imagination and chat.

The man with the paint can owns the Blacktown Arms and takes some pride in its being the hub of most music and dancing in Castlederg's hinterland. It took a certain amount of awkwardness on my part to get his name, Gerry McCay. He might have thought I was trying to gauge what foot he digs with—that is, his religion. Actually, I just wanted to be able to greet him by name next time I saw him; a drink, maybe several, would be most welcome later.

Map 1. Aghyaran within Northern Ireland, the province of Ulster, and the island of Ireland

In the next few weeks I would find this avoidance of stating one's name, to me anyway, to be an almost universal pattern. I would give my name well into the conversation, maybe even shake hands, but would never get a name in return. In time new friends would tell me that not giving a name is perhaps bad manners but nonetheless the custom in this border area where many are wary, still mindful of customs officials and of intelligence officers from the British Army and RUC Special Branch.

With less prompting than it took to get his name, Gerry offered a very helpful introduction to the geography of this parish west of Castlederg. For Anglicans and Catholics, the official name is Termonamongan, but most Catholics use the name of the townland where the Catholic chapel is located, Aghyaran, to refer to the entire parish. Situated on the border,

Termonamongan or Aghyaran is like a peninsula of Northern Ireland jutting into the Republic. It is bounded, roughly, by Castlederg and Killen to the east, Co. Donegal in the Republic to the north and west, and Donegal and a small bit of Co. Fermanagh to the south. The Derg River, which flows from west to east through the middle of the parish, rises in Lough Derg, a renowned pilgrimage site located just across the southwestern border with Donegal.

Exhilarated by one successful chat, I took Gerry's advice and went off in search of John Mongan. Lost in a maze of narrow roads, I stopped several times to ask for directions from people who, to my surprise, would later become my neighbors. The road I took was not the most direct, but it was the best one for piquing my interest in the area. High and narrow, the road wound through the townlands of Gortnagross and Magherakeel. To my left were vernacular white-washed stone houses among more modern concrete block bungalows, and to my right was an abandoned national school with a stone near the doorway reading 1895. Further on to my right was a view down onto the Derg valley, while on the left I passed a lime kiln and a graveyard with headstones dating back to the early 1700s.[5] Opposite the graveyard were the foundations of what I later learned had been Cill Chairill or St. Caireall's Church—the original parish chapel known to have been in ruins by 1622, reestablished by Anglicans in 1693, and abandoned again at an unknown later date. A few more yards away lay St. Patrick's Well, where, it is said, Ireland's patron quenched his thirst on his journey back from a period of Lenten sacrifice on an island in Lough Derg.

When I finally made it to John Mongan's I was greeted by a small hand-painted sign on a telephone pole reading "Ballymongan Museum." Opposite this was a neatly kept two-storey house where John, an energetic elderly man, was fiddling with a hand-cranked corn thresher in his garage, and his younger brother Eddie was pulling weeds in their garden. After some confusion about my presence, John showed me around his museum. In a walled, graveled patch along the roadside he had collected conceivably every type of farm implement known in the area in the last century—several types of horse-drawn plows, grubbers, harrows, reapers, seed sowers, and potato diggers; hand barrows, turf spades, and sally rod creels or baskets; a grain scale, a huge boiler for feed spuds, and even a heavy metal laundry press emblazoned with the ominous name of "The Ulster Mangler." He had also built a small free-standing structure with a

Map 2. Aghyaran's situation in western Ulster

thatched roof that housed an open hearth complete with crane, hanging pots and kettle, and a bread oven. Everything was lovingly and meticulously preserved.

Already quite impressed with his outdoor collection, I followed my host inside to appreciate his grandfather's carpentry tools and the furniture John and his grandfather had made. With firsthand experience of his collection, John could explain and demonstrate the workings of each piece. I was delighted. He lit up when I asked to take photos but seemed a little disappointed that I did not have a video camera, nor was I from the BBC or RTÉ, the British and Irish television networks. After I snapped a few rolls of film, he served me tea. I promised to call back and went on my way to explore a little more before dark.

Further west along Ballymongan Road I passed an Irish tricolor on a barbed wired pole with a sign reading, "Release All Irish P.O.W.S." I passed a thatched house near the Derg and another house with Book of Kells designs in relief on concrete gate posts. Farther on, houses were scarce, some derelict, and the land was more mountainous and covered with rushes. As the stone walls and wire fences petered out into blanket bog, I met a bridge covered in graffiti—"Disband the RUC," "Pigs out," and the decree of 1916 rebel Patrick Pearse, "Ireland unfree will never be at peace."

On my return eastward, I came upon one of the few B&Bs in the parish, run by extremely hospitable and generous people, Danny and Marian McHugh. The McHughs also run a shop connected to their house, so people stopped by throughout the day. My hosts introduced me to many, including Sadie McSorley, a semi-retired primary school teacher who kindly discussed local history at length over tea and lent me books and past issues of *Aghyaran*.

Knowing my interest in his museum, John Mongan stopped by the McHughs' a few days later to invite me to an event at his home. There, on nearly the only bright Sunday afternoon of the summer, about twenty neighbors, mostly middle-aged to elderly men, showed up for a demonstration of his newly refurbished thresher. The demonstration was captured on video like other demonstrations in the past. About half of the men present were old enough to remember using threshers like John's and several other tools there. They seemed eager to get their hands on them for a little entertainment. They made hay ropes and battles, used flails and corn riddles, and crushed oats for feed.

Then there was tea, as always, and chat revolving around past local characters. I knew none of the individuals portrayed anecdotally for the sake of sociable entertainment, but the thought occurred to me—perhaps more readily as an outsider—that in chatting about their peers and predecessors they were simultaneously telling stories about themselves and the spectrum of ways of being human in the midst of shared conditions.

After a week it might have been wise to travel around more. I was quickly being made to feel at home, however, and certain characters and themes kept coming back into sociable chat, piquing my interest in this community as it is imagined through narrative. With Danny McHugh's help, and just in time for Lorraine's arrival, I found a modest house to rent on a nineteen-acre farm in Ballymongan, just a few fields away from John Mongan. The house was situated in what is known locally as the Rookery, a *clachan* or cluster of homes within the larger townland. Previously owned by John McHugh, an irascible bachelor and local character who died in 1995, this house came with a reputation as a house for ceilis, or nighttime social visits among neighbors.[6] After settling in, it was soon clear that there would be no need to worry about isolation. Lorraine and I saw and interacted with our new neighbors far more often than we ever did with neighbors in urban and suburban America, where people tend to live on top of each other.

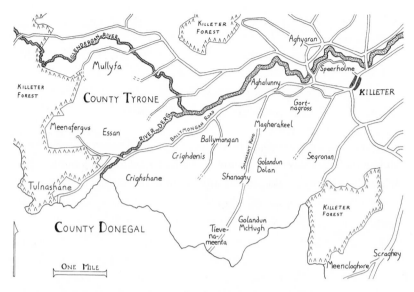

Map 3. Features, roads, and townlands of southern Aghyaran

One of the greatest pleasures of settling in this house was living next door to Danny Gallen, a Catholic hill farmer born in 1944 who raises cattle and sheep and has a "wild interest" in local history and folklore. During his free time on Sunday afternoons, Danny generously took me to and recalled stories about most of the historical and archaeological sites of the parish and bordering areas. Danny may have more of an interest than others in these sites, but his use of the landscape as a vast mnemonic device for narrative is common enough. When people are asked about the relevant past they do not begin with the Neolithic and talk chronologically through the recent Troubles and yesterday's football results. They point you to Aghnahoo dolmen, Carrickanaltar mass rock, and the spots where Willie Bogle was shot dead in 1971 and Patrick Shanaghan in 1991. Narrative inscribes the landscape with meaning, and history in the mind becomes organized in terms of space rather than strict chronology.[7]

Energized by Danny's tutorials I traveled every road with Ordnance Survey map in hand, acquainting myself with major landmarks and interconnecting townlands. These early efforts were a great help in relating to people and perhaps demonstrating that I was serious about learning, not just being an odd sort of tourist. Appreciating context is necessary, but after gaining a degree of familiarity with Aghyaran, I was eager to get to know others and become better known. If one's focus is oral traditions, it is easy enough to collect stories from local authorities in somewhat artificial interview settings, as I had in Omagh, but to grasp how and why people perform narratives in more natural settings requires deeper engagement and more frequent interaction. In my experience, the beginning is rarely the best time for a tape recorder. The first step is familiarity, moving—one hopes—toward neighborly reciprocity, rapport, trust, collaboration, even friendship (cf. Glassie 2006:421–422, Ó Laoire 2003, and Russell 2006).

So I began serendipitously, then moved through the social networks available to me. Gerry McCay led me to John Mongan, Marian McHugh led me to Sadie McSorley, and Danny Gallen led me to Packy Jim McGrath. John, Sadie, and Packy Jim led me to other people, and so on. I met others on my own while buying a used cooker from Sam Crawford at his hardware store in Castlederg and used furniture at Charlie Lynch's auctions at the Border Inn. When it seemed appropriate, I offered new neighbors help moving cattle from one field to another or dropping off agricultural forms when I had errands to run in Omagh. I attended dances and, after Lorraine arrived, invited our neighbors to a party in our nearly completed new home. After I bought a refrigerator that Neil McElhill had ingeniously assembled from his vast collection of leftover parts, Neil brought me along to his regular Saturday night ceili with James Hegarty. Following Barney McGrath, I occasionally ceilied with Jamie Barclay. Danny Gallen, again, was most helpful in inviting me along when he ceilied with Maggie Byrne, Mickey Byrne, Sarah Jane Gallen, Art and Susan Gallagher, Tommy and Paddy Mongan, and John and Eddie Mongan. Keen to revive the Bally-mongan-Shanaghy mummers after a two-year hiatus, Cormac McManus and John Gerald O'Donnell insisted I join them as a fellow mummer rather than as a documentarian. My time in the mummers' van, playing the role of Beelzebub in several local homes and pubs and drinking with fellow actors after our last performance of the night, was pivotal in helping me forge new relationships and comprehend my dual role as neighbor and fieldworker, participant and observer.[8]

Eventually all these interactions culminated in relationships strong enough to withstand the imposition of my recording interviews and group conversations, asking the occasional awkward questions. That said, my questions were gradually more informed, and our work together was not all imposition. We also had a great deal of fun. My social debts will remain no matter how well or how often I express my thanks, but I am sincerely grateful to the many people in Aghyaran who freely offered me their time, attention, hospitality, and friendship. My road to Ballymongan may have been circuitous and unlikely but—permit me this sentimentality—I cannot in retrospect imagine taking any other.

Acknowledgments

Thanks go first and foremost to the people of Aghyaran for their remarkable hospitality and neighborliness. I owe the greatest debt and offer my most sincere gratitude to the people I name in the chapters that follow. There are, however, many people who are not mentioned, or are mentioned only in passing, who deserve recognition for acts of kindness and assistance. They include Will Andrews, Barney Byrne (Grouselodge), Maura Byrne, Gerard Byrne, Stephen Byrne and Liz Sheridan, Joe Carlin, Patsy Connolly, John and Bridget Corry, Fr. Andy Dolan, Thomas Dolan, Eamon and Patricia Dolan, Danny and Joanne Falls, Ali FitzGibbon and Glenn Patterson, Mary Den Gallagher, Art and Susan Gallagher, Dinny and Rosemary Gallagher, Pat Den Gallagher, Colm and Mary Ellen Gallen, Mickey Joe Gallen, Marian Gallen, John and Bernie Gallen, Danny and Fidelma Gormley, Marian Hands, Charley Hilley, Jim Ledwith, Charlie and Rebecca Logue, Mickey Logue, Agnes Lunney, Charlie Lynch, Gerard Lynch, Alan and Ruth McCobb, Breege McCusker, Chris McDaid, Ailish McElhill, Francie McGirr, Bernie McGlinchey, John Myles McGlinchey, Paddy and Peggy McGlynn, Mary McGlynn, Cassie McGrath, Tommy Maguire, Danny and Marian McHugh, Francis McHugh, Sally Kelly McHugh, Cormac and Mary McManus, Mary McShane, Sadie McSorley, Danny McSorley, Jim Macken, Charley and Rose Mongan, Sean Mongan, Alison Monteith, Gerry Montgomery, Dennis Moss, Billy Nevin, Eugene and Isobel O'Donnell, John Gerard and Debbie O'Donnell, Charlie and Claire O'Donnell, Pat and Philomena O'Loughlin, James Hugh O'Neill, Kathleen Owens, Mary Shanaghan, and Gordon and Avril Speer.

Special thanks go to my former neighbor Danny Gallen, who has acted alternately as my guide, advocate, collaborator, patron, editor, critic, and most reluctant photographic subject. Above all Danny is my enduring friend. I thank Danny's wife Susan for being such a welcoming host, and their grown children Fiona, Paul, Louise, and Donal for affably indulging my curious presence.

Sadly, over the course of my research several people have passed on. I miss Maggie Byrne, Johnny Corry, Cissie Dolan, James Hegarty, Mickey Hegarty, Sarah Jane Gallen, Charlie Lunney, Neil McElhill, Paddy McFadden, Fr. Phillip McGarrigle, Fr. Brendan McGinn, Mick Pareroe McHugh, Mick Tom McSorley, James Moss, Mary Alice Mongan, Paddy Mongan, John Mongan, Eddie Mongan, Laurence Mongan, Paddy O'Neill, and Ray Richards. May they rest in peace. Throughout this book I will speak of them as I knew them, in the present tense.

My debts run deep in Ireland but extend farther afield. Three scholars deserve special recognition for their support and guidance. Progressive, insightful, and generous, Gearóid Ó Crualaoich first introduced me to folklore studies, and I credit his scholarship and teaching with the first blinding light moments that led to my conversion. Gearóid also introduced me to Henry Glassie's *Passing the Time in Ballymenone* (1982), the book that convinced me to answer the call. It is my hope that my book about a place not unlike Ballymenone, three decades later, will be read in conversation with *Passing the Time* and *The Stars of Ballymenone* (2006). Henry Glassie has given so much of himself, first as a mentor and later as a colleague, that I can never thank him sufficiently. Henry's critical mind, wealth of experience, and invariable eloquence have enabled me to think and write with greater precision and honesty. I cannot overstate my affection for him as a friend. Finally, Richard Bauman has long been a reliable source of candid and sage advice. Dick's fluid command of an impressive breadth of scholarship has prodded me and many to try to transcend traditional disciplinary divisions of intellectual labor and to attempt more nuanced understandings of concerns central to the humanities and social sciences. Although I am responsible for all deficiencies and failures to heed good advice, I thank these three scholars in particular for their positive contributions and influences.

Many others in Ireland and North America have been instrumental in facilitating or shaping various parts of this project. I have benefited from and am grateful for conversations and correspondence with Mabel Agozzino, Linda Ballard, Jonathan Bell, Harris Berger, Erika Brady, Mary

Ellen Brown, Anthony Buckley, William Cohen, Moureen Coulter, Louis de Paor, Giovanna Del Negro, James Doan, Karen Duffy, John Eastlake, Brian Edmiston, Bridget Edwards, Michael Evans, Michele Forman, Lisa Gabbert, Lisa Gilman, Lee Haring, Julie Heath, Greg Kelley, Andy Kolovos, Christopher Kyle, John Laudun, Elaine Lawless, Carl Lindahl, Danille Lindquist, Críostóir Mac Cárthaigh, John McDowell, Andre Millard, Margaret Mills, Galey Modan, John Moulden, Pat Mullen, Séamas Ó Catháin, Thomas O'Grady, Lillis Ó Laoire, Thomas Dillon Redshaw, James Silas Rogers, Ian Russell, Jack Santino, Jennifer Schacker, David Shorter, Pravina Shukla, Amy Shuman, Sue Tuohy, and Christopher Taylor. Jason Baird Jackson, Tom Mould, and Dorothy Noyes were particularly helpful, going above and beyond the call of duty in commenting with intelligence and charity on previous drafts. Dorry deserves her own sentence of praise for being an extraordinary colleague and intrepid leader. I also thank my anonymous reviewers and the able staff of Indiana University Press for their efforts, and Dan Connolly for his excellent indexing work.

For financial assistance that supported my fieldwork I thank the Department of Folklore and Ethnomusicology and the College of Arts and Sciences at Indiana University, the Academy for Irish Cultural Heritages at the University of Ulster, the School of Social and Behavioral Sciences at the University of Alabama at Birmingham, and the College of Humanities at the Ohio State University. I also want to thank the editors of *The Journal of American Folklore* for permission to reprint portions of Cashman 2006a in chapter 11, of *Midwestern Folklore* for permission to reprint portions of Cashman 2007a in chapter 5, and of *New Hibernia Review* for permission to reprint portions of Cashman 1999 in the preface and chapter 1 and portions of Cashman 2006b in chapter 4.

Deserving tremendous credit and closest to my heart is my wife, Lorraine, who has shared with me the highs and lows of fieldwork and writing. I thank her not only for loving good will and support, but also for her substantial help as a critical thinker. Throughout the conceptualization and writing process, our late-night conversations sustained and inspired me, and I have benefited enormously from her ability to challenge or amplify my impressions of our shared experience. Young daughters Maggie and Nora, lovely and loud, deserve special thanks for as much patience as they can muster and for pretending that picnics at my office are just as good as the real thing.

I am grateful to John and Kathy Cashman, especially, and to the extended Cashman, Trimble, and Watwood clans of Junction, Texas, for taking in a couple of unlikely cowboys.

Finally, this book is dedicated to my mother, Susan O. Cashman, and in memory of my father, Ray D. Cashman, for their lifelong and unconditional support.

Storytelling on the
Northern Irish Border

1

Goals and Orientations

This book examines how local social life and culture are both represented and enacted through storytelling in one Northern Irish community, Aghyaran. Extending language philosopher J. L. Austin's memorable formulation that people "do things with words" (1997 [1962]), we can also say that people do things with stories. What they do depends on who is talking to whom, in what contexts, and to what ends. It also depends on the type of story being told, for different genres implicate different subjectivities and ideological orientations toward the world (Seitel 1999, Bauman 2004). Typically, however, people's stories relay shared beliefs, values, and norms. Stories provide a vehicle through which personal and shared orientations may be passed on, instilled, or indeed critically evaluated and reconsidered. Likewise, stories—especially those that appeal to the authority of tradition—provide powerful rhetorical tools in the construction, maintenance, and revision of individual and group identities. Given that narratives are often commemorative orderings of previous happenings, everywhere people tell stories to depict a meaningful past they can use to assess their present and to bolster themselves as they meet an uncertain future.

If these are some of the typical, universal functions of stories, my goals here are to determine to what ends stories are told in Aghyaran, to contemplate what lasting effects oral traditions have there, and to suggest what the common preoccupations, values, and themes evident in a large body of Aghyaran folklore tell us as outsiders about contemporary culture on the Irish border.[1] Part of my task, in pursuit of these goals, is to demonstrate when and in what recurring circumstances people in Aghyaran tell stories, and how these stories and social contexts mutually constitute each other. This requires investigation of primary situational contexts for storytelling, such as ceilis and wakes, to be discussed in detail in chapters 3 and 4. Another part of my overall project is to investigate what types of stories are told and, in effect, what certain types of stories are good for. This takes us into a consideration of genre as, paraphrasing Richard Bauman (2004), an orienting framework for the production and reception of narrative—one theme in chapters 5 and 6. A third part of this undertaking is to demonstrate what social work is accomplished by certain stories told in particular storytelling contexts, and how this work is accomplished through the ways in which people construct stories. Such contextualized narrative exegesis is the focus of chapters 7 through 10. Brought together in the final chapter, these investigations shed light on how people in one Irish community use stories to sustain and critically evaluate themselves as individuals within a group in the midst of change. Throughout, folklore will be our window into community and identity as they are imagined, articulated, and enacted on the Irish border today.

Through low tumbling clouds the sun shone reluctantly at best, then retired early behind the sodden black tumulus of Mullyfa mountain. September. With days beginning to grow darker I did as my neighbors did. By convention Tuesday was the night for visiting Paddy and Tommy Mongan; there were no scheduled bingo or card games to lure the brothers from home and they had no interest in Tuesday night's television line-up. This particular Tuesday elder brother Paddy was in the hospital for testing, so calling on Tommy was simply the thing to do.

The road from my house to the Mongans' was relatively short. Still, the pitch black coupled with the press of water—not straightforward rain, mind you, but an unrelenting omnidirectional pelting of something too robust to be called mist—left me with the impression of tunneling more than walking. Surfacing from the murk, I crossed the Mongans' threshold into the bright turf-toasted warmth of the crowded living room. "Good man yourself, Ray," Tommy welcomed me as I took my place. "How's Tommy . . . Mickey, Barney, Francis, Mary, Charlie, Mary, Sadie?" Chat focused first on the bad weather, then on reports of Paddy in hospital—not fully "at himself" but "eating like a horse"—followed by concerns over the accuracy of diagnoses and the state of Omagh Hospital.

Tommy shifted gears to introduce me to another Ballymongan man, Jim Connolly, who after making the connection that I was living in John McHugh's old house launched into an anecdote about the time Mr. McHugh gave him a savage "tongue-banging" about a defective tire pump. Apparently Mr. McHugh was enraged that the pump Jim sold him, when attached to a deflated inner tube, was not a sufficient handhold for stopping his Ford Cortina as it rolled downhill during an ill-fated tire change. The story inspired the company to share several related anecdotes about Mr. McHugh and other irascible characters of the recent past. This sustained conversation for about half an hour before tea was served and chat turned to other topics, mostly an oscillation between childhood reminiscences and the daily news.

Later, after the women had gone, it was suggested that Tommy show off his new gift from a friend who spent a holiday in San Francisco. "Oh aye," chuckled Tommy, who produced a box and unpacked a wind-up toy. The plastic clown was about five inches tall with an ear-to-ear grin and half-mast eyes that put me in mind of actor James Spader. With a few turns of the key the toy began to wobble from side to side, lurching forward. More to the point, the front of his striped cloth trousers dropped while his hands jerked up and down, doing to his exposed plastic self about what you would expect of a toy clown named "Happy."

Remarkable feat of engineering aside, that's a tough act to follow. Once our laughter subsided, it was after midnight and our ceili began to break up with a few last bids at repartee and words of farewell: "God bless," "Safe home." Not every ceili—not even every all-male ceili—would make such ribald sport of convention and respectability, but it became a theme worth noting. Tamer nights preceded and followed that night at Tommy's home, but each one progressed toward, revolved around, and was animated by stories.

Having been settled in the townland of Ballymongan for a little over a month, I began to appreciate nighttime ceilis among neighbors as a primary site for conversational storytelling and *craic*.[2] I began to take mental notes on the types of stories told and their plot outlines, writing all this down soon after the event. I was still feeling my way through what my role in these situations should be when one evening my neighbor Danny Gallen presented me with yet another opportunity to meet the neighbors. He offered me a ride to a wake. Having never met the deceased, I was apprehensive about attending her wake, but then I also would have felt awkward declining Danny's invitation. The deceased was a sister of my landlord, so I figured that attending her wake and paying my respects was simply the thing to do.

Danny said little to prepare me, and since I had never been to a wake in Ireland I had little idea of what to expect. When we arrived around 10 PM the house was crowded, and I followed Danny's every lead—whose hand to shake, how to offer condolences, when to pray, when to find a seat and have a chat, when to leave. As we approached the wake house, the widower and male relatives lined the entryway to the home and the stairs in a sort of informal receiving line. Upstairs in the bedroom where the body lay, newly arrived mourners said prayers and expressed their regrets to the female friends and relatives who sat in chairs lining three walls. After paying our respects, Danny and I made our way back downstairs and, finding the house packed, out to chairs in the front garden where we were served tea, sweets, and sandwiches by a young woman. Outside, the company was less somber and entirely male, and we joined Mickey Byrne, our Ballymongan neighbor, for a chat under the stars of a clear night sky.

Soon the widower joined us with a tired but faintly conspiratorial smile, possibly hoping for a bit of craic from Mickey, whose reputation as a character precedes him. My company began to swap stories about local characters whom I did not know, but the themes of these stories and especially the reports of others' battles of wits through repartee were already becoming familiar to me from the conversational exchange at ceilis. The floor was open to anecdotes about past local eccentrics, so with the theme established Mickey took the opportunity to recall one of his favorite stories about a long-deceased fellow bachelor nicknamed Neil the Bucket, a story I recorded Mickey telling several months later during a ceili:

> Neil was a wild drinker, you see. He'd have been an alcoholic, I suppose. And Fr. Doherty, he, he was fond of drink himself, you see.
>
> So anyhow, Fr. Doherty told Neil for to stop the drinking, you see, and this day he give Neil a great deal about drinking so much.

Figure 1.1. Danny Gallen

Figure 1.2. Mickey Byrne

So the following Friday, anyhow, or so, the two of them met up in the town, you see, and Fr. Doherty says to Neil—Neil was very drunk again, you see—and Fr. Doherty says, "Drunk today again, Neil!"

"Well, aye Father, indeed so am I!"

The widower had a genuine laugh, and after a few more minutes of chat, he withdrew to resume his duties in the receiving line at the door. About an hour after our arrival, the crowd had not diminished, and since we were neither related to, nor near neighbors of, the deceased, Danny and I headed for home, our minimal social duty done. Closer friends and relatives would settle in for the night, swapping stories and passing the time until dawn cast shadows from the Sperrin mountains.

Nine years, fourteen wakes, and numerous ceilis and interviews later, I can assert with confidence that both wakes and ceilis are the primary social contexts in Aghyaran for the neighborly exchange of stories from a range of genres—jokes, tall tales, historical and supernatural legends, personal narratives of both everyday and supernatural experience. Close attention to wakes and ceilis have taught me, however, that another genre is most popular: the local character anecdote.

Although relatively little studied by folklorists, with notable exceptions, the most frequent stories at Aghyaran wakes and ceilis are those like Jim's about John McHugh and Mickey's about Neil the Bucket. These local character anecdotes—an outsider's etic term but an insider's emic category[3]—are brief and often humorous biographical sketches of local individuals, living or deceased, especially those affectionately referred to as "characters." With proper contextualization the local character anecdote reveals itself to be a favored channel through which people in Aghyaran engage the past in order to make sense of the present and guide each other toward the future. I cannot deny, however, that at first glance this small genre of short, snappy narratives seems an improbable vehicle of social consequence and an unlikely candidate for serious study.

If the carnivalesque play at Tommy's does not fit the relatively chaste and ceremonious image earlier folklorists wished for the ceili as traditional storytelling session, the local character anecdote does little better to fit the bill of authentic, voice-of-the-nation folklore handed down from time immemorial. In the Irish context, local character anecdotes serve neither as ancient national treasures—as have heroic tales of Cúchulainn and Fionn Mac Cumhaill—nor as evidence of Ireland's contribution to an international heritage of oral literature—as have Irish versions of migratory wonder tales or *Märchen*. Assuming the broader orientations of contemporary European ethnology and the mostly American ethnography of communication, however, the ubiquity of the anecdote demands our attention. Regardless of whatever nationalist, romantic, or conservationist projects and impulses exist in the wider world—regardless of how other people and institutions define, regard, and use folklore—the people of Aghyaran clearly invest a lot of thought and energy in this seemingly modest speech genre when socializing. In the spirit of Franz Boas, founder of American folklore studies, focusing on these anecdotes is a fitting choice for exploring local perspectives and "has the merit of bringing out those points which are of interest to the people themselves" (Boas 1970 [1916]:393).

As we will see, local character anecdotes are not only ubiquitous but also conceptually central in the generic system of Aghyaran storytelling. Detailing the conventions and formal features of this genre and illustrating inter-generic connections can wait for now. Yet having briefly discussed what stories in general are good for, typically and universally, I should anticipate later chapters by delineating the value and utility of Aghyaran anecdotes in particular.

Essentially, local character anecdotes typify the personalities of individuals through reports of behavior treated as representative of those people portrayed. In doing so, any given anecdote—a short report of a single event—does not represent an individual in all of his or her complexity. Rather people are transformed through short narratives into exemplars of certain behavioral types, such as nosey gossips or picaresque drunks. Some types are clearly framed as worthy of emulation. These include the modest saintly bachelor, the good mother, and the "man of words" who is always quick with a clever comeback. Other types are clearly singled out for criticism or rejection. These include the farmer-capitalist who sacrifices neighborliness in his feverish pursuit of wealth, and the fool whose lack of wit marks him or her (but usually him) as the community scapegoat. Still other types evoke ambivalence. These include the wily trickster who is the epitome of wit but who crosses a line into unacceptable behavior when he targets the innocent and vulnerable. Also evoking ambivalence is the socially maladjusted rough bachelor who is no model for proper, modern behavior but who may be prized when he defeats the arrogant outsider in a contest of wit. Quite often the character types depicted in Aghyaran anecdotes are those, such as the rough bachelor, who are associated with the past and symbolic of outmoded ways of being. Stories about these anachronistic characters, then, allow for contemplation and evaluation of change through the contrast of past and present.

Regardless of the personality type a particular anecdote invokes, these stories as a whole put certain ideological orientations and emotional stances on display for evaluation by audience members. That is, local character anecdotes provide a vehicle through which people may contemplate human nature and evaluate a range of ways of being that are found in and shaped by the shared sociohistorical environment of Aghyaran. Moreover, hearers may evaluate their own orientations and stances vis-à-vis those of anecdote characters. In the process, the individuals portrayed in these stories are assigned relative social status and incorporated as exemplars of familiar human types into local collective memory.[4]

Shifting focus from the individual to the collective, this body of oral narrative serves as a community study initiated by locals long before any self-professed ethnographer arrived on the scene. As Clifford Geertz (1973) and Keith Basso (1979) observe, academics are not the only people engaged in ethnography, and oftentimes the stories people tell themselves about themselves are most revealing. As a form of auto-ethnography, local character anecdotes allow Aghyaran residents to represent themselves to themselves, imagining local community through a survey of the types of humanity that comprise and may symbolize that community. At the same time, local character anecdotes bring together narrators and listeners in circles of participation at ceilis and wakes, thus enacting local community while simultaneously representing it in narrative.[5]

If one justification for contextualizing and analyzing local character anecdotes is gaining ethnographic insight into a particular community, another is better appreciation of the politics of culture and identity in Northern Ireland and by extension other plural societies. Much is at stake in imagining specifically local community through anecdotes and related genres of storytelling. Put in proper context, swapping local character anecdotes at wakes and ceilis may be appreciated as a powerful vehicle for challenging the rhetoric and effects of sectarian identity. Aghyaran anecdotes provide a sense of shared identity and belonging based on local community membership rather than on Catholic vs. Protestant ethnic, religious, and political affiliations. Because local identity is imagined as a range of personal identities considered specific to or at least distinctive of Aghyaran as a community, local identity is simply more complicated than sectarian identity, which allows for only Catholic or Protestant as meaningful conceptual categories.

This sort of nuance, a complication of reductive binary thinking, is quite valuable in the midst of violent conflict and sectarian identity politics. Received wisdom about the division of society into that which is Catholic and that which is Protestant is difficult to contest, but given the costs of such received wisdom, revision is urgent. By redirecting attention through storytelling to that which is local and shared, people in Aghyaran challenge impulses toward segregation and difference. Academics should interrogate uncomplicated, romantic visions of "local community" and "local identity," but as we shall see, these are notions that people in Aghyaran embrace, in part, for their potential to transcend the supposedly intractable divisions at the heart of Northern Ireland's Troubles (cf. Cashman 2002).

Community and identity will continually reemerge as themes throughout this book because—Aghyaran folklore attests—they are concepts of interest and value to people in this place at this time. Because community and identity have been much-discussed concepts in folklore studies and related fields, we should review how they are conceived now and have been conceived over time, to indicate where this investigation enters into the ongoing discussion.

In response to a long tradition of thinking of the local community as an extant, bounded entity and a natural focus for study, recent attempts at greater reflexivity within folklore studies have warned against essentializing or reifying community, and have shifted attention to how community is imagined, constructed, maintained, negotiated, and revised (Bendix 1997, Noyes 2003, Shuman 1993). Such a move articulates with the "invention of tradition" school inspired by Hobsbawm and Ranger (1983), Benedict Anderson's "imagined communities" perspective (1991), and postmodernism in general, among other trends in social history, anthropology, and cultural studies (cf. Noyes 1995:466). Here, community is not an essence but an idea appealed to and effected through performance—music, costume, public display events, verbal art.

From this perspective, there is no local community called Aghyaran that conforms to Ferdinand Tönnies's *Gemeinschaft* model (1998 [1887])—fully integrated, culturally homogenous, organized by a unity of ideology and will. Likewise, there is no local community called Aghyaran bounded in space, shielded from the excesses of modernity and the taint of outside influence. While the folklorist may focus on mummers in the home, singers in the pub, or turf cutters in the bog, everyday scenes in Aghyaran also include farmers atop tractors talking on cell phones, construction workers and bank managers beginning their commutes to jobs in faraway Letterkenny and Belfast, and school boys on the street in Killeter sporting Manchester United jerseys made in China. On a recent return trip, I found myself in one of Aghyaran's few shops confronted with a choice between potato chips marketed as "mango chutney with cheddar" and "gently infused with lime and Thai spices." Modernity and globalization are realities and felt presences.

Still, a local community called Aghyaran is regularly imagined and evoked—perhaps in reaction, usually in a commemorative mood—through the annual Killeter Fair, *Aghyaran* magazine, the Killeter and District Historical Society, and indeed the act of neighbors swapping stories about peers and predecessors at wakes and ceilis. In Aghyaran, as elsewhere, the "community of the social imaginary" (Noyes 1995:471ff.) may be a selective and negotiable construction—an appeal made at certain times, in certain situations, to certain ends—but it is nonetheless a favored metaphor and one of great consequence.

While many folklorists have shifted attention toward the community of the social imaginary—in occupational, gendered, religious, or ethnic terms, at the local, regional, national, and transnational levels—there have been other equally useful attempts by folklorists to specify what "community" denotes. Uncomfortable, in part, with the notion that the terms "folk group" or "community" imply homogeneity, Dan Ben-Amos defined folklore as "artistic communication in small groups" and stipulated that these small groups—the social base of folklore—are defined only by frequent interaction and common frame of reference (1972). By extension, community may be understood in sociological terms as a network of communicating individuals. Especially when investigating vernacular speech forms, styles, and registers shared within such a network, we find this definition of community as network overlapping productively with the concept of the speech community developed in sociolinguistics and linguistic anthropology. Expounded in particular by John Gumperz (1968 and 1972) and Dell Hymes (1968 and 1972), the speech community is a regularly interacting network of individuals who are familiar with a given repertoire of speech genres and who share cultural norms and values that shape their discursive practices.[6]

Most communities as networks are mutable. One may opt out of the network and others may join, so while some networks are relatively easy to map geographically they are delimited by participation, not space (cf. Glassie 2005:22, Noyes 1995:459). As Henry Glassie observes in his first community study of Ballymenone, County Fermanagh, Northern Ireland—a sparsely populated rural district with indistinct boundaries—if there had been a village or town he might have mistakenly presumed municipal geographical limits as the boundaries of community (1982a:13). What defined individuals as members of the community of Ballymenone, however, was not the geographical setting of their everyday lives but their willingness to labor and socialize together, helping each other in times of need. As Glassie asserts, "True communities are built not of dewy affection or ideological purity but of engagement" (1982a:282). More specifically, community is "a social arrangement for mutual aid" (2005:27). Glassie's characterization of community is, like Ben-Amos's, sociological at base—an empirically observable network of interacting, mutually engaged people. Glassie, however, takes the further step of identifying the motivation for maintaining this network in a place not unlike Aghyaran: an ethic of reciprocity that cuts across boundaries of age, gender, denomination, and political affiliation.

In Aghyaran the community as network that regularly comes together at wakes and ceilis for entertainment overlaps with the network of those who reciprocate materially through work and neighborly favors. These wake- and ceili-anchored networks include mostly marriage-age to elderly men and women, Catholics and Protestants, but can be characterized as more middle-aged and elderly than young, more male than female, more Catholic than Protestant. Or at least, these were the networks most open to me as a younger, married American male with a recognizably southern Irish surname. Specific demographic details follow in the next chapter, but one larger point is that defining the community as network is not only a productive field method but also a useful step in distinguishing the social base of a given body of folklore.

Following the lead of previous commentary on community, we seem to have two potential Aghyarans—a community of the social imaginary and an empirical network of interacting individuals. Dorothy Noyes is correct to propose that for clarity we should distinguish between these two conceptions of community because "our difficulties with such concepts as 'folk,' 'nation,' 'race,' and so on, may be seen as resulting from the confusion of the two" (1995:452). In a move parallel to Noyes's discussion of "group," what I call "local community" in Aghyaran is in fact the dialogue between the community of the social imaginary and the community of the network; they are mutually constitutive. Reconciling the two, Noyes states:

> The performance that constructs the community ideologically and emotionally also strengthens or changes the shape of networks by promoting interaction. . . . The community of the social imaginary coexists in a dialectical tension with the empirical world of day-to-day network contacts. The imagined community offers a focus for comparison and desire, and, at the same time, is itself subject to re-visionings in the light of everyday experience. (1995:471)

In Aghyaran, storytelling brings people together in enactment of local community—reinvigorating the network—at the same time that the stories themselves envisage and investigate this community, epitomized as it is by a range of richly signifying types of individuals.

Put another way, in agreement with Glassie, community is a network of people brought into engagement by an idea. In Ballymenone that idea was an ethic of neighborly reciprocity founded on Christian principle. The same ethic is still very much at work in Aghyaran, in a county to the north, three decades later. Today, however, another idea that looms as large, binding people together in various imaginings and performances of community, is identity.

Although quite common in our largely self-conscious era, preoccupation with individual and group identities—particularly with the cultural, social, and spiritual wholeness identity promises—is historically situated and culturally relative, as recent reappraisals of the concept of identity demonstrate (Abrahams 2005:198–216; Berger and Del Negro 2004:124–157). Extending an argument made by Elliott Oring (1994), Glassie also explains that identity is not always and everywhere a conscious concern.

Rather, identity is a concept of stress: "The more tense the circumstance, the more likely identity is to rise into articulation" (1994:239). As Bauman explains with his concept of differential identity (1971), folklore does not necessarily proceed from and reflect shared identity; the stress that gives rise to the articulation of identity through folklore often stems from interaction between groups at borders and other contact zones and events.

Invaded and colonized, Ireland has long been "the most distressful country," in the words of the 1798 broadside ballad "The Wearing of the Green." Questions of identity have thus been pervasive in Irish society since at least the sixteenth- and seventeenth-century Plantations. For example, written in the wake of utter defeat, gathering Ireland's oral and written sources into a master mytho-historical narrative, Geoffrey Keating's *Foras Feasa ar Éirinn* (c. 1634) offers a comprehensive early formulation of Irish Catholic national identity (see Cashman 2001, Cunningham 2001, Glassie 2001). Today as then, the tense circumstances that give rise to questions of identity are political. The legacy of colonialism raises the questions "who are we in relation to our neighbor—Protestant or Catholic, descendants of Planters or Gaels—and whose interests are served by the powers that be?"

Another contemporary source of distress and preoccupation is existential. In Aghyaran people who grew up without electricity are now expected to fill out agricultural and financial forms on the Internet. This temporal contrast, apparent in scores of daily manifestations, is jarring. As televisions, labor-saving technology, and other isolating modern conveniences sap the integrating communal impulse, people contemplate losses and gains, and they begin to question the modern teleology of progress that blindly endorses change. The accelerated rhythms of daily life and the seemingly irreversible march of modernization give rise to the questions "who are we in relation to who we have been, and which changes should we embrace and which should we resist?" In Ireland today, as elsewhere, threats to continuity join threats to community.

Pressed, people contemplate identity through their bids to envision some community of the social imaginary. The identity people seek, perceive, and often embrace depends on the type of community they appeal to in performance; it could be local, sectarian, regional, ethnic, generational, gendered, and so on. These performances comprise much of what we term folklore. As Oring argues, the concept of identity has been central to the concerns of folklorists since the eighteenth century, long before the term came into vogue, and the discipline was founded on an understanding of folklore as the artifacts of identity (1994). Extending a more recent trend that reckons identity as situational and relational rather than essential and fixed—seeing folklore as the artifice rather than artifact of identity—Giovanna Del Negro and Harris Berger retain the special relationship between folklore and identity, while recasting identity as an interpretive framework. For them, identity may be appreciated as a set of ideas that academics and non-academics alike use to make sense of folklore and expressive culture (2004).

As Del Negro and Berger write, because "all conduct emerges in a social context and all expressive culture draws on stocks of cultural knowledge, any expressive act may potentially be interpreted as a statement of identity" (2004:142). Through the process of interpreting folklore the world is doubled. In places and times in which identity is a conscious preoccupation, individuals typically interpret a given example of folklore by taking into account its situated performance context, then interpret it again by drawing a connection between that item of folklore and some particular imagined community. The habitual interpretation of folklore as a statement of identity, then, always makes meaning in part sociological. "To interpret folklore in terms of identity means to take the meaning of folklore and project it into the interpreter's vision of the social world" (2004:134).

That vision of how the social world is divided conceptually into different types of community and into specific identity-sharing groups can be figured in a wide variety of ways. In Northern Ireland people quite often conceptualize community and perceive identity in either sectarian or local terms, and these two competing formulations are both reflected and generated by a certain range of folklore genres. Especially in segregated urban areas, many Catholics and Protestants fuel ongoing conflict through symbolic representations of their separateness. Public rituals and commemorations, in particular, continually re-establish two opposing collective identities—on the one hand, Irish Catholic nationalist identity, and on the other, British or Ulster Protestant unionist identity. For example, every summer many Protestants participate in Orange Order parades that can be interpreted both as celebratory expressions of unionist solidarity and as symbolic recapitulations of past military victories over Catholics. Routes chosen for some of these parades purposefully wind through or circumscribe Catholic areas to symbolically claim all of Northern Ireland as Protestant, British territory. Catholics, for their part, have excelled particularly in composing political ballads that commemorate past victories and noble sacrifices. Having appropriated an earlier unionist tradition also practiced by contemporary loyalists, Catholics also excel in painting political murals on the gable end walls of urban public housing. These murals mark Irish Catholic space and commemorate events of importance to collective nationalist and republican identity.[7]

These popular rituals, songs, and works of art are examples of very different genres of vernacular expressive culture, but there are at least three common denominators between them. They are public forms of display meant for wide consumption. They are all invested in the project of commemoration in a place where it would seem, at first, that remembering the past can only remind people of the root causes of division. Finally, all these examples of folklore can be understood as sectarian in the sense that they reinforce separate Catholic and Protestant identities, reifying opposing Catholic and Protestant communities.

Even if certain genres of folklore serve the construction of separate Catholic and Protestant sectarian identities, however, there is no reason to believe that these are the only possible collective identities in Northern Ireland. Other groups are imaginable, and other genres are helpful in imagining them. For example, people in Aghyaran are quite familiar with one striking folk narrative visually anchored and continually brought to mind by a local landmark. In the ancient graveyard of Magherakeel, where both Catholic and Protestant families continue to bury their kin, a stone monument built into the southern retaining wall stands over eleven feet tall. The monument features several carvings in relief: at the top a crucifix and other symbols of a priest's vocation; just below this a neoclassical winged angel; and at the base skulls and bones and a toppled hour glass. These carvings revolve around a lengthy vita in Latin that details the life and career of Fr. Cornelius O'Mongan, who died in 1725. Fr. O'Mongan was the parish priest during the Penal Era, when the practice of Catholicism was by law severely restricted and bounties were paid for Catholic priests who did not abide by strict regulations. According to local legend, Fr. O'Mongan was hotly pursued one day by British soldiers sent into the area to capture him. The priest fled throughout the parish looking for a place to hide, and eventually a miller by the name of Kyle saved him from capture and possible execution. In some versions of the story, Kyle hides the priest in the chaff of his mill, and in others he openly challenges the soldiers and fires his musket

Figure 1.3. Fr. Cornelius O'Mongan monument, Magherakeel graveyard

to disperse them. Kyle, it turns out, was a Protestant. This story is told by many as a sort of origin myth of friendly relations between Catholics and Protestants in the parish.

I first heard a full version of this local historical legend from Mary Alice Mongan when she was entertaining me and others who had come to ceili. As Mary Alice told the story, the affiliations that mattered to Kyle were local rather than sectarian. Kyle's example demonstrated that, sharing the same place and way of life, Catholics and Protestants in this part of the world have many interests and attitudes in common, including an aversion to outside encroachments on local autonomy. Here we have a folk narrative that invites contemporary interpreters—worn down by more than three decades of the Troubles—to reconceptualize community and redefine identity, once again, in local rather than sectarian terms.

Particularly instructive is the fact that in the legend—a genre different from the parade, ballad, or mural—and in the intimacy of Mary Alice's kitchen—a less public realm than city streets and pubs—this more complicated story is possible. To hear the more complicated story that challenges a binary, sectarian vision of the world requires getting to know people, being invited into homes, and paying attention to genres of folklore in a more intimate, communal realm.[8] Once we leave the streets where the marches take place and the murals are painted, once we leave the public houses where the ballads are sung, other genres of folklore become more important and drive at different persuasive ends.[9]

Two young IRA volunteers speeding through the night hit a pothole near the customs hut; their homemade device explodes; the wreckage scatters along the border road, over the ditches, and across the fields. A loyalist gunman riddles a yellow work van as it slowly comes to a halt, veering off the shoulder of the wrong side of the road. The driver, a Sinn Féin supporter, is denied a priest and a doctor by police until after his last breath. A local Protestant and part-time Ulster Defence Regiment soldier stoops to attach a trailer to his car; a mercury tilt switch completes a circuit; the man is blown to pieces; his parents, who witness the explosion, survive with minor physical injuries. A Catholic forestry worker is stopped by armed masked men, pulled from his lorry, and shot twenty times at point-blank range. At the funeral a bishop states unequivocally that the victim was not a member of any paramilitary organization; the Ulster Freedom Fighters claim responsibility for a legitimate assassination. I could go on.

These are the sort of narrative kernels that quite often define Northern Ireland as represented in films, novels, and newscasts. I claim as one of my goals contrasting these images with complicating information gleaned from long-term, feet-on-the-ground research in one border community, and yet each one of the incidents mentioned above took place in or around Aghyaran between 1972 and 1991. In this sense, Aghyaran is not a place apart, a "village without violence" as one hopeful early Troubles ethnography put it (Bufwack 1982). One point to make, then, is that my portrait of border life in Aghyaran is selective; this is both unavoidable and by design. Some may view my portrait as overly optimistic or celebratory, but it is intended as compensatory, emphasizing a side of life that is often ignored, especially stories and practices without which life would be unimaginably worse. Paraphrasing Elliott Leyton (1974: 85), the mystery about Northern Ireland is not why so many people have been killed, but why so few. Folklore—certain genres, certain practices—is part of the answer. Still, even if people ameliorate tensions and appeal to a non-sectarian local community through folklore, individuals may opt out of this version of community and folklore can be used also to reinforce sectarian division, even to provoke violence (e.g., Cashman 2008b).

A second point to make is that in addition to being a case study in the social uses of storytelling, this book joins a wide range of scholarly, journalistic, and artistic representations of Northern Ireland in various media over time. Delineating the full range is well beyond the scope of this chapter, but the reader should be familiar with certain themes in the ethnography of Northern Ireland to better appreciate where this book takes its place, however modest, in a longer tradition.

Thomas Wilson and Hastings Donnan (2006) are correct to point out that whereas twentieth-century ethnography of the Republic of Ireland was long dominated by the theme of residual peasant culture in decline, the ethnography of Northern Ireland since the 1960s has focused on another supposed vestige of earlier times: the discord between warring tribes, Catholics and Protestants (cf. Peace 1989). This tribal conflict theme in scholarship has a prehistory and parallels popular sentiments of journalists, politicians, and other commentators. As Winston Churchill observed with some antipathy in 1922, World War I may have been a great cataclysm of sweeping change, yet "as the deluge subsides and the waters fall short, we see the dreary steeples of Fermanagh and Tyrone emerging once again" (2003:85). This long-held conventional wisdom that nothing can dissuade Northern Ireland's Protestants and Catholics from their ancient hostilities establishes the terms for debate; whether or not it is the intended focus of any given study, sectarianism is an issue no ethnography set in Northern Ireland can ignore. Moreover, whether supported or contested, the two-tribes model reiterates the idea of Northern Ireland as stuck in the past, consigning the people there to a primitive or backward state (Jarman 1997:2).

Posed in response to violent images of anachronistic tribal conflict is a counter-tradition of looking to peaceful Catholic-Protestant relations in rural communities where another set of images is most often reported: Catholics denounce and paint over republican graffiti sprayed on a Church of Ireland parish hall. Protestants donate money and materials to refurbish a Catholic holy well damaged in sectarian attack. A Catholic looks after his Protestant neighbor's dairy herd so that his neighbor can join his local Orange lodge for the Twelfth of July parade. Again, I could go on, but these images—all of them from Aghyaran—are not always as striking as those involving violence. Indeed, at least the first two images cannot be seen as hopeful without the preexistence of sectarian conflict. More to the point, most enactments of neighborliness and local community solidarity are not reactions to trouble. Rather they are a great deal more mundane and routine: a neighbor chats to a neighbor in the shop, neighbors cooperate to win the hay before the weather breaks, a neighbor goes to a neighbor's mother's wake regardless of being diametrically opposed to her family's politics.

One way to interpret this second set of images is to claim that rural society is more genuinely integrated and less confrontational than that of the segregated neighborhoods of Belfast and Derry. In places where Catholics and Protestants share much the same way of life and are more interdependent as neighbors, the argument goes, local identity and affiliations matter more than sectarian ones. This argument applies best to certain but not all periods and to certain but not all rural locations in Northern Ireland. Similar iterations of this argument are made by Henry Glassie (1975, 1982, 2006), Anthony Buckley (1982), Mary Bufwack (1982), Rosemary Harris (1972), and Elliott Leyton (1975). Note that the fieldwork for most of these studies was completed before or during the 1970s.

In Aghyaran at least, paramilitary and state violence from the mid-1970s through the mid-1990s exacerbated and entrenched sectarian divisions at the expense of the traditional non-sectarian common ground afforded by shared local identity and allegiances. Technological change— especially the availability of affordable, labor-saving agricultural machinery—reduced people's daily interdependence in general, and with political tensions at a new high, most but not all people stopped socializing in mixed company. Recent efforts to regain stronger community integration in Aghyaran are self-conscious attempts to undo the damage inflicted most obviously by political violence, through appeals to models of community and identity that were possible and more common before the worst of the Troubles (see Cashman 2006a and 2006b). In this study, my intention is not simply to declare that all is well, that the "good neighbors" template fits Aghyaran. Rather I argue that many in Aghyaran are self-consciously attempting to revive and re-enter a version of the neighborly social reality that earlier Troubles ethnographers described, through both formal community development schemes and informal, traditional practices such as storytelling at wakes and ceilis.

The reasonable question remains: how can both the violent sectarian and peaceful neighborly images be accurate and representative? I have implied one answer already: certain people are more willing to foster a sense of local community and shared identity, whereas others are committed to sectarian division and zero-sum competition. Those republicans who fit this latter description are usually labeled "staunch," whereas their counterparts on the other side of the house are known as "deep." It takes only a small minority of people to keep sectarianism in the forefront of everyone's consciousness, even if for the majority the default for everyday behavior is cooperation.

A more interesting issue, perhaps, is how both sectarian and neighborly impulses can coexist within the same person. Bufwack contends that this internal contradiction is normal, and that the pull toward one impulse or the other depends on the situation.

> [T]he experiences of people, even in crisis situations, are not one dimensional. Sectarianism and violence are pervasive in Northern Ireland. It is part of institutional life and deeply rooted in people's personality structures. However, egalitarian and collective principles govern important areas of institutional everyday life as well. These too become part of an individual's experience and sentiments, contradicting the sectarian reality. . . . This contradictory reality is the norm for people in all situations. People in crisis may thus waver between different political positions. . . . Reality justifies neither a naïve utopianism nor a cynical resignation about the future. (1982:8)

This begins to explain the political complexity of any given individual who responds differently to models for sectarian division or neighborly cooperation depending on both immediate situational context and the broader historical context. Bufwack's perspective also explains a general waxing or waning of these neighborly and sectarian impulses within a larger population as variables change; looking to our Aghyaran case study, the impulse toward neighborly accommodation, not to mention trust, seems to have been most difficult during the violence of the mid-1970s to early 1990s. Still, a more satisfying, generalizable explanation of Catholic-Protestant relations—not to mention an adequate defense of the "good neighbors" strand in ethnography—must address how the two sides can coexist at the worst of times, despite clear provocation and strident public expressions of division.

Here Glassie's most recent account of Ballymenone (2006) helps explain the coexistence of Catholics and Protestants, and of neighborly and sectarian impulses, in rural communities such as Aghyaran in both the best and worst of times. True, behaviors and ideological stances vary with temporal and situational context, but a large part of this equation is governed by proxemics. That is, local senses of place differentiate between the neighborly intimacy of home and the less restricting anonymity of town. There exists an understood but unspoken rule that "political anger must be held in check among the neighbors, but it can be released to erupt, to blow out in public" (2006:338) away from home. In Ballymenone, this meant that the exchange of labor in the fields and the exchange of entertainment in the ceili avoided tension and leveled differences within the local district. Public, aggressive expression of difference, however, was unleashed in the anonymity of the crowd in the removed realm of Enniskillen by the marching followers of King Billy or across the border in the pubs of Swanlinbar by Catholics singing together of bold Fenians and perfidious Albion. This situation parallels that in Aghyaran, where no Orange parades are held, no republican murals are painted, and public signifiers of difference are kept to a minimum and usually away from the eyes of the other side of the house (Cashman 2008b). For those seeking to express party affiliation, there are other more appropriate venues in larger towns or across the border. But within the communal realm of Aghyaran among neighbors—particularly in mixed company—the sectarian divide is either carefully ignored, acknowledged but undermined through play (Cashman

2007b:51–52), challenged head-on with public assertions of local community solidarity (Cashman 2006a:148–153), or made irrelevant through the more intimate social work of stories about local characters and shared experience, discussed here.

~&

Before we enter this world of wakes, ceilis, and characters, a few comments on methodology and presentation are necessary. First, let me identify the steps necessary to present the folklore texts investigated here. Although wakes are a primary performance context investigated here, they simply are not appropriate occasions for using a tape recorder. Although one may certainly take mental notes of the particular stories told at a given wake and how they are offered in response to what has previously been said, none of the stories rendered here in transcription were recorded during wakes. It is possible, however, to record these same stories during interviews. In addition, over time my neighbors allowed and in some cases invited me to record our conversations during ceilis either at my home or theirs. This allowed me to document how the same stories I heard at wakes emerged during similar conversations in similar situational contexts.

Because anecdotes told at wakes are a major focus here, my offering transcripts of stories told in performance contexts other than wakes is admittedly a problem. Given that wakes are not the place for tape recorders and that secretive recording is unethical, however, it is a problem that cannot be solved entirely. Wakes and ceilis are similar, complementary social contexts, and here the reader must simply trust my powers of observation when I assert that the structure and rhetorical uses of anecdotes appropriate at wakes but told during ceilis are by and large the same.

Where possible, I have privileged recorded texts that emerged during the conversational give-and-take of ceilis rather than those recorded during more directive one-on-one interviews in which I occasionally asked my interviewees questions such as "What was the one you told about . . . ?" In some cases, the story told at my request during an interview was more elaborate than it had been at a previous social gathering. Still, versions told during recorded ceilis offer the benefit of emerging more naturally in response to a given flow of conversation, and therefore make it easier to identify how a given story is being used rhetorically to assert a point of view.

I should be quick to point out, however, that I do not claim that the stories presented here are transparent examples of exactly what would be said regardless of my being there. The ethnographer inevitably affects what is said in his or her presence. You will notice in transcripts occasions when narrators take brief tangents to inform me of contextual information about location or family relations, for instance, that I might not otherwise know. I also indicate occasions when narrators follow tangents on subjects such as wraiths or emigration patterns, for instance, that they know I have an interest in but that may not have been entertained were I not present. Having said that, one value of interviewing individuals, especially after a wake or ceili, is that they can provide insight into how typical, in their experience, the conversation was at a given event.

In transcribing texts I have attempted to preserve some impression of language as it is spoken. Folklorists, linguistic anthropologists, sociolinguists, and conversation analysts have developed intricate and illuminating systems of icons and orthographic marks for conveying a range of the linguistic and paralinguistic features of communication. In this project, however, I am most interested in broad expressive fidelity and, like Bauman, wary of "loading the printed text with so much formal furniture that it is inaccessible to the reader" (1986:ix). Here, I have limited myself to one paralinguistic icon, a diamond (◊) indicating laughter, which is borrowed from Henry Glassie (1982a).

Henry Glassie's transcription style in his books treating Ballymenone also influences me in using blank space on the page to indicate silence (1975, 1982a, 1982b, 2006).[10] In some places, I transcribe talk from margin to margin when dealing with more prosaic and unadorned informational speech given in response to my direct questions or as contextual introductions to longer narratives that push in places beyond prose toward poetry. For more poetic and performative speech I pay special attention to pauses, volume, and formal devices such as parallelism in order to make decisions about organizing speech on the page. I use line breaks and indentation to indicate pauses or brief respites in momentum that signal completed conceptual elements in the sequential progress of a narrative. Particles such as "so," "and," or "but" also provide the clues for line breaks because they often, though not always, announce transition or a shift in orientation.

Occasionally I signify emphasis in a speaker's voice by shifting from italics to roman script. No words were omitted in transcription, so ellipses indicate occasions when a narrator's voice trails off. Em dashes set apart asides, informational tangents, or other brief interruptions that narrators find necessary. Words framed by square brackets are my brief editorial intrusions, which I keep to a minimum. My conventions for punctuation will be familiar from the way dialogue is rendered in literature. Bear in mind, however, that in spoken language, very few people speak in complete, grammatically correct sentences. The fact that I have not corrected grammar in my transcripts should not reflect badly on narrators but rather reflect that oral discourse is simply a different mode of language than is found in writing.

Approximating local pronunciation in transcribed speech can be a sensitive matter, so I have attempted a balanced approach. When narrators say "'round" or "'em," for example, I do not alter the rhythm of their speech by rendering these as "around" or "them." Nevertheless, wanting to avoid potentially insulting conventions characteristic of "stage Irish" eye dialect, I have used standardized spelling in certain cases regardless of actual pronunciation. In doing so, I render speech as, for example, "my old mother" instead of "me oul' mudder," "sailing off to America" instead of "sailin' off tee Amerikay," or "wild big brute of a beast" instead of "wile big broot of a baste." Employing standardized spelling in certain cases avoids causing narrators to be seen as less sophisticated than they are, but also makes conveying local pronunciation impossible. Still, readers may appreciate the way English is spoken in Aghyaran through colloquial vocabulary and certain regular syntactical constructions that display the lasting influence of both Irish Gaelic and Ulster Scots on the local dialect. In some cases, a standard word like "idiot" is pronounced locally in a way that has already given rise to an easily recognized and nearly equally standardized spelling such as "eejit." In these cases, I privilege the local pronunciation through spelling because it is easily deciphered and unlikely to cause offense.

Finally, although I have strived for fidelity in representing the speech of others, in some cases storytellers have asked me either to obscure their identities or to change the names of certain story characters. In order to honor these wishes, I have used pseudonyms or disguised identifying information in a small number of stories.

~∂

We begin in the next chapter with an overview of the geography, demographics, and history of Aghyaran. Chapter 2, then, provides background information about the people who share and circulate the stories examined here, and anticipates and explains many local references that appear in the texts that follow.

Moving from broad ethnographic context to typical situational contexts for storytelling, chapters 3 and 4 examine recurring social and discursive patterns that are common in ceilis and wakes. As important as broader context is, the intended and potential meanings of a particular story cannot be understood fully except in its specific performance context. For this reason, chapters 3 and 4 tack back and forth between establishing typical patterns for social interaction and considering the social uses of particular stories during specific ceilis and wakes. Likewise, in following chapters the interpretation of scores of transcribed stories is informed by the ethnography of communication and by performance studies, which challenge the division of text and context through holistic analysis of communicative events. In discussions of specific transcripts I provide as much information about their situational performance contexts as is necessary to support the level of interpretation attempted.

In general, conversation at ceilis covers a broader sweep of topics and encourages narratives from a broader range of genres than is common at wakes, but ceilis and wakes have much in common as contexts for storytelling. Particularly when past locals are raised as topics for discussion, wakes continue much of the social work accomplished at ceilis, and vice versa. Unlike ceilis, however, wakes are occasioned by death, and as Lawrence Taylor observes, people in Ireland often use death as an opportunity to imagine community (1989b). By investigating wakes in Aghyaran I intend to complement Taylor's research in Donegal, which is particularly eloquent of the "metaphoric role of death in coming to terms with historical change in the character of the community" (1989a:152). Influenced by Arnold van Gennep's classic formulations about rites of passage, I demonstrate how through both custom and narrative, people in Aghyaran enact community while incorporating the dead into a body of local collective memory.

Chapter 5 begins a shift in attention from common patterns in the situational contexts of wakes and ceilis to the generic contexts of the stories told on these occasions. More than categories for classification, genres are shared sets of communicative conventions for artistic and rhetorical expression. Once identified, locally specific generic expectations provide a window into the dynamics and preoccupations of a given speech community. Being the most popular genre at ceilis and wakes, the local character anecdote deserves special attention. Taking into account a large body of Aghyaran anecdotes, we see how these stories use individuals to delineate a range of personality types that may be understood as a bid to imagine community and define identity.

The local character anecdote is not only popular in Aghyaran but also conceptually central in the local expressive system of both fictional and nonfictional narrative genres that includes historical legends, supernatural legends, personal experience narratives, jokes, and tall tales. As chapter 6 demonstrates, the formal features and rhetorical functions of local character anecdotes overlap, either directly or indirectly, with all other genres popular at wakes and ceilis. Reliant as it may be on other genres, the local character anecdote is most useful for meditating on present identity and recent change. Featuring remarkable individuals while identifying shared concerns, local character anecdotes offer commentary on both shifting and stable relationships between the individual and the group in the local community over time.

Attention paid to local character anecdotes reveals that these stories inevitably typify or epitomize individuals through literary-like strategies of characterization. Given that through anecdotes individuals are transformed into the sorts of characters familiar to us from literature, in chapter 7 I look to scholars such as Roland Barthes for insight into the nature of characters as personas that serve the needs of narrators and audiences. Benefiting from a vocabulary developed by E. M. Forster and David Fishelov to discuss literary characters, this chapter explores the notion of character from an outsider's etic or analytic perspective. Although this perspective illuminates strategies for narrative representations of individuals, it does not necessarily correspond with an insider's emic or local perspective on what a character is.

Transitioning from etic to emic perspectives, chapter 8 defines what people in Aghyaran mean when they use the term "character." A character in the literary sense is broadly conceived as a persona—the more or less psychologically realistic representation of a fictional or actual individual. A character in the local sense, however, is always an actual individual and is usually an eccentric. Not everyone may be considered a character in the local sense, for characters—often pronounced "char-ACT-ers" in Aghyaran—are people who embody traits such as wit or gullibility in the extreme. Further, it is their extremity and often their transgressions that make them most memorable, entertaining, and story-worthy. One goal of chapter 8 is identifying what personality types and traits are considered most worthy of narration in Aghyaran. Although characters in the local sense are most often featured in anecdotes, it is important to note that even if not everyone may be considered a character in life, everyone will eventually be treated as if a character, if only temporarily, through anecdotes told about him or her at his or her wake.

As Linda Ballard observes, characters as defined in local communities throughout Ulster "express themes and ideas highly significant to members of the community." She continues, "They permit the statement of how members of the community view themselves and those around them, and they air attitudes to life past and present" (1986:69). If characters, in the local sense, are used in Aghyaran folklore to typify certain attitudes or ideological stances, then anecdotes told about them are used as tools of rhetoric to assert or contemplate certain points of view of value to narrators and audiences in the midst of communal social interaction.

While chapter 8 delineates a wide range of reoccurring personality types in Aghyaran anecdotes, chapter 9 considers that one individual may exemplify more than one commonly appreciated type of character if the entire cycle of anecdotes told about him or her is taken into consideration. Therefore the notion of character types as rigid categories must be qualified. When dealing with cycles of anecdotes revolving around certain individuals, we will focus more narrowly on personality traits rather than types as the more appropriate narrative constructs for comparison and analysis. Individuals as characterized in entire cycles of anecdotes may be seen as unique combinations of familiar traits that portray a more psychologically realistic individual subjectivity. Still, these characters are not transparent representations of individuals but linguistic and rhetorical constructs answering to the needs of those who shape their memory through narrative. Characters, as represented in Aghyaran anecdotes, give expression to collective concerns whether they are characterized as a certain personality type in one anecdote or come to be understood as a unique combination of personality traits by virtue of personal experience and a more complete cycle of anecdotes told over time.

Chapter 10 reviews the most popular character types and traits in Agh-yaran anecdotes in order to formulate more assertive conclusions about how community and identity are imagined and enacted in Aghyaran. Re-iterated again and again in local character anecdotes are certain contrasts between, for example, iconoclasm and conformity, wit and foolishness, a non-competitive communal ethic of industry and a more aggressive entre-preneurial spirit. Such contrasts allow narrators and audiences to evaluate their own personal behaviors and identities vis-à-vis those of other com-munity members, past and present. Clarifying these contrasts recasts sto-ries commemorating personal character as stories articulating collective concerns in contemporary Aghyaran.

Swapping local character anecdotes at wakes and ceilis is but one form of commemoration in this community and in Northern Irish society as a whole. Indeed, the broad range of commemorative practices evident in Aghyaran and across Northern Ireland indicates that the backward glance is a shared preoccupation of thousands of people. Like many other forms of commemoration, swapping local character anecdotes at Aghyaran wakes and ceilis derives a great deal of its rhetorical impact from contrasting past and present ideological orientations and ways of being. Accordingly, chap-ter 11 considers what is at stake in telling these stories by defining the role this form of storytelling plays within the wider range of commemorative activity popular in Aghyaran.

From Orange Order and Ancient Order of Hibernian parades to grass-roots historic preservation projects, commemoration in Aghyaran estab-lishes competing versions of the past and collective identity. On the whole, different genres of commemorative activity gesture either toward a sense of community based on province-wide sectarian affiliation or toward a sense of community based on shared experience within the local area. Like other forms of commemoration that imagine and enact local community, swapping local character anecdotes at wakes and ceilis allows for at least two crucial accomplishments: coming to terms with modernity by weigh-ing the relative advantages and disadvantages of sweeping socioeconomic change over the past century, and asserting a collective identity based on local affiliations, which potentially moderates the divisive rhetoric and ef-fects of sectarian identity politics. In reviewing the range of commemora-tive practices in Aghyaran, the activities of the Killeter and District His-torical Society deserve special attention because they are essentially an institutionalization of the twin impulses of the anecdote: contrasting past and present for the sake of evaluation, and asserting an anti-sectarian local identity. Paying attention to less-often-publicized commemorative practices such as storytelling and amateur historic preservation not only offers ethnographic insight into the issues that most concern ordinary people every day but also poses a challenge to a conventional media-driven image of Northern Ireland as a society dominated by unthinking intolerance and hopeless conflict.

Figure 1.4. Summer

Figure 1.5. Autumn

Figure 1.6. Winter

Figure 1.7. Spring

2

Aghyaran: A Sense of Place and History

Storytelling in Aghyaran is always informed by and in many ways a response to a changing social, historical, economic, and cultural environment. Understanding the contents of but also the motivations for these stories requires appreciating a certain amount of prior context. In order to situate ourselves in space and time, we need a thumbnail sketch of geography, demographics, and history.

In geographic terms, Aghyaran is a rural parish in the upper Derg River valley. Distinctive on maps as a spit of Northern Ireland protruding from its western border into the Republic of Ireland, this area includes sixty-nine townlands[1] comprising a little over 34,000 acres or about fifty-three square miles. In the east, the fields tend to be large and well drained, supporting mostly dairy herds and "suckler" calves fattened for sale to farmers in areas boasting better land. In the west, the fields tend to be smaller, rockier, and more saturated, supporting some cattle but more sheep. These higher elevations in the west yield naturally to blanket bog, and more recently to state-run forestries. The main roads of the parish stretch like five fingers on either side of the Derg and its tributaries, the Glendergan and Mourne Beg rivers. At the palm lie four churches, all a short distance from each other—St. Bestius Church of Ireland in the village of Killeter, the First Presbyterian church in Magheranageerah townland, and St. Patrick's Catholic chapel and the Methodist church in Aghyaran townland.

The parish is home to roughly 2,500 people, and the most common occupations are in local agriculture and in building trades, the latter taking workers over the border into Donegal, where new construction is flourishing in the "Celtic Tiger" economy.[2] Second to these occupations are those in manufacturing and health care and social work, which often require Aghyaran residents to commute to work in the nearby towns of Castelderg, Sion Mills, Strabane, and Omagh.

While only about 15 percent of Aghyaran residents are full-time farmers, more than half of the population is involved in agriculture, and many of these people piece together several jobs. Typically a farmer with modest land resources may supplement income through occasional carpentry, welding, road maintenance, or other forms of specialized labor and services. Likewise those who are primarily auto mechanics or civil servants may maintain a family farm, raising small numbers of sheep or cattle on a part-time basis. Those who own land but make a full-time living in some nonagricultural occupation typically "let out" or rent their land to full-time farmers who must maximize grazing resources to remain economically viable. Although "farmer" is the preferred term, most Aghyaran farmers are really pastoralists or what Americans would call ranchers. Commercial tillage of grain crops mostly disappeared after World War II because Aghyaran cannot compete with other more productive areas of the British Isles and European Union, areas better suited to modern mechanized agriculture.

Over two-thirds of Aghyaran's population is Roman Catholic, the rest Protestant, with exceptionally high church attendance in all denominations. (For comparison, according to the 2001 census, 44 percent of Northern Ireland's total population is Catholic, and 53 percent is Protestant.) The vast majority of Protestants are either Presbyterian or Anglican, with roughly equal numbers for both denominations. Only about 10 percent of Aghyaran Protestants are Methodists or members of evangelical groups. On the eastern peripheries, the village of Killen is almost entirely Protestant, and Castlederg's population of roughly 2,800 is about 60 percent Catholic and 40 percent Protestant. The further west one travels along the Derg valley, the more Catholic the land ownership, with the exceptions of some Protestant farms on the flat, fertile river banks. The western half of Aghyaran is 90 percent Catholic.

The parish boundaries may at first seem to circumscribe an easily identifiable social unit. Indeed, Aghyaran is bounded on three sides by an international border, and from 1971 to 1994, during the worst of the Troubles, cross-border roads were cratered or blocked by the British army, artificially creating an isolated peninsula and reinforcing a sense of Agh-

Figure 2.1. Scottish blackface ewes, Mullyfa

yaran as a place apart. However, several smuggling routes were never suc-
cessfully closed, and even after twenty-three years of relatively restricted
movement, people maintain strong economic, kinship, and sentimental
ties across townland, parish, county, and country borders. It seems that

county and country borders in particular are not nearly as significant when you live on the margins, compared to when you live in Omagh or Belfast, at the centers.

While Aghyaran as a simultaneously geographical/administrative/ecclesiastical/social unit is conceptually meaningful to locals, I should make clear that this study focuses on less than the entire parish. Over time, I reached out from one person to another through networks of neighborly, friendly, family, and commercial relationships. Of course, such social networks can spin out into space indefinitely, especially in an age of commuting to distant cities for work and entertainment. Eventually, though, it became clear that the core of social networks available to me from my home in Ballymongan townland was spatially situated south of the upper Derg in the southwestern end of the parish. This area, defined more by social interaction than by administrative boundaries, includes Killeter and surrounding townlands and occasionally spills over the border into the sparsely populated Lettercran area of Co. Donegal.

Although comprised of a dozen inhabited townlands, the southwestern end of the parish is sometimes referred to as Ballymongan and Shanaghy (also locally and perhaps originally spelled Shanaghey), two relatively densely populated townlands connected by a low mountain of rough common grazing land. Because the two main roads in this area are named after these two townlands, people have begun to use "Ballymongan" and "Shanaghy" as shorthand referring to several townlands clustered along these roads. Choosing one name for the community connected by these roads to Killeter is a slightly vexed problem that requires acknowledging a little more complexity before committing to an informed simplification.

Whether Catholic or Protestant, most Derg Valley residents identify their home place with a townland name when speaking to someone familiar with local geography. When speaking to an outsider from Belfast, for instance, they usually favor a regional term, saying they come from West Tyrone or the Castlederg area. However, when identifying home and community at a more intimate level than region but at a less intimate level than townland, they choose terms that identify them as either Catholic or Protestant. Of the Presbyterians I came to know, many refer to their home as the Killeter area or the western Derg Valley. Many Anglicans, too, use these terms or their parish's official name, Termonamongan. Due mostly to the demographics of this area south and west of Killeter, however, the majority of the people I came to know best are Catholics. Although aware of differences in the parish north and south of the Derg and differences from east to west along this river valley, most of my Catholic neighbors refer to their home as Aghyaran, after the townland in which their shared place of worship is located.

Recognizing how the majority of people refer to their home in the southwestern end of Tyrone's Derg Valley, I have chosen to use the term Aghyaran as a community label. I do this for the sake of brevity and in order to reflect demographics rather than to proclaim partisanship. Furthermore, when I speak of Aghyaran identity or of Aghyaran as a community, I am depending mostly on the perspectives of those engaged in social networks that cluster in the southwest of this larger area.

If naming this area can be so vexed, it will come as little surprise that the history of this area is equally troubled. A conventional history of Aghyaran would highlight, among other things, local events during the early Christian and medieval periods, the Plantation, the Penal Era, the Famine, and Land League agitation of the late nineteenth century. Bear in mind, however, that history as a chronicle of political transition and conflict is only part of a larger story that encompasses both change and continuity, both internal division and solidarity. For our purposes the local past that is most relevant—the past that informs the majority of commemorative discourse in Aghyaran—is the last eighty to ninety years. This period is within the living memory of the most elderly, the people who as they pass away become the focus of conversation at wakes and ceilis. During this period people in Aghyaran have witnessed Partition, the waxing and waning of the Troubles, and a massive and possibly unprecedented amount of social and economic change.

What follows is not a comprehensive history of the last century in Aghyaran but a synthesis of several oral histories that is chronologically organized and occasionally supplemented or corroborated by written academic histories that offer accurate dates and necessary contextual information. Topics discussed are the events, trends, and themes continually reiterated in a number of local personal accounts, rather than the entire range of topics of interest to academic historians. Selected topics identify the local past that people in Aghyaran, more Catholics than Protestants, find most relevant from their contemporary perspectives. More specifically, the temporal context for these perspectives on the past is the period between the signing of the Good Friday Agreement in 1998 and the cessation of the Provisional Irish Republican Army's armed campaign and the withdrawal of British combat troops in the summers of 2005 and 2007 respectively.

In the midst of wranglings between native clans, ecclesiastic spheres of influence, and Planters and Gaels, Aghyaran has always been border country. Despite being home to relatively few resources and, in places, only marginally productive land, Aghyaran would again become the site of controversy over boundaries during the political upheavals of the early twentieth century.

After the execution of leaders of the failed 1916 Rising in Dublin, nationalist sentiment solidified in Tyrone as elsewhere. During the 1919–1921 Anglo-Irish War, or Irish War of Independence, the Irish Republican Army increased its support and presence in Aghyaran, drilling openly in Ballymongan. Faced with civil war, the British government supplemented the local police force, the Royal Irish Constabulary, with troops fresh from World War I. Known as the Black and Tans because of their makeshift uniforms that combined army trousers and police tunics, this quasi-military force soon gained the animosity of many Aghyaran Catholics who were badly treated by them. For example, John Glackin, a native of Segronan townland, recalls the Black and Tans rounding up Catholic men after Sunday mass and forcing them at gunpoint to dig trenches that severed cross-border roads. Danny Gallen recollects being told about a wake raided by the Black and Tans, who appalled mourners by lifting the corpse to search for weapons. Cissie Dolan, born in Crighdenis, clearly remembers the Black and Tans and Ulster Special Constabulary storming into her home one night in May of 1922. Shouting orders from the Ministry of Home Affairs, they arrested her older brother, Patrick, whom they suspected of republican activity. Stories of midnight executions had traveled throughout the country, and as Patrick was dragged outside, young Cissie waited in terror to hear a single gunshot. Instead Cissie's brother was taken, along with ten others from Aghyaran, to be interned without trial in inhumane conditions on the prison ship *Argenta* in Belfast Lough.[3] As these local dramas unfolded, British and Irish negotiators arrived at fateful compromises, and the new state of Northern Ireland came into being.

Finally accepted on both sides of the Irish Sea in 1922, the Anglo-Irish Treaty divided six northeastern counties of Ireland, including Tyrone, from the other twenty-six and allowed these six counties to remain part of Britain. The Treaty also appointed a Boundary Commission to redraw the border county boundaries that would separate the newly founded British province of Northern Ireland and the Irish Free State, "in accordance with the wishes of the inhabitants, so far as may be compatible with economic and geographic conditions."

The Commission anticipated ceding the majority Catholic parish of Termonamongan, if not more of Tyrone, to the Irish Free State. However, in 1925 the Commission announced that the traditional boundaries of the border counties would remain intact, with the exceptions of a part of East Donegal becoming part of Northern Ireland and part of South Armagh becoming part of the Free State. Infuriated, the Free State representative to the Commission resigned, and the Commission collapsed soon after.

Despite repudiations from the fledgling Free State, the boundary between Northern Ireland and the Free State then reverted to the established, traditional boundaries between the six northeastern counties and the Free State border counties in accordance with the Government of Ireland Act of 1920. This state of affairs left significant, disaffected Catholic minorities within Northern Ireland along the Tyrone, Fermanagh, and Armagh borders and significant, disaffected Protestant minorities within the Free State along the Donegal and Monaghan borders.[4] As the limits of territory were debated and finalized, a new parliament for Northern Ireland got under way outside Belfast at Stormont, where in 1934 Northern Irish Prime Minister James Craig would proclaim, "We are a Protestant parliament and a Protestant state."

In Aghyaran social and commercial relationships between Catholics and Protestants remained largely the same in the aftermath of Partition. Protestants continued to own the largest farms on the most productive land, and they often hired Catholic laborers from Aghyaran and the poorer sections of surrounding Donegal. For the majority of people, more Catholics than Protestants, widespread poverty and few opportunities for amassing capital continued to be the norm.

Less affluent Catholic and Protestant hill farmers in Aghyaran tended to have more in common than they had differences, being of roughly the same class and sharing the same routines of daily existence. Before widespread access to tractors and other labor-saving technology, cultivating oats (known locally as corn), potatoes, flax, and hay for fodder was labor-intensive, requiring a certain amount of interdependence between farmers. Neighbors regularly engaged each other in labor- and equipment-trading arrangements, and many found that "swapping," as it is called, with farmers they were not related to ensured more equitable relationships. This often meant swapping with someone from the "other side of the house" and resulted in greater integration among neighboring Catholic and Protestant hill farmers in Aghyaran, as it did elsewhere in mixed areas of rural Northern Ireland.[5]

In such a context, differences in political opinion and affiliation did not necessarily result in open friction, despite nineteenth-century and earlier precedents for sectarian conflict. Several stories are currently told to describe the period between the world wars as peaceful and ecumenical. For example, in 1936 Protestant farmer Sam Clarke donated building stones to Catholics refurbishing St. Patrick's holy well in Magherakeel. Local Orange and Hibernian bands borrowed each other's instruments and simply substituted green ribbons for orange ones and vice versa on the appropriate days. Catholic and Protestant children attended the same schools until the late 1950s, when the Derry Diocese put increasing pressure on Catholics to send their children to Voluntary or Maintained schools whose curricula were supervised by the local Catholic clergy. Today many middle-aged to elderly people in Aghyaran look back on integrated schooling as a major contributor to greater cross-community solidarity between the world wars.

For nationalists and republicans eager to see the north unified with the south in an independent state, one's immediate Protestant neighbors were not necessarily the enemy, for the most obvious recent aggressors, the Black and Tans, had been sent from Britain. However, genuine rifts in Aghyaran resulted from growing awareness by Catholics of inequities perpetuated by the Stormont parliament, the domination of local politics by members of the Orange Order, and especially the introduction of part-time security forces, known as the B Specials or B men, drawn almost exclusively from the local Protestant population.

In 1970, the B Specials were effectively replaced by the Ulster Defence Regiment, which was in 1992 amalgamated with the Royal Irish Regiment. Despite name changes and shifts in purview between the B Specials, UDR, and RIR, a common complaint Catholics had about all three bodies was that their employment of local Protestants posed a threat to community by putting one neighbor in a position of power over another. The same man you worked with all day in the fields could afterwards don a uniform, strap on a gun, and ask you your name while searching your person or car at a nighttime checkpoint. As divisive as this could be, many Protestants considered it a necessary evil. The B Specials and later locally constituted security forces were a response to the concerns of northern Protestants about further republican violence and the prospect of becoming second-class citizens in a unified, independent Ireland. Privileging Catholics and claiming sovereignty over the six northern counties, the Free State did nothing to allay Protestant fears.

Republican discontent continued in Aghyaran and throughout the six counties, but the IRA had virtually disappeared as an organized force in Northern Ireland by the mid-1920s. Although the IRA reemerged in the 1950s, there were no incidents in Aghyaran associated with the IRA border campaign between 1956 and 1962.

Concerning the local economy, the more robust cattle trade and the higher prices for agricultural produce caused by World War I began to falter in the mid-1920s. By the late 1920s, worldwide economic depression reached Aghyaran, and many remember activity at Killeter Fair on the 21st of each month coming to a near standstill. People in Aghyaran, however, were soon to benefit from political and economic emergencies that crippled their neighbors across the border.

In 1932, Eamon de Valera, a surviving leader of the 1916 Rising and the Taoiseach or Prime Minister of the Irish Free State, withheld funds owed to the British government. Before Partition, a series of Land Acts starting in 1870 allowed Irish tenants to buy the holdings they farmed at drastically reduced prices over extended periods and effectively dismantled the landlord system, a legacy of the seventeenth-century Plantation. The Anglo-Irish Financial Agreements of 1925 and 1926 determined that the Free State would pass along outstanding land annuities to the British Exchequer, but when De Valera's government withheld these annuities the British Parliament imposed duties on Free State livestock and agricultural produce. In response, the Free State imposed tariffs on British goods such as coal and metal, and the ensuing escalation of import tariffs on both sides of the border became known as the Economic War. Already impoverished, farmers in Donegal were in dire straits and resorted to smuggling sheep and cattle into the north with the paid assistance of both Catholics and some Protestants in Aghyaran. Subsistence farmers in Donegal found markets for their stock, and those in Tyrone enjoyed an opportunity to amass capital for the first time.

Those with well-located farms in Aghyaran often vouched for smuggled Free State stock, drove them to fairs in Killeter and Castlederg, and kept a fee for their services. Other young men on the Tyrone side of the border such as John McShane and Alec Byrne became professional smugglers, having an intimate knowledge of local geography and a familiarity with the movements of customs agents and the Royal Ulster Constabulary, successors to the RIC. For men on both sides of the border, smuggling became both a survival tool and a way of life. As Barney Byrne of Grouselodge, Donegal, put it, "Oh, it got to be a habit. Some just wouldn't be happy only you're smuggling."

The Economic War was resolved by 1938, but smuggling continued and expanded with the coming of World War II and shortages of or dramatic price differentials in certain goods on either side of the border. In the Free State, renamed Éire in 1938, tea, rope, high-quality flour, and sulphur-ammonia (used for fertilizer) were either scarce or expensive, but they were readily available and cheaper in the north. Conversely, tobacco, butter, sugar, bicycle parts, and clothing were scarce or expensive in Northern Ireland but readily available and cheaper in Éire. These price and availability differentials contributed to extensive smuggling of goods back and forth across the border by a wider range of men and women, Catholics and Protestants alike.

Many invented ingenious schemes to transport goods. Ballymongan man Johnny McCay, for example, filled his bicycle frame with sprigs (small nails for shoes), pedaled to Pettigo in Donegal, and sold his contraband without incident. War rationing had little initial effect in Aghyaran, for few people had the money to fill their allotments. However, Johnny's wife Cissie and others were wise to invest in tea and sell it to the many small shops that sprang to life just across the border in Lettercran. In addition, although eggs were plentiful locally, they soon became too valuable to eat and, through both smuggling and lawful sale, became one of Aghyaran's most profitable commodities during the war years.

Widespread smuggling declined in the early 1950s with equalization of prices on either side of the border. However, some continued to smuggle cattle and sheep as subsidies were introduced, sometimes higher in the Northern Ireland and sometimes higher in what was by 1948 the Republic of Ireland. One legacy of smuggling is that many subsistence farmers were able to pay off debts and increase their holdings. Others diversified their economic activities or got out of farming altogether, buying a pub or setting up a shop or grocery.

Nevertheless, there was a pervasive belief that smuggling money somehow never went as far nor had the same "luck" as money earned through other means. During fairs in Killeter and Castlederg, much of the cash earned from smuggling never left the pubs. As Alec Byrne, Eamon Dolan, Jim Falls, and Danny Gallen pointed out to me on separate occasions, many Catholics in particular grew up in a cultural and socioeconomic environment that simply did not prepare them for the concept of investment. Furthermore, one enduring lesson of the landlord system was that debt is to be avoided at all costs, so negotiating with banks for a loan was for many Catholics a foreign concept. A man such as James Mulreany, who started with almost nothing in the 1910s but made his fortune buying local cattle and shipping them to Scotland, had to develop a sense for business on his own. He and others like him might be seen as cultural aberrations or perhaps as men ahead of their time. However, the fact that the occasional entrepreneur was not universally admired by his fellows during this and later periods speaks to local ambivalent attitudes toward the ambition and enterprise that sets one apart by advancing one's economic interests and social status. Less evident today, these attitudes were perhaps fostered by centuries of a more communal subsistence culture and a very gradual transition to a cash economy.

By the late 1940s Britain had adopted social welfare policies from which many in Aghyaran benefited, but in retrospect some recognize in these policies a sort of trap. As Jim Falls observed, a man with a family of six and no substantial land holdings earned more on the dole than he would have as a laborer and thus had little incentive to work. Once his children had reached the age of sixteen, however, his dole money was halved, and with little work experience or skills, he had few job prospects at his advanced age. In addition, the introduction of agricultural subsidies now seems to some to be another sort of trap. At their peak in the 1970s, subsidies in conjunction with more mechanized agricultural methods encouraged over-production, but now that subsidies are being gradually phased out, full-time sheep and cattle raising is untenable for all but a few.

Although government subsidies for education, heath care, and some housing removed many burdens from poorer families, at least in the short term, the new welfare state did little to counteract widespread, endemic unemployment in Aghyaran. By 1960, a limited number of relatively well-paying jobs were available in what would become Killeter Forest, a state forestry that expanded to over 12,000 acres. However, while new sources of employment were welcomed, there remained few jobs to be had. Jim Falls remembers working as a farm laborer for the Andrews family in 1965 for £1 a day, earning at most £9 a week if he worked overtime and on Sundays. These were decent wages by the standards of the time, a period when a pound had considerably more buying power and there was little to spend the money on. Electricity was not available in more remote parts of Aghyaran such as Tievenameenta until the mid-1970s. Few had phones or cars, and no one dreamed of spending money on food that could be grown at home in even the smallest garden plot. Still, before minimum wages were standardized in the early 1970s, wages such as Jim's could support a bachelor but not a large family. Women helped make ends meet by selling eggs and fowl, embroidering (known locally as sprigging), and later knitting, but even with the help of social welfare, the income brought in by women alone could not sustain a large household.

For those who could not expect to inherit the family farm—the majority of men and virtually all women—at least temporary emigration to England, Scotland, the United States, Canada, and Australia was the norm. There had been a steady flow of emigrants from Aghyaran since the nineteenth-century Famine, but the number of emigrants fluctuated and the reasons for emigration changed over time. As during the Famine, emigration was a matter of urgency and necessity for many, especially for women, during the depression of the late 1920s that segued into the Economic War of the 1930s. During World War II, many emigrated to England and Scotland to fill jobs vacated by men and women engaged in the war effort. Twenty and thirty years after the war, young people emigrated for at least a few years, not because they were desperately needed in Britain or because they had absolutely no prospects in Aghyaran, but because London and Glasgow promised a certain amount of adventure and freedom.

Although several Aghyaran Catholics and Protestants permanently relocated abroad, many others who left after World War II returned after a few years to buy farms or after several decades to retire. Having seen the wider world, those who returned to Aghyaran brought with them new attitudes toward money and new expectations about living standards. Work in construction, factories, and pubs provided them with disposable incomes

Figure 2.2. Aghyaran women Anna McGlinchey and Anna Gallen tending bar in London, 1965

spent on consumer goods such as cars, clothes, and various luxuries previously beyond their grasp. Due in large part to the return of emigrants, a more thorough acceptance, even embrace, of consumer society was well under way by the late 1960s in Aghyaran.

The late 1960s also witnessed growing, province-wide discontent among Catholics impatient with a Stormont government that had failed to institute promised political reforms. Public housing allotment, gerrymandering of electoral divisions, and voting rights predicated on property ownership all privileged Protestants, who also enjoyed markedly higher percentages of employment. Some liberal Protestants and a new generation of Catholics who had taken advantage of free university education began to organize demonstrations that were inspired, in part, by the example of Martin Luther King Jr. and the civil rights movement in the United States.

The RUC failed to protect civil rights demonstrators from often violent counter-demonstrating loyalists who were convinced that the civil rights movement was little more than a front for republicans. The IRA had in fact been virtually defunct since the failure of their 1956–1962 border campaign. When the RUC used excessive force to contain a demonstration in Derry in 1969, rioting broke out and spread to Belfast. With the situation out of Stormont's control, the British government sent troops to keep the peace. Initially, thousands of Catholics, many of whom had been burned out of their homes by loyalist gangs, welcomed the troops. However, most Catholics soon regarded the army, like the RUC, to be biased in favor of Protestants, and some Catholics felt the need to provide for their own protection by reviving the IRA.

At Stormont's request the British government reintroduced internment in August of 1971. In a massive joint operation between the army and the RUC, 342 Catholics, including several from Aghyaran and Castlederg, were swept up, interrogated, and imprisoned without trial. Internment and the fact that no loyalists were arrested led to a greater sense of disenchantment and alienation among Catholics, more province-wide demonstrations, and in some quarters increased support for the IRA.

As elsewhere, tensions in Aghyaran were high in the aftermath of internment. Danny Gallen recalls driving home late at night from Omagh with two friends when they were stopped in Aghyaran by the police and army at a series of checkpoints. They searched Danny's car and found an ear tag for cattle, a clothesline peg, and a safety pin. The officer in charge maintained that these could be used for making a bomb. After two hours of interrogation and radio contact back and forth with Omagh barracks, they eventually let the three men go. As Danny remembers:

> *I never was so scared in my life, you know. At that time, Ray,*
> *it didn't take much to get you put away, you know. In fact, you*
> *could've been taken for nothing. I remember going home and*
> *going to bed, and boy, in the morning at five o'clock, I could*
> *hear the Saracens [armored personnel carriers] coming up the*
> *road—I was dreaming. You know, you could hear them coming*
> *all the time. Well, they scared the life out of us. They were just*
> *looking for someone.*

Also in 1971, the army used explosives to destroy cross-border roads in an attempt to make movement more difficult for the IRA. The result for many Aghyaran farmers was that they were cut off overnight from livestock they kept on land owned or leased in Donegal and in some cases land owned or leased within Tyrone adjacent to the border. Under cover of darkness, many repeatedly gathered with tractors to fill in massive road craters, only to have their work undone by army explosive teams within a few days. In 1972 eleven men met to fill in a border crossing near the Shanaghy road. Soldiers swarmed in and arrested eight who did not leave earlier or manage to escape the ambush. The army treated the men as political dissidents, and republicans in Castlederg cheered them on as heroes when they were released on bail from the Castlederg RUC station the next day. Charges were eventually dropped, but with their tractors impounded, the farmers among them were severely inconvenienced. In 1974 Danny Gallen was awarded government compensation for his inability to use thirty-one acres of his land on the border due to army cratering, and the court case served as a precedent for compensations to other farmers in Aghyaran and elsewhere along the border.

The repercussions of other major political events across Northern Ireland would be felt in Aghyaran after Bloody Sunday in 1972, when the army opened fire on civil rights demonstrators in Derry, killing thirteen; the resumption of direct rule from Westminster; the introduction of successive, severe anti-terrorism acts; and the 1981 deaths of ten republican hunger strikers in the Maze prison. In this context, previously apathetic Catholics became politically involved, and some either joined or provided support for the IRA, which had gone on the offensive through assassination and bombing campaigns in Northern Ireland and England.

Despite relatively peaceful cross-community relationships from the 1920s until the 1960s, Aghyaran was not immune from the political and sectarian violence that plagued Northern Ireland as a whole.[6] In the mid-1970s, the IRA began a bombing campaign in Castlederg, exchanged fire with the army from the safety of Donegal, robbed the dole from what was then Killeter Orange Hall, and destroyed government property including postal vans and buses. In 1972, a car bomb destroyed several buildings in Killeter and killed a young Catholic woman as she was posting invitations for her wedding.[7] Although no one claimed responsibility, it is widely believed that loyalists, who detonated similar bombs in nearby Pettigo and Ballyshannon, detonated the Killeter bomb in retaliation for the shooting death of a local Protestant and part-time UDR soldier in front of his family nine days before in the village.

Local Catholic deaths during the Troubles included three IRA men who died in two separate incidents in 1973 and 1989 while handling bombs of their own making. Although widely believed not to have been involved with the IRA, two members of Sinn Féin—the political party most closely associated with the IRA—were shot and killed by loyalist paramilitaries in 1977 and 1991. In both cases, there is evidence of collusion between the RUC or army and loyalists. A Catholic and alleged informer from Derry was executed by the IRA and left on an Aghyaran border road in 1986, as were two other Belfast Catholics and alleged informers in separate incidents in 1993.

Whether targeted by local IRA volunteers or those from other areas, at least eighteen Protestant civilians, RUC officers and reservists, and UDR soldiers from the Aghyaran and Castlederg area were killed by gunfire or bombs between 1972 and 1991. The majority of these victims were members of the Castlederg First Presbyterian Church, and the majority of these deaths occurred during the 1980s as part of an IRA assassination campaign on the West Tyrone border. This campaign has had a devastating and lasting effect on Catholic-Protestant relations in Castlederg in particular (see McKay 2000:207–208).

Oral historical accounts of the recent local past revolve in large part around the issues of modernity and community. Of great concern in Aghyaran are, first, the massive and possibly unprecedented amount of social and economic change wrought during the last century and, second, the competing impulses toward neighborliness and toward sectarian division in the midst of the Troubles of the 1920s and those of the last thirty years.

Political division and violence in particular are not topics of conversation in mixed Catholic-Protestant company. Since the late 1980s, however, there have been several efforts to increase cross-community contact and to ameliorate division through organizations such as the Killeter and District Historical Society and the MourneDerg Partnership, and through annual public events such as local talent shows, Killeter Fair, and Killeter Show. One common subtext to these organizations and events has been a focus on shared concerns and an appeal to local as opposed to sectarian identity. Even if overt talk of divisive politics is to be avoided, such grassroots efforts allow for gestures toward reconciliation. Even if overt talk of the history of local violence is to be avoided, the social and economic changes of the last eighty to ninety years are a shared experience. The changes associated with modernity are often discussed in mixed company at ceilis and especially at wakes. By focusing attention on a life that spanned the better part of a century, storytelling at wakes for the elderly encourages meditation on the contrast between past and present ways of life.

Whether accomplished through formal acts of preservation by the Killeter and District Historical Society or through informal conversation at ceilis and wakes, commemoration of the local past is not a form of uncritical nostalgia (Cashman 2006). As Day Marshall observed, "There have been terrible changes this last seventy, eighty years. We're spoiled with machines now." Born in 1923, Alec Byrne refuses to romanticize the poverty of his youth but recognizes that the gradual influx of capital increased competition to the detriment of a certain amount of neighborliness. "Oh, people were far friendlier when they had nothing." His general impression is of overwhelming change for everyone, not all of it favorable.

> *The changes, Ray, around here this last fifty years and more,*
> *I just couldn't explain it to you. Oh, you could go all day, all*
> *night, through all them changes. It's hard to believe what we've*
> *seen. If they change as much in the next fifty years, well, God*
> *help us. A lot of things were for the better and a lot of things*
> *were for the worse.*

Known for his extensive repertoire of jokes, anecdotes, and songs, Patrick McElhill recited at a singing session at my house a well-known poem composed by Drumquin poet Charlie Kearney, probably in the late 1980s. The poem encapsulates what I found to be the general mood of people's evaluations of social and economic change over the last century.

> *I was sitting at the table through the window gazing out,*
> *And I thought of all the changes that has lately come about.*
> *And I thought about the old folk and what they'd have to say*
> *If they seen us sitting idle in the middle of the day.*
>
> *For the old man's life was slavery, a living was hard to get,*
> *And I don't think they would change it if they had been living yet.*
> *Do you mind the way they grumbled, and they said it was a curse*
> *When they saw the tractors plowing. They'd far rather have the horse.*

They said that it'd ruin the land, it made it far too tight.
Sure I sometimes think that those old fellows could be right.
For the corn had all stopped growing, they filled the soil with lime.
Now you hear no one talking on the good old harvest time.

For the soil it grows great docks [weeds] and rushes, too, galore,
And the cattle takes diseases now that they never had before.
The food that we are eating, we hardly know its name.
It comes in plastic packages from China, France or Spain.

But man, but we were healthy when they made the good kale broth,
And they tipped the pot of praities [potatoes] on the meal bag tablecloth.
They say that we are all spoiled now, we're living far too soft.
Sure we're running to the doctor if we only sneeze or cough.

We've seen a lot of changes, there's no penny saving now.
What used to buy the farm, wouldn't buy us the cow.
And how the old men wonder when this spending spree will stop.
They say it takes a fortune every time you go to shop.

But no matter what the changes, the farmer must go on.
He's got to work the seven days, and he rises with the dawn.
No matter how he struggles, more riches for to gain,
The sons that come behind him will have to do the same.

Despite the many changes, there remains a certain continuity in general attitudes toward centralized authority, attitudes fostered by the experience of living on the border. After Partition, the state sought to extend its control over border areas such as Aghyaran by expanding bureaucracy and surveillance and by cracking down on activities such as smuggling and illicit distillation. Today, however, smugglers and poteen makers (moonshiners) speak openly of their exploits to audiences known to them, and their reminiscences and the occasional smuggling ballad are regularly published in *Aghyaran*. Not only do attitudes that allow people to rationalize smuggling as less than criminal survive; smuggling itself continues.

As long as there is a border, there will always be price differentials. Today as markets fluctuate and opportunities arise, a handful of inveterate smugglers deal in everything from diesel and heating oil to cigarettes, strawberries, and eels. Interestingly, though, contemporary smugglers tell me that since fewer customs agents were posted after the reemergence of the Troubles in the late 1960s, smuggling is simply neither as much of a challenge nor as much fun as it had been. These younger men share with their fathers' generation a sense that smuggling was and is not only an economic activity but fundamentally a contest of wits. Whereas smuggling and stories told about smugglers' exploits used to be, in part, a way to express that "we may be poor but we are intelligent," today in the midst of greater prosperity smuggling remains an assertion of autonomy from centralized authority, whether British or Irish.

In addition to the traditions of smuggling and poteen distillation, there are many other instances of people on the Tyrone border, Catholic and Protestant alike, either completely ignoring external authority or selectively complying with the law. I recall asking a Donegal native who had moved to Aghyaran what differences between this border community and his homeplace were most striking in his first impressions. He asked me if I had noticed anything peculiar about local attitudes to the law. I was not sure what he was driving at until he offered as illustration an account of his attempt after moving to the parish to obtain the supposedly necessary licenses for his television and his dog. His efforts were in good faith, but no one at the post office in Killeter could supply him with the proper forms. For him, the experience was instructive of a local casual attitude toward the law and in some cases authority in general. He also mentioned the common practices of "doing the double"—collecting unemployment benefits while getting paid in cash for unrecorded work—and "doing the quadruple"—doing it on both sides of the border (cf. Wilson 1998). As he characterized the situation, some and perhaps many people in Aghyaran do not understand lawful obedience in terms of civic obligation, much less morality. Many pick and choose which laws they consider reasonable. On the margins, in border country, much of the bureaucracy imposed from the centers of power is perhaps consciously or unconsciously understood to be arbitrary, even transitory. Moreover, if the government hands out something for free or leaves loopholes in its regulations, there is no shame in taking advantage. As we will see, an appreciation of wit, a sense of independence, and an ambivalence toward outside authority continually reemerge in a range of Aghyaran folklore.

Figure 2.3. X marks the border for air surveillance and checkpoints, 1998

Figure 2.4. Cross-border road, improved and unrestricted, 2007

3

Ceilis as Storytelling Contexts

In Aghyaran, people are more likely to tell stories in certain situational contexts, but even in those contexts stories are not usually planned for, much less scripted, in the way that homilies are at masses. Given the right occasion, conditions, and moods of individuals present, storytelling is the result of a progression in sociability. When entertainment is the goal or when sustained reflection on a given proposition is desired, storytelling is of a piece with the discourse that leads up to and surrounds it. As a form of speech, the story can sum up or challenge a proposition that emerges in conversation. Full of rhetorical potential, the story is often pivotal in peoples' invitations to social accord; the story is central in appeals made for a sense of collectivity in small groups.

The best ethnographic description in an Irish context of the progression from conversation to storytelling and beyond is found in Henry Glassie's description of ceilis in his second and third chapters of *Passing the Time in Ballymenone*, "Silence, Speech, Story, Song" and "Ceili at Flanagans'." Glassie raises issues that will be addressed later, such as the utilities of different storytelling genres. For now, I cannot improve on his characterizations of storytelling as a possibility in the flow of discourse and of the story as a bid for meaning among people socializing. His observations apply equally well in the case of Aghyaran.

> The shape of Ballymenone's concept of sound can be imagined as a terraced sequence leading upward from silence to music and from separation to social accord. Silence, talk, chat, crack, story, poetry, song, music: with each step, entertainment increases, sound becomes more beautiful, and the intention of the creator of sound becomes more clearly to please the listener. Individual creations and

> whole events feel as though they shift from plateau to plateau along
> a flight of steps that lift people simultaneously toward aesthetic per-
> fection and social union. Central and crucial to this rising sequence
> is the story. (1982:37)

Conversation primes the pump for storytelling, and conversation is possible in a range of contexts from chance meetings in public to regular or
planned social occasions in more intimate settings. Conversation brings
to mind ideas worthy of further investigation; it forges or re-establishes
relationships of exchange between people willing to take responsibility for
more complicated narratives through performance.

Although conversation is natural in a wide range of social situations
and is the prerequisite for storytelling, I should note that not every conversational context is conducive to storytelling. For instance, stopping
off at the grocery or hardware store for supplies during the day, a person
customarily exchanges a few remarks with store clerks and customers
about the weather or local events. Yet the purpose of stopping is to gather
materials to continue work, so the interaction remains brief and may be
interrupted by others also in the process of gathering what they need to
remain productive. In most conversational contexts that allow for storytelling, there are a limited number of people interacting and a shared
notion that they are at least temporarily at rest. The storytelling contexts
most available to me were predominantly but not exclusively male domains, so I will focus on these. As such, I should reiterate that this exploration of Aghyaran storytelling is heavily weighted primarily toward
male expressive traditions, verbal skills, and contemplative concerns. In
terms of ethnography, this acknowledgment should also serve to qualify
observations and conclusions about life in Aghyaran as being viewed from
a specific perspective.

Male work situations such as bailing silage, winning turf, and shearing
sheep require individual attention and coordination of efforts, but workers
often take breaks for tea in which conversation and storytelling is possible.
Some forms of work require little concentration, so men digging a grave, for
instance, may entertain each other with stories. More often, storytelling is
found in the places and at the times set aside for leisure. One common site
has been the pub after work, on Sundays, and on holidays, but such public
space allows fewer opportunities for more intimate dialogue. In addition,
even in rural areas televisions have encroached on the social interaction of

the public house, drawing eyes, numbing minds, and relieving people of the responsibility to entertain themselves.

Many storytelling contexts are the result of unique and rarely repeated circumstances. For instance, one of the richest storytelling contexts I experienced was waiting night after night with fellow Ballymongan-Shanaghy mummers for absent troupe members. Although nightly rendezvous times and places were agreed upon during our mumming season in mid-December of 1998 through early January of 1999, up to a dozen mummers regularly sat together drinking tea and smoking for at least an hour before the group fully assembled. Mummers were already energized and in a sociable mood. Anticipating a long night of public performance, and perhaps impatient to begin, we allowed discussion about the weather, news, and previous mumming escapades to lead quickly into a fast-paced exchange of jokes and anecdotes. Storytelling and occasionally singing continued in the van between performances at various homes and pubs, and well into the next day at whichever pub saw the conclusion of our night's work.

During late December of 1998 and early January of 1999, a winter storm knocked out the electricity in most of the western Derg Valley, thus recreating what is now a less frequent situation. Huddled around grates and cookers for light and warmth, people in search of entertainment on long nights had no choice but to converse and tell stories. Middle-aged parents teased their often bored teenage sons and daughters that they were lost without television and radio. Several of my elderly neighbors remarked how socializing had returned to the pattern of their youth—the majority of people returned to ceiliing.

Visiting certain houses at night for the entertainment of tea, conversation, and occasionally singing and storytelling is known in Aghyaran as "ceiliing" or occasionally as "raking," as it is called farther west in Donegal. Ceiliing is not exclusive to, but is more regular during, the darker and colder months from October through February. Ceiliing is often said to be almost a thing of the past. As Cissie Dolan, my most senior neighbor, remarked, "We were sitting by the fire telling stories, singing songs, days gone by. There was nothing else to pass the time. There wasn't television. You see, radio and television killed all that." On another occasion, Cissie's near contemporary Mary Alice Mongan echoed her, saying, "Oh aye, television has cut down on the raking." Her son, Sean, expanded on the point: "Nobody goes anywhere now unless they're looking for something, you know, that sort of a thing. Back in the time of John McHugh and Francie [McHugh] and them, they would have come in for the craic, a night's chat and a couple of drinks."

In addition to the isolating effects of television, car ownership—virtually universal since the 1980s—has played a major role in the decline of ceiliing. Mobility allows people in search of entertainment to bowl in Killeter Hall, dance at the Blacktown Arms, play cards or bingo at the Aghyaran GAA center, or travel farther afield to Ballybofey, Letterkenny, Omagh, Strabane, or Derry for movies, discos, and shopping. Yet despite undeniable change, ceiliing and storytelling are not entirely things of the past. People's impressions that they are lost customs may be exaggerated to convey what many consider—and what very well may be—an unprecedented amount of social and economic change in such a short period since the early twentieth century.

Ceiliing is not dead. In Ballymongan, Tommy Mongan's house has long been a ceili house, as was John Mongan's house through the beginning of my fieldwork. Also in Ballymongan, Jamie Barclay regularly hosts ceiliers on certain nights, as does James Hegarty not far away in Magherakeel. A little further east toward Killeter, Robert Cunningham hosts a number of neighboring farmers on Sunday nights. In most of these houses certain ceiliers are expected on certain nights. What is common about these ceili houses is that the hosts and many of the regular guests are middle-aged to elderly bachelors.

Ceiliing is largely but not entirely an activity for single men. Art and Susan Gallagher in Golandun Dolan often host ceiliers, as do their near neighbors, Michael, PJ, Marian, Anne, and Kathleen Gallen, the grown children of Sarah Jane Gallen. Living in John McHugh's old house, which had long been a draw for ceiliers, Lorraine and I had nighttime visitors, men and women, between two and four times a week during the winter months. When asked about the custom of ceiliing, most of my middle-aged to elderly neighbors recalled that the two most hospitable and most frequented ceili houses of the previous generation were hosted by women, Cassie O'Donnell and Bella Mongan. The ceili houses mentioned are not the only ones in the parish, but the ones in the social circles most available to me.[1]

Although ceiliing continues, Cissie Dolan, Mary Alice Mongan, and Sean Mongan are correct in noting that it has diminished and altered to an extent, and that this is due in part to television. Danny Gallen often poured over Ordnance Survey maps of the parish with me, offering anecdotes and local legends brought to mind by place-names, natural features, and the rectangular outlines representing households and, for him, family histories. The last thing that could be said about each rectangle was whether it was a "television house" or not. For him, when it came to socializing, there were two types of people—television people and ceiliers—and it was clear whose company he preferred.

I found myself distracted during nightly conversations in households where the television remained on, sometimes muted and sometimes not. However, I was also surprised to find that the television can have a place, like an extra guest, deaf and unresponsive to his audience but nonetheless bearing news from farther afield. In a few ceili houses, the ticking away of minutes and hours was entirely irrelevant until the mantel clock chimes reminded us that it was time for the nightly news. After the news, the television was switched off or muted again, and conversation was reinvigorated by the wranglings at Stormont, the latest political scandal from the White House, or the collapse of the Asian and Russian pork markets. Occasionally discussion of province-wide and global issues would strike a local chord, leading ceiliers to recount the reactions of past locals to adversity, to retell the stories about past neighbors that provide comment on human nature and the nature of community.

Television is not always the enemy of storytelling. Once after a Saturday night mass, James Hegarty, ever generous and open-handed, fed me and Neil McElhill a meal of sausages, freshly baked bread, butter, sweets, and tea. Afterwards, Neil seemed tired when I pressed him, perhaps more than I should have, to describe changes in farming practices during his lifetime. Having never farmed I failed to register all of his explanations. My questions were confused, and understanding my trouble, James quietly moved across the room to remove the front of a drawer in his dresser. Behind the drawer front sat a VCR, and into it he fed a video of men near Maghera, Co. Derry, sowing and harvesting oats with equipment from the 1950s. All became clear. I needed the visual demonstration. Watching was not a silent, isolated activity, for throughout Neil lit up in recognition of the tools of his youth. "Hu-hoh!" was his response when the grubber appeared; "There's the boyo!" at the sight of the rake harrow. During the

Figure 3.1. Jamie Barclay and James Patrick Collins

slower sections of the video, Neil became animated, telling me of the time a Ballymongan man, John "Caper" O'Donnell, died from a threshing accident, and reminiscing about the feats of great plowmen sixty years before. Soon our ceili expanded with newcomers. Lessons learned, I suppressed my urge to gather information and eased back into my chair. Chat rolled on past midnight.

One clear Friday evening in July, I walked to Jamie Barclay's house. Jamie usually hosts ceiliers on Friday nights, so I knew I stood a good chance of meeting his Ballymongan neighbors for several hours of chat. Judging from past experience, that night's ceili at Jamie's seemed fairly typical of a good, lively, and well-appreciated ceili and can stand for us as a model.

I met with Mickey Byrne on my way to Jamie's, and together we arrived around nine o'clock to find James Patrick Collins already there. James Patrick and Jamie had become friends while working together in Killeter Forest, and although James Patrick lives on the northern side of the Derg, he has a car and makes a point of ceiliing with Jamie twice a month. Within the hour, Barney McGrath and Tommy Mongan arrived separately. Both opened the front door and walked straight into the sitting room without knocking. Those of us already seated greeted them with "How's Barney" or "How's Tommy?" and, in a teasing mode, something along the lines of "Ah God, there goes any chance of a civil conversation now."

Raffle ticket sellers, insurance salesmen, and those who consider themselves to be authority figures knock. Friends and neighbors waste no time coming in to take their seats. The sitting room or kitchen may be technically inside the home, under the same roof as private bedrooms, but in every house—whether modern bungalow or traditional room and kitchen—some room remains communal unrestricted space for those already known by the host. When I first arrived in Aghyaran, I was unable to entirely adopt local etiquette for entering a house, and I somehow settled on the compromise of knocking while walking through doors. At Tommy Mongan's one night early in my initial fieldwork, my confused entry ritual elicited hoots of laughter, and even before the assembled company could see me, one ceilier called out: "There's Ray now!" At the ceili at Jamie's, almost two years after meeting those gathered, I had a better grasp of the largely unspoken rules of behavior and speech at such gatherings.

Certainly my presence, my additions to the conversation, and my company's knowledge of my interests both affected and effected what was said that night. Unlike in the beginning of my research, however, I was relaxed about letting the evening unfold without asking premeditated questions, searching to fill gaps in my knowledge about the local community, or awkwardly and perhaps selfishly baiting people to narrate stories so that I could reassure myself that there are Märchen or memorates or what have you to document. This ceili was not a directed group interview in an "induced natural context," in Kenny Goldstein's phrase. It was a social occasion that I both observed and took part in. I had no tape recorder but made mental notes at the time and wrote down observations and select, short quotations immediately afterward. Acknowledging my influence on the night, I would characterize the ceili as what Goldstein termed a "near-natural context" (1964:87ff.).

When the sixth ceilier arrived, Jamie quickly gave up his seat and brought in a wooden chair from the kitchen for himself. With all assembled, we had taken up Jamie's comfortable seats in his stuffed, upholstered settee and two matching arm chairs. Jamie's sacrifice caused me to remember and repeat an anecdote from my own family lore. One evening my grandfather returned home to find all the seats in his house occupied by his six children and their debris. Exasperated, he scratched his head and turned to my grandmother, saying, "Well Maw, looks like we've screwed ourselves out of a place to sit." My short bid for humor complete, I had made a contribution. All chuckled, some genuinely and others politely, but none as hard as Jamie who usually gives his guests the benefit of the doubt, laughing generously whether attempted comedy is achieved or not. Talk shifted thematically to the modest size of families today in Aghyaran. Not counting myself, the ages in the room ranged from late fifties to mid-seventies, and although only one other man in the room was married, most grew up in families of six or more children.

Before the room had filled, talk about the recent decline of the weather and comparisons of Irish and American weather and geography had sustained us—Jamie, Mickey, James Patrick, and me. To think country people have nothing better to discuss than the weather would be uncharitable, for in a farming community weather talk is not simply idle chat. The state of the weather is just as important for farmers as changing public opinion is for politicians or fluctuations in the stock market are for brokers. The topic was our warm-up for other topics to come. After Tommy and Barney arrived, and after chat about family sizes ran its course, the topic of constant unseasonable rain resumed so that the two late-comers could weigh in on the subject. I took the opportunity to look around the room again, refreshing my memory of the scene.

Although I did not think to inquire, Jamie had probably had his sitting room redecorated within the previous five years. On one wall is the mantel and small fireplace, fueled with local, machine-cut turf. No longer sites for cooking, most open hearths in the area have been closed in to accommodate a metal cooker or, as at Jamie's, an abbreviated, decorative metal opening that houses a smaller elevated fire in a metal grate. Across Jamie's mantel are symmetrically arranged ceramic and brass ornaments. Above the mantel hangs a framed print of Da Vinci's *Last Supper,* reinterpreted in broader brush strokes and bolder, more vivid colors. Above the door to the left of the mantel is a likeness of Pope John Paul II reproduced on a reflective metallic background, and above the door to the right of the mantel is a holy picture, the Sacred Heart of Jesus. The fire itself competes for visual distraction with the recent-model television, glowing but set to mute, in a corner cabinet on the opposite wall. These other walls are decorated with additional holy pictures and family photos: Jamie's five brothers in color, his five sisters in color, his parents in black and white. All four walls are papered with navy and beige vertical stripes from the floor to a six-inch-wide stylized border about three feet up, and from the border to the ceiling with beige paper punctuated with navy fleurs-de-lis. These details in addition to the large floral-print carpet, dark wooden accents polished to a shine, and general plushness of curtains and upholstery give an overall impression of newfound prosperity and communicate a significant, lasting influence of Victorian aesthetics.

I brought my attention back to the ceiliers as weather talk again found its conclusion. Soon, one ceilier contributed news: an account of his encounter that day with a local eccentric and fellow bachelor who was not present at our ceili. Others recounted recent meetings with the man, which added to the group characterization of him as an eccentric, but he soon proved too easy a target. Quickly, counterevidence of the man's finer qualities was produced. In part, this impulse to strike a balance fit with the unspoken ethic in social conversation of avoiding overt criticism of neighbors, the people one sees and must deal with on a daily basis (cf. Glassie 1982:41).

In addition, chat about the eccentric bachelor tapered quickly, perhaps, because one of the ceiliers is related to him. Slight tension seemed to hang in the air during a short silence after the counterbalancing flow of praise. Would it be enough to neutralize any implied criticisms? Would it be enough to appease the eccentric's relative if he had been offended? Although the topic of conversation could easily have switched at that point, the eccentric's relative concluded the silence with a story about the man in question and his failures at courting a particular younger woman. Appropriate in the small circle of ceiliers, the anecdote is not appropriate in a wider circle of potential readers, but the utility of the story that night is relevant. Whereas previous chat about the eccentric came amid quick changes in turn-taking, the failed courtship story went uninterrupted, the responsibility entirely of its narrator, the eccentric's relative. He implied that the story was "safe" because the eccentric had told it about himself. As he was seen to be properly self-effacing, the eccentric's modesty and integrity were reasserted. The story also put us ceiliers at ease by demonstrating that some entertainment at the eccentric's expense was acceptable to his kinsman. Having reestablished social accord, the story had performed important, pragmatic social work by reaffirming the bonds of those gathered to pass the night together.

The air was cleared and local bachelors remained an acceptable topic for discussion. Given the opportunity, Tommy reported that he had seen another absent local bachelor in the company of an attractive young woman. Bachelors such as Tommy often make comments and tell stories that highlight their single status. For instance, choosing fiction and humor to avoid offense, Mickey has a habit of claiming "the Missus" will not let him out of the house when, in fact, he wants to decline an invitation to a given event. Other older single men fabricate news about fellow bachelors involved in scandalous affairs. Unlike gossip, such fabrications are not intended ultimately to be believed. Moves like these allow bachelors to poke fun at themselves, while using humor to call into question others' perceptions of them as marginal, undesirable, or disadvantaged.

In claiming to have seen the bachelor and woman together, Tommy had switched tacks from storytelling to "codding." A "cod," in local terminology, is a bid to fool listeners into believing an exaggeration of the truth or a pure fabrication.[2] Stories have the potential to support or cinch a proposition in the flow of discourse, defining a moment in the progression of sociability. Cods offer a representation of events that reopens the floor to debate. Although lacking the veracity of news, cods are more like news in their elastic form and structure than they are like stories, and cods may be no longer than one sentence: "I saw X with Y." Codding is an invitation for a contest of wits and verbal sparring, for at its base is a challenge. As a piece of entertaining gossip, the cod is tempting to believe, but at the same time a trap is set. If the information is a cod, rather than news, acknowledging your belief will demonstrate your gullibility. The man doing the codding will become the victor, and your gullibility will then become the source of entertainment.[3]

In making his claim, Tommy pitched his voice to Mickey, and it is well known to those present that Tommy and Mickey have a friendly but competitive relationship of trying to cod each other. James Patrick and I sat next to Tommy on the settee, and Tommy jabbed us with his elbows to reiterate that he had thrown down the glove. Even without Tommy's signals, ceiliers know to be guarded about entertaining news that seems too good to be true, and Ballymongan men in particular have a reputation in Aghyaran for codding.

At first, Mickey would not be drawn into discussion of Tommy's sighting. As Tommy added more detail, ceiliers offered mock interest in or acceptance of Tommy's account: "Man dear," "Boys a boys," "Oh, he's a boyo." Some winked to ensure that others were aware of their complicity. Mickey countered by claiming, with a straight face, to have seen the two together. We waited to see if Tommy was gullible enough to believe that Mickey was gullible enough to believe the original cod. Tommy ignored Mickey's counterbid and upped the ante by claiming to have seen the bachelor with a second woman. "Oh aye, I saw him with that one, too," Mickey assured everyone. As at the end of a tall tale when the bounds of believability have been stretched to their limits and the story is discovered to be fiction, Tommy had pushed his codding to the point where disbelief could no longer be suspended and the codding was about to collapse under its own weight. Wishing to prolong the fun, Barney asked Mickey, "Was that the blonde one?" Mickey let out a quiet sigh, then gathered himself up and claimed the floor:

> *Well . . . I don't know, now, if she's a blonde, but she could be very ready making herself a blonde. They're all blondes these days, you know, with the bottle. It'd nearly be a holiday to see a black haired one now.*

Everyone laughed genuinely, and a few congratulated him with "Good man" and "That's a good one, now." Contributing to the night's entertainment, Tommy had had his fun at Mickey's expense, and, challenged from many sides, Mickey rose to the occasion to defuse the situation. Mickey's quip submerged implicit competition in shared laughter and cleared the way for new topics of conversation. Tommy turned his attention to Jamie by wondering aloud to the room would we ever get tea in a house such as this. Jamie laughed . . . and did nothing.

Tea is to be expected at a ceili, usually around eleven o'clock or, regardless of when it arrives, at least a half-hour before people feel comfortable making the first motions to leave. On a long winter night, tea may be offered early and late. Tommy's jab that night came a bit early and too directly to be taken as a serious request for tea, but it laid a foundation for teasing that would reoccur through the rest of the night.

Soon after Tommy's jab, there was a knock at the window. A young boy of about seven was sobbing, frightened by some cattle he believed were chasing him: "It was two black ones and two ginger ones after me, and they make a right team!" Amused but sympathetic, Jamie drove the boy home a short distance up the hill.

When Jamie returned, Mickey complained to the room, for Jamie's benefit, that he had just searched the cupboards and found no bread. Others chimed in, wondering out loud if we should take the ceili somewhere more hospitable. Jamie laughed harder and again did nothing. For the rest of the night, even after the appropriate time for tea, each time the hint for tea reemerged, Jamie laughed and "got his own back" by delaying it for another fifteen minutes.

Conversation wandered for a while among a range of topics: models of chainsaws and their varying merits, cars owned and the crafty deals made to sell them, a rise in the number of tourists seen in the area, and the recent decline of local emigration. Perhaps in part for my benefit, we lingered on the topic of emigration. Mickey and Barney took turns informing me how locals in the early 1900s, their relations, would walk to Derry for the boat to America or elsewhere. The night before leaving there would be a party for them, called a convoy, that served as a living wake, for it was unlikely an emigrant traveling as far as New York or San Francisco would ever return. They had told me the information before, but I was happy to fulfill my role as student, which facilitated their rehearsing for me and perhaps for themselves a chapter in local history, an aspect of local identity.

As it did on other nights, the topic might have sparked anecdotes about specific emigrants, historical tales of local oppression and deprivation, or personal experience narratives of time spent working abroad. However, the nightly news glowed in the corner, broadcasting the image of a young girl missing and thought to have been abducted in England. Although all eyes turned to the screen, no one reached to turn up the volume. Everyone recognized her face from previous newscasts, and we provided our own editorial commentary. "What sort of lunatic . . . ?" "Who could do such'n a thing?" "What the parents must be going through I can't imagine."

The images changed, but with abduction and uncertainty about the fate of loved ones still on the mind, one ceilier proposed a related moral question:

And then, *what about all those people the IRA killed and wouldn't let their families know where they are? I mean how could you justify that, like? Oh you just couldn't know, now. No you just couldn't know.*

There was no effort made to take on the morality of republican violence as a topic for debate. Ceilis are made of equals, so ceiliers may raise problems but do not seek to impose conclusions upon each other (cf. Glassie 1982a:79). The question called only for shared contemplation of the unkindness of allowing bereaved families to live on in ignorance. Offered a topic such as the justness of armed struggle in the midst of a fledgling peace process, ceiliers may find a way not to attack the problem head-on. The potential for disagreement is significant, too threatening in a context where men take every opportunity to assert agreement and oneness. All could agree that not being able to bury a loved one is a "hateful" situation and that the dead, regardless of their actions in life, should be afforded more dignity.

James Patrick and Jamie remembered a time in 1986 when a man was found executed by the IRA in Killeter Forest on the Tulnashane border. Fr. McGinn had been called out to administer to the body and was shaken by the experience. It seems the man was an informer from Belfast who had been taken to Pettigo in Donegal for interrogation, marched barefoot back across the border, and shot in the back of the head, left for the RUC to take care of. Whether or not the man deserved death was not discussed, but there was a shared sense of pity given the way he was abandoned in the wilderness, "the poor creature."

Coincidentally, the BBC kept pace with the turn of our conversation toward politics by showing images of British Army engineers erecting a barricade to keep the Orangemen at Drumcree from marching down the Catholic Garvaghy Road. "It's that time of year again," muttered one. In file footage that panned a line of Orangemen in their dark suits and bowlers, the sun peeked out and flashed off of ceremonial cutlasses and sash badges. Harold Gracie stood aloft, bellowing into a microphone to his cheering supporters, unaware of the fact that in our presence he would remain mute. The Twelfth was less than a week away.

Based on his experience working in London, one ceilier observed that the average Englishman was not a bad sort. Another who had spent time working in England agreed. The first man ventured another opinion that the common English foot soldier in Ireland was an innocent forced into an impossible situation, just doing a job. The impulse toward agreement seemed to elicit general affirmation, but this characterization of the English soldier was slightly risky in a room of men representing a cross section of persuasions from apolitical to nationalist to republican. Striving again for a sense of balance, yet another ceilier mentioned the Ulster Defence Regiment and before them the B Specials as the worst of the lot that the BBC, unionists, and British government collectively refer to with the non-neutral term "security forces."

Although B Specials, a fixture of post-Partition Northern Ireland, were later replaced by the UDR, who were recently amalgamated with the Royal Irish Regiment, these groups are often alluded to interchangeably, ahistorically in discussion. The conceptual link between the three bodies is their threat to local community. Their ranks were and are filled almost exclusively with Protestants, but more important to the ceiliers is the fact that these part-time and later full-time soldiers, armed and authorized to search and interrogate at will, were and are locals, neighbors, and co-workers.

Most hateful thing about them was they were your neighbors.
They could have been working with you all day, lifting praities
[potatoes] maybe, then stop you at night with their red torches
and guns and ask you your name. Your name *when they know*
damn well.

Jamie disappeared into the kitchen to butter scones and boil water for tea. Perhaps seeking to align himself with the present course of conversation, the man who had excused the English foot soldiers as innocents asked Mickey for a story he knew him to have. "Mickey, what was that one you told about the priest and the B men?" Mickey fumbled for a bit, protesting that the story was well known. Pressed further, he told a halting version of the story; throughout he deferred to the memories of men, some dead, from whom he had heard the story, apologizing that they could have told it better. Told in many versions, the story is one that we will have occasion to revisit in more detail in chapter 7, but the essential details of the plot are relevant here. One night local members of the B men stop an Aghyaran Catholic priest, and they are less than respectful to him. Before letting the priest pass, one of the B men asks him in a patronizing tone if he will be at the Castlederg Fair later in the week. The priest replies, "I'll be there surely, but you won't." Before the fair, the B man takes to his bed and dies. The cause of death, either implied or sometimes made explicit in a sort of coda to the story in other tellings, is that the priest put a curse on the B man to pay him back for harassment. Mickey ended his version by saying he thought it "rare" that a Protestant relative of the B man had told him the story. For Mickey, the fact that the original teller had little to gain by sharing this story that did not reflect well on his family or his coreligionists indicated a kernel of truth in the story. Others agreed, "There must be something to that."

Jamie returned with the tea. Conversation began again in contemplation of Protestant neighbors, which ones were ecumenical "good sorts" and which ones were aloof, bigoted, "bitter." I listened as they discussed how it was sometimes difficult to gauge the intensity of their Protestant neighbors' politics except through small actions that, for keen observers, speak volumes. There was general disapproval of one Protestant family that refused to enter the Killeter post office and shop ever since the ownership changed from Protestant to Catholic. In general, people play their cards close to the chest in part, I imagine, out of fear, and some Catholics and Protestants feign impartiality when true partisan convictions lie beneath the surface. Catholics refer to bitter Protestants, staunch unionists, and committed loyalists as "deep"; the passion of their convictions has roots stretching beyond what can be seen.

There was particular distrust of another Protestant who, it was claimed, went out of his way to conduct business in the nearby Protestant village of Killen. Moreover, he had been kicked off the UDR, had become a preacher for a short time, and had been briefly married for a few weeks. "Sure, he'll try anything the oncest." Inconstancy seemed to be his most intimidating trait in a place where people depend on minute signals to convey larger messages, to help them negotiate social interaction, and to perceive the limits of trust and goodwill, the boundaries of community. Sensing a turn toward the negative, the ceiliers revived their appreciation of their near Protestant neighbors, with whom and for whom they have worked all their lives. Among these neighbors are Orangemen, but most tolerate the loyalties of neighbors precisely because they are neighbors. "You can't condemn a man for what he's born." "They may follow Paisley, even, but here they're just not the same crowd as that Gracie fellow. They're neighbors, like." A hopeful tone reestablished, they agreed that despite the tensions that remain, the Troubles will not be as bad again as they have been, not for a while at least.

In the past, I had made no secret of having both Protestant and Catholic relatives or of having been confirmed first as an Episcopalian—a compromise between Roman Catholic and Southern Baptist traditions in my mixed family—and later before marriage as a Catholic. James Patrick was curious about religion in America. I characterized many American Christians, more often Protestants, as willing to "shop around" for a denomination that suits them, and this elicited some interest in the contrast. Pressed further, I described the various theological stances and types of worship services I had encountered in different congregations in America.

Mixed marriages, they told me, are on the rise in the North, and fewer people convert to one side or the other at marriage. For the most part people remain members of the denomination into which they were born. James Patrick noted that the one chance Catholics have to enter other churches and experience other denominations is at funerals. Conversation quickened again as ceiliers compared their impressions of Anglican and Presbyterian funeral services. All remembered how in the past the Catholic clergy discouraged them from entering other churches, then relaxed that position to allow Catholics to enter other churches as long they did not take an active part in the services. Having been to funerals at St. Bestius, the Anglican church in Killeter, the ceiliers agreed that there seemed to be only a paper-thin wall separating their religion from that of Anglicans. Still, some wondered why certain Protestants, I assume Presbyterians, would not cross themselves at Catholic funerals. "It's the sign of the cross. Surely they would believe in the cross, like."

Time had passed quickly, bringing us past midnight. Once an adequate silence permitted it, talk of leaving began. Comical, exaggerated, and again teasing bids for a suitable exit emerged in conversation. "What time do you go to bed around here, Jamie?" "Well, boys, are we staying the night?" "It'll soon be clearing again." We rose collectively, and Jamie conveyed us out to the street. "Good night." "God bless." "Safe home."

The next day, some who had ceilied together would chance to meet and rehearse particularly interesting points or humorous turns of phrase. A few who missed out on the ceili would wish that they had been there. Tommy would be praised for keeping Mickey on his toes. Mickey would be praised for thinking on his feet. Witnesses would narrate the two men's interaction and structure it in a familiar way, with the narrative sequence ordered by the dialogue leading up to Mickey's quotable punch line. Whether or not people will retain some version of the repartee as an anecdote remains to be seen.

We have lingered on this ceili to gain a better understanding of the dynamics of ceilis as primary storytelling contexts. If we look at the ceili at Jamie's in outline, we see ebb and flow in the progression of discourse toward stories. Looking only at time spent in different types of discourse, conversation and repartee rather than storytelling dominated. This is not uncommon. Storytelling is rarely sustained for long periods except in intensified circumstances, such as at wakes where many talkers have a stake in memorializing the deceased and being entertaining for gathered mourners, or during interviews when I elicited certain stories that naturally led to others.

Consider when stories emerged at the ceili. Talk began with the weather and took a brief tangent into reflection on the nature of Aghyaran today in terms of change in the family unit. The first successful bid for entertaining chat came in the form of news about the neighbors, which invited anecdotes about a local character that might have damaged harmonious interaction. A sense of neighborliness restricted storytelling about that character until the one man qualified to resolve the tension—the potentially offended party—carefully selected a safe anecdote to tell about the man being discussed. It was a story sanctioned by the protagonist and original teller of the story and a story that portrayed him, modestly, as the loser in an attempt to woo. The ceili had reached its first peak when one man took responsibility for narrative. Then the ceili transformed into a friendly battle of wits and verbal repartee. Codding built up to a point at which it simultaneously climaxed and dissipated in the wake of Mickey's quip. Enjoying each other, the men continued to tease, offering mock criticisms of their host in order to entertain and at the same time reassert affinity and an appreciation of the hospitality that structures their assembly. News from the television sparked reflection on the nature of a good death and on the nature of community in a divided society. Faced with politics and potential dissension, efforts to once again achieve agreement called for one man to tell a tale. In the story of the priest and the B man, harassment was met with swift and devastating force, leaving listeners to consider matters of correct behavior, justice, even divine intervention. The story led us to topics too large and complicated to be summed up in one story. Conversation continued to explore the nature of community and difference, but time did not allow further stories.

Only twice during the three hours did talk lead to chat that led to what locals would consider stories—the one about the eccentric bachelor and the one about the priest and the B man. Both stories served to lessen potential discord among ceiliers in the moment. Both stories left us not with didactic conclusions but with issues to think about at the time and in the future. That night, among these people, the underlying, pressing issues concerned the maintenance of dignity in the relationships between those of opposite genders and those of opposite religions. The first story I would refer to as an anecdote because of its structure, style, and content. The ceiliers have no other label for this type of story than "a story about X [a character]." Because all the characters in the second story are long dead and the content illustrates a previous but still relevant historical period, I would refer to the story as a local historical legend. If the efficacy of the priest's curse were emphasized in a particular telling, I might also call it a supernatural legend. If it were told in a series of stories about the same priest, I might call it an anecdote or personal legend. The genres are not mutually exclusive. Regardless of how I might label the story, the ceiliers would call it history, a story about the past, or a story about Fr. Floyd or Fr. McCrory, depending on which protagonist was selected in the version told. These two tales are locally considered "stories" because they are memorable narratives with beginnings, middles, and ends that have been told before and will be told again to illustrate or make certain points in discussion. They are part of local oral tradition, a potentially shared Aghyaran repertoire.

Note the patterns in the discourse of the ceili: from talk to chatty news culminating in storytelling, then from repartee to chat to storytelling and back to chat again. Storytelling has long been understood as more than the reporting of set types of narrative that one might label folklore. It is a stage achieved in the progress of sociability, a behavioral mode in face-to-face interaction. To understand the motivations behind and the intended or potential meanings of particular stories, we must have an understanding of storytelling as part of a process of communication and negotiation in intimate settings. At Jamie's, that process was guided by patterns of and conventions for sociability already established and mutually understood in its particular, conventional, recurring social setting—the ceili.

Conversation rose to storytelling and left us with ordered instances of speech, identifiable as stories, which could be transcribed and transformed into publishable texts by a folklorist. However, stories are more than items, more than the bones of plot conveyed by words folklorists once scrambled to document and then render into lifeless plot summaries. Stories are situated instances of verbal skill and intellectual labor wrought to link past events with the present situation in an attempt to sustain us in the future. Ceili stories are artful bids for meaning and order given propositions made in conversation. Exegesis of ceili stories requires attention to individual social actors involved in a specific storytelling event, and to the communication that proceeds, follows, and is transformed by their performances. In order to better appreciate and interpret more storytelling events, performances, and narrative texts, we should turn our attention now to the other primary situational context for storytelling in Aghyaran—the wake.

4

Wakes as Storytelling Contexts

One Saturday morning, about three months after settling in Ballymon-gan, I woke a bit late and groggy having been to a music session at Eugene O'Donnell's house the night before. I wandered outside to appreciate some rare sunshine and was greeted with a flat tire. Resigned, I crouched down to try replacing it without the benefit of proper tools and soon saw my neighbor Danny Gallen coming to greet me. Self-centeredly, I assumed that he was coming to offer me a hand.

"Did you hear about John?" he asked without any apparent inflection.

"John Mongan? I heard he was in the hospital."

"He's dead."

"Jesus." I fell back from my crouch to land on the ground with a thud. "I wasn't prepared for that.... I really wasn't...."

"No, none of us were."

For a moment, Danny simply had nothing more to say. He then glanced over the car and led me back to one of his outbuildings to look for the right spanner. With Danny's help some part of me went through the motions of replacing the flat, but all the while I was preoccupied, stunned by the sense of loss. Widely recognized as Aghyaran's unofficial curator of local oral traditions and material culture, John Mongan had long helped his neighbors make sense of the complicated present by offering lessons from the equally complicated but very different past. He was such a force in and embodiment of the community, perhaps I assumed he would live forever, like the very names that give the landscape meaning—Ballymongan, Trie-namongan, and Termonamongan. At John's wake that night, neighbors and relatives from far and near would articulate a similar impression of John, memorializing him through one anecdote after another.

Although many people's deaths have greatly affected me over the years in Aghyaran, I was most involved in the events surrounding John Mongan's death. Here I want to offer first my impressions of John's wake, funeral, and burial. From these particulars and from my experiences at other wakes I will then sketch the general patterns of customs and social interaction at wakes, with special attention to how wakes not only invite but also revolve around storytelling. The larger goal is to better appreciate wakes, in addition to ceilis, as primary situational contexts for storytelling, but first sufficient context is necessary.

At two o'clock in the afternoon after John Mongan's death, Danny and I joined a column of cars traveling to Omagh to accompany John's body home from the hospital morgue. At the morgue, roughly fifty men and women, predominately from Ballymongan and adjoining townlands, gathered to offer their condolences to two of John's brothers, Eddie and Laurence, as they stood bravely at the head of the coffin. Undertaker and publican Charlie Lynch led us through a decade of the rosary. Afterwards we all had an opportunity to say a silent prayer, individually, over John before following his coffin back out to the waiting hearse. Our line of cars followed the hearse through a long and purposefully indirect route from Omagh through Drumquin, Castlederg, Killeter, and finally to John and Eddie's home in Ballymongan. In the car, the tinny voice of Highland Radio announced that "The death has taken place of John Mongan, Ballymongan, Castlederg."

In Ballymongan, the wake house was very crowded, and those who had not been to the morgue offered prayers over John upstairs in his bedroom where he lay in an open coffin on trestles. Downstairs, industrious young women relatives made the rounds with tea and sandwiches to everyone inside and outside on the street. Exchanges remained brief and were often interrupted in the flow of people back and forth.

The character of the wake would change later that night after an especially full eight o'clock mass in which Fr. McGinn announced John's death. Though the wake house remained crowded after mass, most could find seats in various rooms and cluster into conversations. People exchanged accounts of how they had received the news of John's death.

Figure 4.1. John Mongan surveying his open-air museum

One farmer had made his way to the cattle market in Newtownstewart where an Aghyaran man informed him about John, and he immediately returned home, his cattle still in the trailer. Another neighbor and long-time friend of John's described how he reacted after hearing the news.

"Boys, I went inside and do you know what I did? I fecking broke down. I fecking broke down."

For the next two and a half hours, groups of people chatting expanded and contracted. Rooms remained too crowded for extended conversations, and trains of thought were punctuated and altered by new faces and fresh rounds of tea, sweets, and sandwiches. Occasionally one group of mourners whose conversation had faltered would look to another more animated group and then renew their chat along a new tangent.

Some who hardly knew John had come to pay their respects and enjoy the chat and company, knowing that a wake is one of the few social gatherings left in which conversation, without the interference of television and radio, is the sole entertainment. In the course of my fieldwork, I had become accustomed to asking people about the local past and to eliciting their evaluations of change, but at John's wake there was no call to press people with such questions. These topics seemed the natural focus of conversation at the wake of the local historian, the erenach and seanachie of a modern era.[1] Preoccupation with the past was the case at other wakes as well. More than a strategy to pass the time or create a general mood, commemoration was the purposeful task at hand.

Near midnight, John's brother Charley and his wife Rose arrived from England. The crowd had thinned to about thirty. The term wake suggests staying awake in vigil, and many of those who remained would sit up all night. Frs. McGinn and McGarrigle came to lead us through another rosary. Afterward the roughly twenty people who remained split into two groups—one in the upstairs room with John, and the other downstairs in the main sitting room. As is customary, the family offered alcohol to those who remained to sit the night, yet perhaps out of respect for John's sober character and his having been a Pioneer,[2] few indulged and none did so to the point of drunkenness.

Danny, Barney McGrath, Mickey Byrne, and I had been in the same sitting room a few weeks previously for a night's ceili with John, and our rehearsal of the stories told then sparked similar stories along similar themes among others in the room—anecdotes of past local characters, accounts of pranks, and jokes that naturally followed these narratives of people's wit, gullibility, modesty, and eccentricity. Consideration of the character of known individuals was a strong current in the flow of our chat, and it regularly brought us back to John and what a great loss we faced.

Humor overlapped with serious appreciation, laughter with occasional tears, irreverence with homage. Downstairs, this oscillation continued for hours, as did the rounds of tea and tobacco. Upstairs, where John lay, conversation was slightly more reserved, allowing more quiet reflection. People switched between rooms throughout the night until dawn, when women relatives and neighbors offered to make breakfast for those who remained.

After a heavy sleep I was up again in a few hours by eleven. I had neither cattle to fodder nor houses to build, nor would public work have been appropriate. The townland was still; tractors were silent. Only close family remained at the wake house, so I offered to run a few errands for the Mongans, including delivering refreshments to the five Ballymongan men—Seamus Mongan, John Collins, Charlie Logue, Pat Logue, and his son Patrick—who were beginning to dig John's grave in St. Patrick's grave-yard. In the parish, neighbors and more distant relatives of the deceased, rather than professionals, have always undertaken this task.

Wanting to be useful, I helped shovel the white quartz gravel from the surface of the family plot into recycled meal bags. After removing the black plastic sheets underneath, John Collins marked a roughly three- by-seven-foot rectangle with his spade, and we took turns digging in pairs. The first foot or more was dry, but the next few feet were thick, gluey clay that was more difficult to raise to the surface. At about three and a half feet we hit soft fragments of wood from the coffin of the last Mongan buried in the plot a couple generations before. We gathered a brass crucifix from the previous coffin's lid, two metal handles, and a scattering of bones into another meal bag to be reburied in a corner of the grave. We continued digging for at least another foot and a half.

Throughout the digging Charlie and Seamus repeated what they considered the funniest stories from the previous night to those who had not been there but would attend the second night of the wake. John and Pat then added their share of different versions and similar stories. After finishing the grave, we adjourned to Duffy's pub for a "quick pint" that lasted over three hours, as is the custom after digging a grave, and Pat Logue generously left me home, a bit worse for having declined the offer of breakfast after the wake and having skipped lunch. Although it seemed to amuse my neighbors, I had every intention of returning to John Mongan's for the second night of the wake. "He must think dying's the best part of living here," Charlie quipped. Apparently only a few people beyond the next of kin are expected both nights. Despite my intentions, after a hot bath I simply passed out. My inability to handle the combination of sleep loss, not eating, and alcohol provided a few good laughs for the second night of chat.

Monday morning a little after nine, the majority of Ballymongan residents and those of adjacent townlands gathered for tea and prayers at John's house for one last time before the burial. It was standing room only. Downstairs we could make out only the faintest trace of someone beginning the rosary upstairs in John's room: "Hail Mary, full of grace . . ." Volume increased as prayer spread like a wave. The crest of the wave had reached the top of stairs by "Holy Mary, Mother of God," and it gathered momentum as it rolled downstairs. We were all together for "the hour of our death. Amen." Over and over the wave of Hail Marys and Our Fathers spread through us.

After the rosary, the coffin was closed, and family and friends carried John downstairs and outside. The hearse waited, back door open, some thirty paces down the road. The funeral procession began on foot, giving a nod to a past era when bearers often walked the coffin all the way to the graveyard. A long line of cars slowly followed the hearse to the chapel and gradually grew longer as cars from other townlands joined. Inside, family sat up front, and Frs. McGinn, McGarrigle, and Sproule concelebrated the requiem mass. In his eulogy, Fr. McGinn commended John's piety and good works, and in a departure from many eulogies, referred to John's loss as a personal one. After the procession to the grave, there were further prayers. I recognized a significant number of Protestants who had come to pay their last respects. Family, neighbors, and the wider community waited, whispering praises and regrets, until the last shovel of damp clay was packed into place. "John would have done a tidier job," I heard someone say.

The customs and events from John Mongan's death through burial followed the general contemporary pattern for coming to terms with the loss of an elderly person among Catholics in West Tyrone and surrounding areas. Although the death of anyone is of course sorrowful, people in

Aghyaran recognize such a thing as a "good death," which includes being emotionally and spiritually prepared and dying among loved ones at
or near home.[3] It is important to note that accidental, tragic, violent, or
otherwise untimely deaths, especially those of the young, are observed by
almost entirely somber wakes and funerals. Our focus will remain on how
people pay their respects to and memorialize the elderly who have died a
good death.

My account of the three-day period from John Mongan's death to his
burial provides details from which we can begin to abstract a general chronology of customs, the local cultural script from which people draw in the
face of death. In the process, we will better appreciate the centrality of
storytelling at wakes and take note of how the same individual is memorialized through narrative in different ways at the wake and funeral.

News of the death disseminates by word of mouth, phone, and local
radio announcements. Near neighbors almost always attend the wake, regardless of religious affiliation. Once, a middle-aged republican proclaimed
to me that since the beginning of the recent Troubles there has been little
substantial mixing of religious communities in Aghyaran. His mother in-
terjected that he had just been to the wake of an elderly Protestant woman.
He paused, then offered, "Well, that's different. She's a neighbor." Whether
recognized or not, there remains an "equalitarian" impulse governing behavior, if not attitudes, among Catholic and Protestant neighbors of roughly
the same class. Anthony Cohen (1982:11, 17), and after him Crozier (1989:
73), define equalitarianism as a belief in "masking or muting social differentiation," which is different from egalitarianism, "the belief in equality
as a moral principle" (cf. Glassie 1982:137–138). This equalitarian ethic
allows for contact during work and social situations, such as wakes, even in
times of province-wide political tension. In addition to cross-community
contact, most feuding relations reconcile at wakes, at least temporarily, out
of respect for the deceased. As Jim Falls mentioned, "I think death here is
one of the things that nearly would draw people together, you know, even
families that would have fell out for years. As soon as somebody dies, they
seemed to forget all their arguing."

Sociability at wakes helps reassert the solidarity of the mourners as
a community, even across the religious divide. Disparities in status, denominational affiliation, and opinion are at least temporarily irrelevant,
leveled by shared grief or at least a sense of neighborly obligation. As Cro-

zier observes in her study of contemporary wakes in Co. Down, the extent of attendance and the suspension of disputes "implies a solidarity which is not generated locally by any other event." In Crozier's Ballintully as well as in Aghyaran, the assembly of kin, neighbors, and a wider social network "does not necessarily represent real cohesion: participation in the wake represents an ideal of co-operation which may, or may not, be true in reality" (1989:89). Despite disengagement from normal activities, social life does not stop but rather intensifies within the frame of the wake. Far from retreating from society, the next of kin prepare for society to come to them and to reconstitute itself in idealized form.

If one's religious denomination has little bearing on whether to attend a neighbor's wake, when, and for how long, gender and age do. Women tend to come in pairs or groups during the day, and men at night. However, couples occasionally arrive together if they live far enough away to travel by car. Children related to the deceased are expected to attend, but not necessarily to stay long. Girls may attend with their mothers and boys with their fathers, but today wakes are mostly the domain of adults from marriage into old age. This is a significant change, according to many middle-aged people who remember that when they were in their early teens and even younger they pleaded with their parents to accompany them to wakes. When I asked about this, Danny Gallen, Jim Falls, and Sarah Falls became quite animated:

> Jim: *It was a big job to get to a wake when you were very young. I remember myself, if my father was heading off walking to the wake, we'd have been pestering him can we go, so he would have taken someone. And he might have taken one brother somewhere to a wake, and then it was your turn and you reminded him, you know. My brother, Mick, was older than I was, and I would say Mick got to the last wake and I'm due to get to this one, you see.*
>
> Sarah: *Now you'd never see a ten-year-old, an eight-year-old, a six-year-old, except they're part of the family.*
>
> Danny: *You know why? They'd have more entertainment watching the television than a wake, a house full of older people, you know. They don't want to go, but we did want to go. It was a chance to get out for a night.*

Jim: *To see the pipes and the snuff, and all this, you know. A different thing altogether. And to get the tea, sit and get a cup of tea, and usually there was some cake or something that you wouldn't have normally got.*

Danny: *And you met people that you wouldn't normally have met.*

Jim: *That's right, that's right.*

One draw of the wake is clear: entertainment (cf. Narváez 1994: 288–289). On the whole, people's choice of daily entertainment has shifted now toward the effortless, asocial distraction provided by television. However, for those who grew up without television, not to mention household electricity, entertainment was—and in many cases remains—conversation, a sweet milky cup of tea, and a break in routine. For a child in the 1950s the entertainment of the wake was participating in adult society, being served rare treats that are now commonplace, and enjoying the spectacle of strangers, the women and their snuff, and the men and their white clay pipes, which had gone out of fashion except at wakes.

As night approaches, a wake becomes crowded, and neighbors or family may be called upon to help direct traffic and parking. Usually close male relatives greet newcomers at the door and accept their handshakes and brief conventional condolences, usually a simple "Sorry for your loss" or "Sorry for your trouble." They then direct the mourners to the room where the body lies. In the appointed room, mourners often have to wait in line for the coffin, so they offer further condolences to relations, more often women, sitting in attendance. Once their turn has come, mourners view the remains, say a silent prayer. If the deceased and the mourners are Catholic, mourners typically leave a mass card[4] in the coffin or on a surface designated for their collection.

The room where the body lies is often crowded with family in chairs lining the walls, so after paying their respects most mourners usually find a seat in another room, or outside if the house is crowded and the weather is good. Up to a half-dozen young women and girls, usually relatives of the deceased, are vigilant about offering newcomers a cup of tea and refreshments.

Just as there is a space set aside for sacred rites—the room where the body lies—there are times set aside for sacred rites: one's arrival for individual prayers, midnight for a group rosary, and the moment before processing to the chapel for a final rosary. Yet as Lawrence Taylor has noted, most of the wake experience is "patently communal and conversational." The sacred rites "do not set the tone for the general occasion, which is rather marked by the general sociability of neighborly exchange. It is not an occasion for pronouncements about religious belief, certainly not more than a few vague words of reassurance" (1989b:177).

Early on, each new arrival to a group of talkers occasions a brief mention and appreciation of the deceased but then a return to the news of the area. The demeanor of individuals and of the group may be affected by grief, especially when in the presence of the next of kin, and mourners may occasionally be moved to tears. However, since the wake allows for a larger gathering than usual of a broad range of people in a sociable setting, most of the time leading up to the midnight rosary is spent trading news, and the general demeanor is outgoing and gregarious. Many appreciate wakes specifically because they are a now-rare occasion for social interaction with near and far neighbors.

As at ceilis, there is a progression of sociability at wakes that leads up to storytelling. Types of verbal exchange at the wake can also be conceptually envisioned as steps leading from talk to chat to storytelling. Still, the progression of speech during a wake is not unilinear but admits both escalation and oscillation between types of speech due to a number of patterns specific to the event. In many ways, the wake is a ceili writ large: a ritual of neighborly exchange in forms of reciprocal hospitality and entertainment that reasserts solidarity in a communal forum. But key differences from the ceili such as the larger scale, the fluidity of participants, and the length of time committed to the wake affect the progression of sociability that makes storytelling possible.

As seen during John Mongan's wake, there is a discernable relationship between the number of mourners, the time of night, and the type of verbal exchange at wakes. Before the midnight rosary, the house is crowded and may be loud, so people do not often attempt longer narratives because they will be interrupted and cannot be appreciated. Initial remarks about the pity of losing the deceased or how one heard the news are sincere and reverent but brief and often conventional. Further topics of conversation are often light and subject to sudden change in the shifting boundaries of groups of talkers. Those who know each other cluster and discuss the local news as they would during any chance meeting in town, a break from work in the fields, or a ceili after the day's chores. If a group exhausts the local news and remarkable happenings gleaned from the newspapers, radio, and television, the focus shifts to discussion of strangers who are present but out of earshot, mostly concerning how they are acquainted with or related to the deceased. Danny Gallen and Jim Falls explain:

> Danny: *You know, the thing about wakes even nowadays, it's a time when everybody gets to know who everybody is, who their relations were. You get to know who people are and who they're married to, the whole relationships.*
>
> Jim: *And you would inquire at a wake and somebody come in. You could sense if they're talking or crying or if they're going around to their relations. You will inquire if you don't know, why is this person in the line and so on.*
>
> Danny: *You do learn a lot at wakes. There's hardly a wake you go to that you don't learn something like that.*

So after paying respects to the dead and next of kin, and after discussing local events, people push chat toward the spectacle around them. They note the many known and unknown faces. Unlike in the ceili, the crowd of the wake provides visual cues for further news. Those unknown are like puzzle pieces, their appearance and behavior are clues, and placing them is like a game. In the process, people reevaluate the boundaries of their local and familial communities, enjoy learning something new, appreciate a fresh or reaffirming perspective on the familiar.

At this point, sociability is in its most public, least intimate phase. As in a public house, there are several simultaneous conversations in different rooms and areas. With chairs circled and backs turned, brief pockets of intimacy are possible. Relationships are reestablished, conversational foundations are laid, and now entertainment becomes the object of sociability. News and discussion of new faces may give way to genres of shorter, humorous narrative that lead quickly to punch lines. Narrators must be abrupt and economical in their bids to entertain because they cannot hold the floor for long. At John Mongan's wake, Danny Gallen, Barney Byrne, Patrick McElhill, and I sat together for a short period discussing John's fine craftsmanship and that of his grandfather Hugh Shiels, a master carpenter. Those men could turn a hand to anything, we agreed. An association must have flashed in Patrick's mind, and he told a joke that I recorded him telling again during a later ceili.

> *This other man went to confession, and he says, "Father,"*
> *he says, "I've been working in the timber yards," he says, "for*
> *this last twenty years."*
>
> *"And all these years," he says, "I've been stealing wood and*
> *selling it," he says. "God forgive me."*
>
> *Aye.* ◊
>
> *The priest says till him, he says to him, "Can you make a*
> *novena?"*
>
> *"Well, Father," he says, "If you've the plans," he says, "I*
> *have the timber."* ◊

We erupted in laughter, but then toned it down so as not to offend anyone who had not been privy to the joke, its relevance to the previous conversation, and the appreciative spirit in which it was offered. Humor becomes safer, more appropriate, when there are fewer people and all are within earshot or when those trading jokes and humorous anecdotes have a room to themselves.

After the midnight rosary, the crowd at a wake thins, and more stable groupings of talkers are possible. Those who will remain until dawn usually come together into one conversation, more like a ceili. Because sociability has been occasioned by death, the range of relevant topics and genres tend to narrow, but not to the exclusion of humor. Humor often becomes a preferred mode of expression later in the night, but it is important to note that humor does more than entertain with a distracting laugh. Simultaneously, humor provides an indirect but meaningful channel through which to express genuine emotion and affinity. Whether offered in terms of humor or serious reflection, conversation and storytelling tend to assert shared feeling and pool shared knowledge. Unlike the ceili, the wake is not always the most appropriate place for genres such as memorates and supernatural legends, which leave open for debate fundamental conceptions about the nature of reality.

With a smaller core of people remaining to stay the night, a few sit up in the room with the body, and occasionally mourners who have been engaged in chat elsewhere in the house relieve the sitters to allow them a chance to join the larger group. The room where the body lies is not without conversation, but understanding the room to be sacred space—no less so than a holy well, chapel, or graveyard—often restrains overtly humorous or lively talk.

During this later period, turns taken in conversation are longer and more animated, and may be dominated by fewer people. Talkers take responsibility for more complicated narratives, and conversation often elevates into a more performative mode.[5] This later period of conversational exchange involves more intimate and personal reflection, and storytelling focuses on the deceased, past local characters, and other themes that follow from narrated reminiscences. This period stretches until dawn.

Although all mourners are treated to hospitality throughout the wake, those who stay the night are given special treatment with the offers of alcohol after the midnight rosary and a breakfast at daybreak. Men rarely serve guests except perhaps to pass around whiskey and beer. All this hospitality, then, can put extra pressure on the women of the house, but usually there are enough women present to distribute the burden. Women I spoke with did not seem to mind serving food and drinks at wakes, partly because it is not far different from their normal experience, at least of more formal family gatherings such as at Easter and Christmas. In addition, serving allows them to mingle and socialize in a way that men cannot without inventing an excuse to leave one group for another.[6] Sometimes, having a task such as serving can be a welcome distraction from grief. At other times, however, it is simply an imposition. Two women in their mid-twenties recalled being expected to cook breakfast for a dozen men when caught as the only women left at a wake as the sun rose. Never again, they vowed. One rolled her eyes, affecting a thick country accent: "Och-aye, it's very important for the men to get their fry after a long, hard night of staying up drinking."

Eventually, after dawn, those who sat up retreat to their beds, but the wake will continue for another night after a period of calm in the morning as more-rested relatives and neighbors replenish supplies and tidy the home. Having wakes last two nights allows news to travel, far-flung relations to return, and the maximum number of people to attend. The second night is usually better-attended and livelier, with more people staying the night. It is a minor source of pride in Aghyaran that they retain the custom of having two nights of a wake. At different times in surrounding areas in Donegal and Fermanagh, and especially in larger towns, the clergy have enforced that after the first night the body must be brought into the chapel, which is not conducive to socializing, drinking, or storytelling.

After the second night of the wake, family and neighbors gather again in the morning at the wake house to pray a rosary before the funeral, as previously described. The family surrounds the deceased during the rosary, and after the prayers they close the coffin and, with neighbors, carry it to the hearse. At the chapel, mourners wait until family carry the coffin inside before filing into pews. The funeral mass follows the same order and structure as any mass, though with a eulogy in place of the normal homily and a final commendation of the soul of the deceased instead of parish announcements. Readings may be delivered by family members or other lay people, but in Aghyaran only priests deliver eulogies, which by and large comment on the spiritual qualities of the deceased. After the priest sprinkles the coffin and family with holy water, the congregation follows the coffin outside to the graveyard or follows the hearse in their cars if the burial is to take place in the farther graveyard of Magherakeel.

In the graveyard, voluntary grave diggers lower the coffin into the ground, and the priest leads mourners in a final decade of the rosary and offers a final blessing over the deceased. The grave diggers then replace the soil over the coffin, and most mourners remain until the job is finished. In the past, the undertaker always had the honor of saying the last prayer, but this is not always the case today. Mourners leave the graveyard after offering handshakes, occasional hugs, and condolences to the next of kin.

After the burial, it has been customary for the family to host close neighbors and friends for a meal at the wake house or in a restaurant. Within the last decade Catholic families have begun to host teas for all mourners in the large gymnasium space of the Gaelic Athletic Centre not far from the chapel, as did John Mongan's family. At first only tea and sandwiches were served, but over time refreshments have grown into full catered meals for as many as four hundred people. After the tea, close relations of the deceased gather one last time at the wake house for conversation that provides a final opportunity to freely express grief with the family assembled. I am told that at this last family gathering people are often exhausted, but the mood can be light-hearted depending on circumstances.

Wakes are natural draws for ethnographers interested in ritual and custom, but equally important is what is said at wakes and how memory is constituted in the face of death. In social settings of everyday life, the actions and remarks of neighbors and acquaintances provide the material for narratives that form a significant portion of local discourse. These actions and remarks are memorable because they entertain, and relevant because through narrative local characters can be made to exemplify values and propositions that people find worth contemplating. Mourners at a wake rehearse known stories or occasionally create new ones about the deceased. This intensifies the process by which the deceased—an actual, multifaceted individual—is conceptually transformed into a characterizable type of person.

At the wake of Bridie McMenamin, a woman who lived more than one hundred years, mourners praised her as a mother, wife, and ceaseless worker. Several attributed her longevity to her undaunted faith and calm acceptance of the good with the bad. From this discussion emerged an anecdote about Mrs. McMenamin performing her usual daily chores, despite being very pregnant with her last child. Three months after the wake, I asked Danny what stories he remembered, and he recalled the following anecdote in particular:

> *They were talking about her and the way the family was raised, and some of the boys said that Gerard was the youngest of the family.*
>
> *And they said that she had gone out one evening swinging a bag of turf, which was quite normal. She was expecting, but the turf would have been stacked somewhere near the house, or maybe not so near the house. And it was generally the woman of the house took in the turf for the fire.*
>
> *But she went out for a bag of turf and she came back in carrying a baby boy. That was Gerard. And Gerard would be over sixty now. That would have happened about 1940.*

I had mistaken the anecdote for fiction, perhaps a tall tale, and I asked Danny if he thought that the story had been made up on the spot.

> *It wasn't made up. It was true. But it wouldn't have been chatted about, you see. It's something you wouldn't hear.*
>
> *You hear these things at a wake, about all the things that happened to people in their lifetime, you see—you know, who they were related to and everything else. Oh, you're going to hear the lot at a wake, you know.*

Being remarkable, the story stayed with Danny and circulated widely after the wake. At the wake itself, the story brought home a certain image of Mrs. McMenamin that rang true to those who knew her. "Boys a boys, you wouldn't find a woman like that the day." She had mastered the role of mother, made it look impossibly easy, and faced the toil and exertions of everyday life with a courage and stoicism almost unthinkable today. According to Danny, conversation that followed focused on how much easier Mrs. McMenamin's life would have been if she were born now, how much we have to be thankful for in an era of labor-saving technology, and how we have forgotten what truly hard work is. In part, the story provided commentary on change and evaluation of the present.

Immediately at stake in telling anecdotes about Mrs. McMenamin at her wake was searching through narrative for a way to sum up her personality, to pay tribute to her strength of character. The effort to epitomize or to locate individuality in narrative at the wake, however, can also have a depersonalizing effect. At the wake, anecdotes of Mrs. McMenamin led to anecdotes of others who epitomized self-sacrifice and industry, and from this implicit comparison a character type is constituted and reinforced for the audience. In time, Mrs. McMenamin may be best remembered only for actions and characteristics attributed to her that exemplify values worth considering. For those who never knew her complexity in life, she will stand in for a type; she will serve as an exemplar of valuable and perhaps increasingly rare qualities.

Exchanging anecdotes about the deceased takes part in the wake's overall project of transition by simultaneously evoking the presence of the deceased and bidding the deceased farewell. At the one time, storytelling keeps the deceased alive in narrative during grief and prepares a place for him or her in local collective memory of past neighbors and relations. Stories at the wake about the deceased easily lead narrators into stories of other characters of similar or opposite types, reviving the memories of others. There is a double movement of focusing on the character of the individual and gesturing toward the character of the community comprised of such individuals. On the one hand, the process of reminiscing about the deceased pays tribute to individuality. Mourners use shared knowledge to construct narratives that serve as memorials to individuals. On the other hand, anecdotes can characterize the deceased in already meaningful tropes as character types. This may detract from an individual's uniqueness to an extent by integrating a selective memory of the deceased with those of others. Memorializing the deceased through anecdotes, then, is in part a secular act of incorporating the deceased into a vernacular body of memory, an act that can be contrasted to the sacred act of incorporation achieved by the more elaborately ritualized funeral to follow.

If storytelling at the wake creates for the deceased a secular life after death in local folklore, the requiem mass seeks to ensure a very different kind of afterlife. The priest's eulogy rarely extends beyond a consideration of the deceased as a Christian.[7] At stake in the ritual of the mass is the soul and salvation. The funeral incorporates the deceased not into a sort of pantheon of past local characters but primarily into the collective anonymous corps of the "faithful departed." The community whose continuity is most explicitly reasserted is not the web of acquaintances, friends, and family that formed the social world of the deceased. It is the parish congregation and, more broadly, "one holy catholic and apostolic Church," as identified in the Nicene Creed and Apostles' Creed. These two communities, one geographically and socially based and the other religiously based, may overlap but are not necessarily coterminous. The community into which the deceased is incorporated by the wake is locally specific and understood in terms of personality traits and types. The community into which the deceased is incorporated by the funeral is universal and undifferentiated. Anecdotes about the dead may elide personal particularities because of a shift over time toward typological characterization, but the community of the dead memorialized in local folklore is far more differentiated than that to which the funeral mass commends the soul of the deceased. As Taylor observes, unlike the wake, the funeral places emphasis not on singularity but on "the depersonalizing generality of one more soul joining all the others—the Church Invisible" (1989b:178).

Both the wake and funeral provide, in Arnold van Gennep's terms, gestures of incorporation, as narratives told at wakes and funerals seek to incorporate an individual into different conceptual bodies of the dead.[8] Thus the individual memorialized by the wake may seem very different from the one memorialized by the funeral. Taylor, again, is astute in noting that "The wake and funeral seem to some extent less like stages in the same rite of passage than separate rites dealing with different aspects of the deceased" (1989b:178). Wakes and funerals deal, respectively, with social and religious aspects of the deceased, thus providing distinct frameworks for conceptually reconstituting the individual in death. Usually, for the bereaved both frameworks are necessary for making sense of loss; the wake and funeral can join in an effort to construct a meaningful death and to memorialize a broader, more holistic range of the deceased's qualities.

However, to what extent wakes and funerals overlap, complement, or even compete with each other in their gestures of incorporation ultimately depends on the individual memorialized. John Mongan, for instance, was known in life and remembered at his wake for his daily mass attendance and volunteering at various church functions. He was quietly proud of his family's historical role as keepers of Church lands in Termonamongan. So the social aspects of John Mongan's life remembered at his wake and the religious aspects remembered at his funeral overlapped considerably. At his wake he was appreciated as the epitome of the "modest wee bachelor," exemplary in his decency, honesty, and industry. At his funeral he was appreciated as a model Christian. These two visions of John Mongan are difficult to separate. His incorporation as the modest bachelor into a collectively remembered pantheon of past local characters and as the model Christian into the body of the "faithful departed" dovetails.

John McHugh was an entirely different sort of bachelor. Fond of drink, cards, darts, and sleeping until noon, Mr. McHugh is valued in chat today, a decade after his death, as the irascible eccentric, stubborn iconoclast, and untamed bachelor who knows how to have a good time. As portrayed in anecdotes, he fits easily into the known character type of the rough or untamed bachelor, but his singularity also reanimates and fleshes out that type. As a foil to John Mongan's embodiment of duty and sobriety, the John McHugh of anecdotes provides a certain vicarious enjoyment of life outside of convention, even outside of conventional respectability. Contrasting the two men and the character types they have come to exemplify provides the relief needed to witness a range of possibilities for human actors sharing the same environment and conditions.

Indeed, making this contrast seems a natural thing to do. It was precisely when we were digging John Mongan's grave that one man, Charlie Logue, brought up the subject of John McHugh. While digging we had exhausted a string of anecdotes appreciating John Mongan's piety. Perhaps out of a desire for balance or comic relief, John Collins offered his account of the time John McHugh, drunk, made a visit to the women's bathroom at the GAA Centre. While McHugh relieved himself, an older woman came in, saw him through the open stall door, and shrieked at him, "Goodness, John! This is *strictly* for *ladies!*" Without missing a beat, McHugh whipped around waving his "lad" and retorted, "Christ, cutty [girl], so is this!"

Danny, PJ Gallen, and John Gerald O'Donnell tell me that there were plenty of anecdotes like this one told at John McHugh's wake in 1995. The wake was particularly valued as an occasion for people to share their favorite John McHugh stories, hear ones new to them, and occasionally embellish story fragments and apocryphal elements into fuller narratives. In contrast, John McHugh's funeral mass proposed another vision of him, focusing on his record as a Christian and candidate for forgiveness and salvation. This contrast does not amount to evidence of tension between wake and funeral and specifically between their respective gestures of incorporation into different conceptual bodies of the dead. Indeed, the offices carried out by the Church for the salvation of John McHugh's soul probably comforted his friends and family. However, we can infer from stories about him that anecdotes told at his wake came closer to emphasizing where John McHugh centered his energy and attention.

Interestingly, Fr. McGarrigle included in his eulogy a characterization of John McHugh as having a "short fuse," which elicited widespread tittering and some open laughter. The priest's remark may seem inconsequential, but eulogies rarely shift focus from the religious qualities of the deceased to commentary on his or her personality. The remark further illustrates that John McHugh's relevance in collective memory resides in his particularity as a character, so much so that this image of John McHugh as character carried over into his funeral. The gestures of incorporation offered by wake and funeral may focus on different aspects of the same person, complementing each other, but in the case of John McHugh the aspects memorialized at his wake dominate by coming closer in popular opinion to what makes him memorable.

To amplify the distinctions and potential competition between wake and funeral memorializations of John McHugh, consider Taylor's observations about the death of a similar character he knew in southwest Donegal. Conny the Gap was a "wildly amusing man whose exploits, real and apocryphal, were favorite topics of local talk," and thus Conny's company and example were central, even crucial, in local social life (1989b:176). The sociability at a nearby pub during his wake served as "a natural consummation of a life-time of such occasions" (1989b:178). Within the domain of the Church at his funeral, however, he was transformed from Conny the Gap into Conal O'Beirne. The two can seem to be distinct individuals who were members of "two quite different communities of both the living and the dead" (1989b:178). The eulogy characterized Mr. O'Beirne's demise as a "good death" because he had received Extreme Unction, and the priest informed the congregation that it was now their responsibility to remember the deceased in their prayers. At the graveside, musicians who had played for Mr. O'Beirne at his deathbed and who had hoped to "give him a proper send off" with a last reel or jig were not allowed to play, and thus the rituals of the Church prevailed.

Such overt competition is not apparent in the case of John McHugh's wake and funeral. Moreover, Taylor's contention that the "continuous struggle for control between the Church and the people" is now "to some extent subsumed in the contest for prominence between wake and funeral" (1989a:152–153) only applies, at least in my experience, to rare instances in contemporary Aghyaran. Yet stories of both John McHugh and Conny the Gap, and others like them, potentially subvert efforts made by the Church in the funeral mass to fix the identity and memory of the deceased in its own terms. The stories of whiskey and music, petulance and rancor are potentially subversive in expressing the joy of disobedience and the charm of flawed humanity. Moreover, these stories make a competitive bid for which community of the dead better welcomes the bachelor home and which community of the living is better reconstituted by celebrations of the bachelor's death. What Taylor says of Conny the Gap also applies to John McHugh:

> The gentle death of old Conny the Gap is an opportunity to invoke another sort of community, whose existence and cultural character are particularly well defined by such bachelors. Men like Conny are less 'civilized,' in Elias' sense of the term; they stand at the center of—and can thus stand for—the occasions and styles of sociability not successfully contained and tamed by the middle class Catholicism of Church and proper household. The rural wake, no longer wild, continues to express just this social world. Perhaps ironically, it is a collectivity based on the celebration of peculiar individuality. (1989b:184)

Local conventional wisdom holds that television is firmly established and that ceilis, socializing, and storytelling in general have suffered for it. Yet many in Aghyaran are proud that storytelling flourishes at wakes. As Patrick McElhill told me at John Mongan's wake, "Wakes in this country, all down the years, was a great time of storytelling. All them stories, aye. Only a night like this recalls all that type of craic." Danny Gallen reiterates that this is still true because "It's nearly the only time when there's not a television on." Day Marshall, Paddy McGlynn, Packy Jim McGrath, and Mick "Pareroe" McHugh agree that the wake is the last social occasion that provides an ideal context for storytelling. Some of what ceilis have lost in the process of modernization remains, shielded, within the frame of the wake. In describing the wake as a storytelling context people in Aghyaran use words like "pure," "unspoiled," "true," and "authentic." Of course, wakes, too, have changed.[9] Wake games died out early in the twentieth century. Pranking, card playing, music making, and singing are no longer considered appropriate at wakes. Besides eating, drinking, and smoking, talking is the only entertainment, and it becomes the natural focus of people gathered to stay up and pay their respects to the dead.

Conversation may lead in many directions and rise to storytelling in different genres, but the centripetal force of discourse is appreciation of the deceased and, secondarily, appreciation of those brought to mind by the deceased. Content with representations of wakes by famous writers, and overly confident that "wake culture" is a thing of the past, Nina Witoszek and Pat Sheeran dismiss the focus of discourse at wakes on the deceased: "The wake functioned as a theatre of social rehabilitation in which useless praise was expended on those who were denied a good word during life" (1998:28). Praise is the more common but not the only mode of discussing the deceased, for it is also tempered by careful criticism that is often subtle but unmistakable and all the more arresting in its understatement. As we saw in action during ceilis, criticism must be balanced with praise and plainspoken ridicule is shunned. Only the most wicked would be denied a good word during life. Still, the assertion by Witoszek and Sheeran most important to dispel is that praise is useless. Identification of the deceased's qualities, and shortcomings, is both an appropriate expression of affection and more. Characterizing the deceased either begins or intensifies the transformation of an individual from neighbor or relation into an exemplar of notions, principles, and attributes that the community who remain find useful to discuss.

The genre that best serves as a vehicle for contemplation of the individual's character is the local character anecdote. The exchange of anecdotes about the deceased plays a role in the grieving process by evoking his or her presence. If the deceased was recognized in life as a "character"—in Aghyaran parlance, a sort of local celebrity noted for conspicuous traits such as intelligent humor or innocent gullibility—people most likely already have a cycle of anecdotes about him or her to trade at his or her wake. By rehearsing known stories, mourners continue and make explicit the individual's transformation into a personality type. Through anecdotes over time Johnny Owens, for example, comes to exemplify the timeless sly trickster; Dennis Corry, the consummate unassailable smuggler; and Sarah Jane McGlynn, the classic curious neighbor in search of scandal. Each can serve as a model through which to contemplate larger issues such as the value of wit, the local ambivalence toward outside authority, and the potential claustrophobia of tight-knit community. Even if an individual was not particularly remarkable in narrative terms during life, there is nonetheless an effort by mourners at that individual's wake to typify him or her through anecdotes. Perhaps this typification turns a John Mongan into the archetypical quiet wee man who exemplified modesty and decency or a Bridie McMenamin into the dutiful, self-sacrificing mother from whom listeners should learn a lesson.

Whether recognized as a "character" in life or not, the deceased is resurrected through the exchange of anecdotes that amounts to a character study, in the literary sense of an examination of a given persona. Given form in narrative, the memory of the individual as embodied in anecdotes is as much community property as it is familial property. Character studies continue through the wake and beyond, intensifying a process of turning the individual into an assemblage of characteristics and occasionally into a recognizable personality type in local collective memory. Anecdotes focusing on personal character will be rehearsed again and again at ceilis and other social settings after the wake for as long as a given individual may be used to typify issues of concern to those who gather to evaluate shared experience through storytelling.

Interpretation of any given story depends greatly on attention to how and why it is told to certain ends in specific situational contexts. Further clues to intended and potential meanings in a story may come from attention to its genre, understood not only as a category of classification but more importantly as a set of conventions for the production and interpretation of discourse within a given speech community. Attention to generic contexts and their influence on meaning and performance will occupy us in the next two chapters. We begin with a more detailed consideration of the central genre discussed here—the local character anecdote.

5

Local Character Anecdotes

Storytelling at wakes, ceilis, and other social occasions has directed our attention repeatedly to a particular genre: anecdotes about neighbors and local characters, sometimes living but more often dead. Given the centrality of local character anecdotes to our investigation, we should review first popular and then folkloristic understandings of what anecdotes are.

Anecdotes can be understood to be both oral and literary. On March 11, 2001, the Sunday edition of the *New York Times* ran a short piece entitled "It's the Pith: Short Yarns that are Long on Legend," by Tom Kuntz. "Everybody loves anecdotes, which reminds me of a story…" begins Kuntz, who continues with seventeen of what he considers the best examples from the updated *Bartlett's Book of Anecdotes.* The subjects of these anecdotes include the likes of Muhammad Ali, Princess Diana, and Richard Nixon, which indicates that in common usage the term "anecdote" refers to short biographical stories about the rich and famous.

E. 'Nolue Emenanjo reviews several English-language definitions of the anecdote over time and identifies one commonality that "the anecdote is seen chiefly as something written" (1984:171–172). In the Irish context we have *The Book of Modern Irish Anecdotes: Humour, Wit and Wisdom* (1872), compiled by novelist and folklorist Patrick Kennedy. His work demonstrates a common understanding of the anecdote as a literary form taking for its subject the witticisms and story-worthy character attributes of contemporary celebrities and historical figures. As literature, anecdotes are most often collected for the expressed purpose of light entertainment.

Samuel Johnson's 1775 characterization of the anecdote as "something yet unpublished" (in Emenanjo 1984:171) reminds us that anecdotes often begin life as oral tradition, circulated in face-to-face interaction—hence one potential attraction for folklorists. Benjamin Botkin (1949) and Laurits Bødker (1965) provide brief encyclopedic references, demonstrating folklorists' recognition of anecdotes in the mid-twentieth century, but Archer Taylor correctly characterizes the state of folkloristic research into anecdotes up to 1970 in the title and argument of his "The Anecdote: A Neglected Genre." A few years later, Richard Dorson published a chapter entitled "Legends and Tall Tales" (1972) that defines the anecdote as a comic type of personal legend that highlights common eccentric character traits. Dorson ends his contribution to anecdote study with a helpful, lengthy note identifying sources for and collections of American anecdotes of local characters. Ronald Baker (1982:11–23) and Jan Brunvand (1986:173–176) adopt similar understandings of the anecdote as a form of personal legend focusing on locally known figures.

Sandra Stahl, now Dolby, refines folklorists' thinking on anecdotes by emphasizing their local orientation and their focus on the issue of character, hence her label "local character anecdote" rather than simply "anecdote" (1975). She also illustrates how the local character anecdote is a permeable genre with links to genres in addition to the legend. Patrick Mullen's *I Heard the Old Fishermen Say* (1988) treats regional and occupational lore on the Texas Gulf Coast, and includes an analysis of local character anecdotes in the seventh chapter. His investigation of rhetorical devices specific to the genre and the role of the social deviant in local folklore is particularly useful. Catherine Peck, too, highlights the role of the social deviant, or scofflaw in her terminology, in constructions of local identity through folklore (1992). She also notes how the local character anecdote may provide a frame for examples of other genres, such as the tall tale and supernatural legend, that are no longer as popular on the North Carolina coast. Henry Glassie's investigation of exploits and bids in Co. Fermanagh (1982a:44–49; 2005:85–91, 335–344) covers similar generic and cultural territory and will provide points of comparison and contrast as we proceed. Finally, Richard Bauman's treatment of West Texas anecdotes is quite helpful in extending investigation beyond generic definition to the formal features and rhetorical devices common in anecdotes and their efficacy in storytelling contexts. Specifically he draws from Mikhail Bakhtin's notion of the dialogic nature of discourse to focus on reported speech in anecdotes and its role in fusing narrated and narrative events in oral performance (1986:54–77).

With this previous research in mind, one way to approach anecdotes is to sketch the shape of the genre, with special attention to how anecdotes are constructed and used in Aghyaran in particular. There, oral anecdotes are brief and usually humorous biographical narratives. They relate reportedly factual incidents involving known or knowable, living or deceased individuals, often those people locally referred to as "characters." Told as firsthand personal narratives and as third-person accounts, anecdotes tend to focus on the interaction and dialogue of two people, usually during a single episode or scene. Dialogue often structures anecdotes, so reported and especially quoted speech, rendered in direct discourse, is a common formal feature of the genre. Anecdotes often climax or end with an individual's memorable statement, such as John McHugh's "Christ, cutty, so is this!" Such quotable remarks often serve as humorous punch lines, similar to those of jokes. Anecdotes can also share generic features with tall tales, historical legends, and personal experience narratives. Attempting a genre definition cannot be the end of study, but as a starting point it invites careful description and can lead to a more critical understanding of folklore in practice (cf. Stahl 1975:283).

Aghyaran anecdotes are firmly localized and most often foreground the notion of character and representative character types and traits, the focus of chapters 8 and 9. I have already described the local character anecdote as a reportedly factual, brief, first- or third-person narrative about known or knowable local individuals. To that description I would add that anecdotes in Aghyaran tend to break down into two thematic types— contemplative and comic—that correspond to the genres of the exploit and bid, respectively, which were identified by Glassie in terms provided by Ballymenone local Hugh Nolan (1982a:44–49ff.). In Aghyaran there is considerable overlap between these two types in form, content, and effect. Contemplative anecdotes that are told well, articulately summing up a personality or an idea relevant to conversation, can cause people to laugh, and comic anecdotes that climax in joke-like punch lines often have serious messages. Perhaps, in the case of Aghyaran, it is better to consider anecdotes as located somewhere on a continuum between the contemplative and the comic depending on their content, their structure, and especially their use in context, rather than splitting the genre into two sub-genres.

Both contemplative and comic anecdotes use individuals as exemplars of ideas, but contemplative anecdotes tend toward the serious in their telling and reception, and in the ideas exemplified and offered for consideration. It is tempting to call contemplative anecdotes "appreciative" because they foreground individuals' admirable qualities, such as perseverance and courage, which by implication are worthy of imitation. As we will see, however, comic anecdotes also offer appreciation of individuals' finer qualities, especially wit and verbal acuity, or evaluation of their lack of these qualities.

Sometimes contemplative anecdotes are followed by commentary and discussion that directly identifies the personal qualities worth appreciating and emulating, such as in the case of the wake anecdote about Bridie McMenamin giving birth in the midst of daily chores. The most basic form of contemplative anecdote is the simple remembrance: Paddy Boyle of Magherakeel was so strong that he transported a pig in a wheelbarrow all the way to Castlederg. Patrick McElhill of Shanaghy was so athletic that he jumped uphill over the gate of Magherakeel graveyard. Eddie McHugh was so kind and modest that he let the wee'uns (children) win when playing cards. Dennis Corry was such a prolific cattle smuggler that he spent more nights lying out than he did in bed, and that life made him so tough that he never thought to complain. Circumstances and actions, rather than quoted speech, comprise what is memorable and reportable in such basic contemplative anecdotes.

More complicated anecdotes, both contemplative and especially comic ones, are often structured in a way that leads up to a climax in the form of quoted speech. During a recorded nighttime gathering at my house, discussion turned from past and present funeral customs to the previously contentious system of assigning plots in St. Patrick's graveyard. Danny Gallen's offering to the turn of conversation was an anecdote about Fr. McKeague, parish priest from 1966 to 1983.

> *Well, they say the last big row about a grave would have been in Father McKeague's time.*
> *And two people differed about a piece of ground.*
> *And Father McKeague got them together.*
> *And he sorted it out very handy.*

He says, "You two people seem to be claiming the same
grave," and he says, "All I can do," he says, "is whichever of yous
wants it first can have it."
  And that's the way it was settled. Whoever died first got it.
  They say there was never a row about a grave since. Didn't
that man make great sense, you know?

Drawing from Labov (1982) and Bakhtin (1981), Bauman has demonstrated how in many anecdotes reported speech, especially the appropriated words of others rendered in direct discourse, is the "maximally reportable act recounted" and serves as the climax and point of the narrative
as a whole (1986:54–77). Drawing from Goffman, Bauman also observes
how anecdotes, like other narratives drawn from experience, are highly
"end-oriented stories" (Bauman 1986:59) that tend to be "organized from
the beginning in terms of what will prove to be the outcome" (Goffman
1974:559).

  Danny begins his story with a sort of claim about the traditionality,
and thus the authority, of the anecdote by starting with "they say." Authority resides in the collectivity of "they," previous narrators. Moreover,
"they" are ostensibly more reliable for having come before, for being closer
in time to the events narrated. With Fr. McKeague's retort in mind, Danny
tells us only as much as we need to know about the people involved and
more importantly about the situation that leads to conflict, in order for
the coming retort to have an impact. Properly contextualized, the quote
from Fr. McKeague dissolves social conflict in the narrated event by challenging the presumptions upon which tension is based. I will return to
the issue of how climactic, quoted speech in anecdotes comments upon
and often subverts the contextual information that proceeds it. For now,
we see an example of how many anecdotes are sequentially organized in
terms of an opening section that provides contextual information, then
the main action that often climaxes in direct discourse, and occasionally
a coda in which the narrator identifies the relevance of his story to the
present conversation, offers interpretation, or invites further discussion.
In this case, Danny's coda repeats his original "they say," thus framing the
anecdote with two efforts at traditionalization, the "active construction of
connections that link the present [text] with a meaningful past" (Bauman
1992a:136). Moreover, the coda reiterates the relevance of his story as an

explanation of how a conflict was resolved and as an appreciation of a man who made "great sense."

Responding to situational context, Danny offered the story as an illustration of the topic of conversation and ended with an appreciation of Fr. McKeague's wisdom. The anecdote was not offered primarily as an attempt to entertain through humor, but Danny's rendition of the priest's final statement elicited short, forceful laughs from his audience in recognition of Fr. McKeague's wit and perhaps in approval of the priest's perspective that the quarrel was senseless. Death comes to us all, Fr. McKeague argues, and as long as burial in sacred ground is assured there is no need to be in a rush to claim a specific plot.

This particular anecdote could be pushed more toward the contemplative or more toward the comic depending on its use in context, and by no means are these two extremes mutually exclusive. As a more contemplative anecdote in this context, the story remembers the sagacity of a popular parish priest while simultaneously exposing the potential pettiness of local bickering. Perspective and common sense are necessary to resolve quarrels that are relatively superfluous in a place where other conflicts take priority.

The vast majority of anecdotes told are intended to be humorous. Quite often, comic anecdotes highlight an individual's wit as demonstrated through verbal repartee, and they contribute to a communal sense of pride in the intelligence of locals. In order to illustrate how anecdotes memorialize the wit of past and present locals, let us continue with a couple of stories that are somewhat thematically related to the last one about Fr. McKeague. Always at issue along Ireland's internal border is discerning which issues are worth fighting over and which are not, whether conflict be between neighbors arguing in the rectory over grave plots or between groups of people divided by the legacy of colonialism.

In a state originally established to privilege Protestants, and particularly in reputedly republican areas such as Aghyaran, Catholics were long subject to seemingly prejudicial scrutiny and occasionally patronizing treatment by police and soldiers at permanent and temporary checkpoints on the roads. On such occasions, Aghyaran Catholics had to choose between conciliatory behavior and confrontation—or something in between—which often amounted to choosing between minimizing their delay and maintaining self-esteem through some show of defiance. Asked about his experiences with the RUC, UDR, RIR, and British army, Danny recalled instances of harassment and inconvenience but moved quickly into comic anecdotes about how others have dealt with the authorities at checkpoints.

The first of theses anecdotes concerns a middle-aged farmer, Willie Duffy, confronted about a road tax sticker missing from his windshield. Understand as basic context that being interrogated at a checkpoint can be rather intimidating. As one soldier or policeman handles the interrogation and determines whether or not to search your car and your person, other soldiers or policemen have their weapons trained on you. Verbal sparring and general cheekiness are therefore rare. With that in mind, consider Danny's account of Mr. Duffy's checkpoint confrontation.

> *Willie Duffy was stopped in Killen, and I think Tommy Doherty was with him. He had a trailer on, and he was carting hay or something. He was stopped at a checkpoint in Killen anyway.*
>
> *And, eh, the soldier asked him—everything was right, you see, his license and all.*
>
> *And he says, "You've got no tax up."*
>
> *"Ah," Willie says, he says, "she's taxed all right." He says, "I'm right for the road. Everything's right with me. I'm never on the road and me wrong," he says, "There's five or six kids in our house, and they just pulled it down."*
>
> *And the boy says, he says, "There was five or six kids in our family, but we wouldn't have been allowed to do things like that."*
>
> *And Willie says, "Whatever about that," he says, "your father didn't think much about you when he let you over here with a gun in your hand." ◊*
>
> *Ah, they kept him for hours, Ray, pulling the car, the trailer to pieces. He annoyed them and that would be it, you see.*

Parsing this anecdote, we see that the narrative is ordered in a way that builds up to Mr. Duffy's retort. Danny introduces the dramatis personae, sets the scene, and stops himself before reporting the soldier's interrogation to establish, in his role as omniscient narrator, that Mr. Duffy was in the right. Then Danny lets the story unfold in dialogue that is crucial to the outcome and point of his story. The anecdote climaxes in reported speech: the farmer's reply that allows him to save face when he feels the soldier has crossed a line by questioning his competence as a father.

Looking to the dialogue, we find that Mr. Duffy, challenged about the missing tax sticker, gives the soldier a chance to trust him as a man with a reputation for and commitment to responsibility: "I'm never on the road and me wrong." To that he adds an explanation for his appearance of negligence: the kids "just pulled it down." The soldier refuses to treat him with empathy, man to man. Dismissing the farmer's explanation as a typical lame excuse, the soldier makes a personal attack, tapping into stereotypes of Irish Catholics as lax and undisciplined. But Mr. Duffy—as Danny conjures him—will have none of it and turns the attack on its head.

By saying that he grew up as one of "five or six kids," the soldier sets up the comparison between his own father and Mr. Duffy, and implicitly between himself and Mr. Duffy's children. In a flash of wit, Mr. Duffy uses that parallelism as an entry into counterattack, by treating the soldier as an unruly child talking back to his elder. Note how Danny may be appropriating Mr. Duffy's perspective, calling the soldier "boy." Moreover, seizing the role of father, disciplinarian, and teacher, Mr. Duffy demonstrates that he cares more for his children than the soldier's father does for his. "Your father didn't think much about you when he let you over here with a gun in your hand." Mr. Duffy argues that the father who wastes his energy ensuring impeccable behavior but allows his children to endanger themselves by meddling in the lives of others has misplaced priorities. Serving as punch line and climax of the anecdote, Mr. Duffy's retort completely subverts the soldier's criticism, and lays it back at his feet. This response both dismisses the soldier's bureaucratic concerns and trivializes his authority as contingent upon merely having a gun in his hand. Rendered a child out of his depth, the soldier is an outsider to a community that resents his intrusion for the political tensions it exacerbates.

Pushing beyond close reading to focus on formal structure, we should note how the punch line of this or any anecdote serves as a reflexive comic corrective. As Bauman observes, punch lines "loop back to reconstitute or rekey (Goffman 1974:79–81) what has come before. In this process, the antecedent portion of the narrative, which has built up a context for the punch line, is itself recontextualized" (1986:59). Inherently reflexive and subversive, punch lines effect an ironic, relativistic shift in our understanding of the situation previously described; punch lines appropriate what has come before to put forth an alternate perspective. By virtue of their formal conventions, anecdotes, jokes, and any punch line–driven narratives are dialogic, heteroglossic, and perhaps contrarian by nature. More specifically, by virtue of revolving around punch lines, anecdotes are bound formally and structurally to challenge assumptions, to subvert received hierarchies of power and value. Being subversive, punch lines allow both the anecdote narrator and the protagonist whose words he appropriates to "take on a skepticism and relativism that takes pleasure in refusing to take ideal, normative moral expectations too seriously" (Bauman 1986:75).

The West Texas anecdotes Bauman examines revolve around issues of morality and subversively leave open to question the cultural norms underpinning social tension, such as the local work ethic and attitudes toward public drunkenness. In contrast, the anecdote about Mr. Duffy at the checkpoint, like many Aghyaran anecdotes, has more to do with leaving the issue of authority open to question. By establishing an alternative to the perspective that the armed men at a checkpoint are in authority, Mr. Duffy's retort is a victory for locals who see themselves as harassed. Rendering the soldier a child out of his depth, the anecdote gives voice to resentment at the presence of outsiders who exacerbate political tensions. In this way, an otherwise comic anecdote conveys serious messages and potentially shapes collective attitudes.

Moreover, Danny's coda is no mere afterthought but an artfully constructed statement that further complicates the potential message of the story. In formal and referential terms, there is a parallel between the coda and the dialogue that sets up the punch line. Consciously or not, Danny uses the same verb, "pull," when quoting Mr. Duffy's explanation that his kids "pulled down" the sticker and when describing how the soldiers further inconvenience Mr. Duffy in response to his show of defiance, "pulling the car, the trailer to pieces." This word choice in the coda recapitulates Mr. Duffy's earlier implication that the soldier is acting childishly. In Danny's characterization, the soldier and his colleagues pulling apart the car and trailer is just as arbitrarily destructive and ultimately as trivial as Mr. Duffy's children pulling down the road tax sticker.

However, Danny's coda serves not only to reiterate Mr. Duffy's perspective that British military presence is capricious and prejudicial in its intrusion, but also to project part of Danny's personal perspective. His coda in this version of the story puts a damper on whatever vicarious enjoyment we might have in Mr. Duffy's victory. On the one hand, the punch line—which is a structural necessity and is the same in all versions of the anecdote I heard—upsets the apparent direction in which the gist of the story was leading. On the other hand, Danny's personal coda offers yet another perspective on both the reported events and the subversive success of the punch line. Mr. Duffy achieved a successful challenge to authority, but it was short-lived.

Danny is the sort of storyteller who only reluctantly tells a fairy legend and never without distancing himself from superstition or offering rational alternatives for supposed mysteries. As one of my guides to the political landscape of Aghyaran, he wants to convey what he knows to be truth. As an intellect, he tends toward skepticism. As a narrator, he embraces realism. So in telling anecdotes that deal with political tension, he is unwilling to end at the entertaining, optimistic punch line. The truth as Danny understands it is that tension remains, and questioning authority, even conceptually overturning unfair social structures through verbal wit, does not necessarily lead to justice at the end of the day.

Mr. Duffy's is not the only way to deal with the indignity of checkpoints, and Danny continued with an anecdote about his neighbor and contemporary Paddy O'Donnell. The events remembered took place at a time when the army and police were suspicious of members of Comhaltas Ceoltori Éireann—an organization that promotes traditional Irish music, song, and dance—and they were especially suspicious of CCÉ members found in the vicinity of Carrickmore, a staunchly republican area.

> *After we got the branch of Comhaltas going in Aghyaran— that would've been in 1974—the following summer, the first fleadh [music festival] in Tyrone for a long time was going to be held in Carrickmore, you see.*
>
> *So having a branch in Aghyaran, they'd expect help, you know. So Paddy decided we'd go to a meeting—that had been decided at a branch meeting that we'd go, like, and Paddy and me would've been delegated maybe to go. . . . I don't know how it happened, but we went anyway, went to the meeting in Carrickmore, and on our way back, a couple of miles out of Carrickmore we were stopped at the checkpoint, and it was UDR and policemen . . . no, soldiers, like, and this bloke says,*

"*Where are ye coming from?*"

Paddy says, "*Carrickmore.*"

"*And where are ye from?*"

"*We're from Aghyaran.*"

"*And what are ye doing in Carrickmore?*"

Paddy says, "*We were at a meeting.*"

You'd see their faces light up, like, you know? ◊ *That bloke's gonna tell it all.* ◊

"*Right,*" *they said,* "*get out.*"

And we got out of the car. He got a book and pen, started writing down our names and addresses and all this.

"*Where abouts in Carrickmore was the meeting?*"

Told them it was in the old school.

"*What was the meeting about?*"

Paddy says, "*fleadh ceol.*"

He says, "*What, mate?*" *[in a high-pitched Cockney accent]*

Paddy says it again, and that went on, he said it about three times.

"*What's a fleadh ceol?*"

And Paddy started telling him, you know, about the competition for Irish music, you know, and dancing and everything else.

And he says, "*You know, it starts off with the under elevens on a Saturday, and then the twelve to fifteens, and the fifteen through eighteens. On Sunday,*" *he says,* "*you have the senior competitions: banjo, fiddle, accordion*"—*and by this time, the boy was ready to stick his fingers in his ears.* ◊

"*And then,*" *Paddy says,* "*on Sunday,*" *he says,* "*there'll be street music sessions on Sunday all day, and it'll finish up in the Patrician Hall with a final ceili, you see.*" ◊

And the bloke was trying to push us away, you know. ◊ *They were trying to get rid of us. We were really sickening them, and Paddy kept going, you know*—"*Any of yous with an interest are more than welcome to come.*" ◊

He nearly had to shove him into the car again. That was a
great approach, you know.

But meeting two blokes from Aghyaran in the middle of
the night up there coming from a meeting in Carrickmore, they
really thought they had something, you know.

Paddy had politely answered all the questions asked of him, but at the same time had "got his own back" by "torturing" the outsider—and reiterating the soldier's outsider status—with more esoteric detail than he could possibly have been interested in. Following the letter of the law in his absolute compliance while simultaneously making himself a nuisance was a masterful, underhanded strategy for repaying the soldier in kind for his annoying intrusiveness. For an audience sympathetic to Paddy's predicament, the anecdote offers a lighter take on a customarily tense situation and potentially provides its receivers vicarious enjoyment of another minor victory. It is another example of how most anecdotes that are structured through dialogue foreground verbal contest, showcase wit, and tend toward the comic.

Again, however, the victory is short-lived, and in a following story, Danny brought us back to a more somber view of everyday reality. There is no doubt that the soldiers logged the exchange, for at subsequent checkpoints Paddy was subjected to hours of interrogation for information in minute detail about his family and neighbors and their distinguishing characteristics, jobs, and addresses.

Aghyaran comic anecdotes highlight not only the verbal wit of locals, but also gullibility or lack of wit and especially nonconformity and eccentricity, demonstrated through accounts of individuals' actions and memorable sayings. As we will see in the following chapters, both comic and contemplative Aghyaran anecdotes provide commentary on several issues and serve several functions. As a body of oral narrative they amount to character studies through which people think about their neighbors and themselves. They assign people and their memories varying levels of social status and offer meditation on the nature of a community composed of such memorable individuals. As "equipment for living" (Burke

1973 [1941]), anecdotes facilitate reflection on human nature, historical change, and the validity or vulnerability of cultural norms and social structures. For now, though, we have sufficient information about the common formal features and thematic ground of anecdotes to make comparisons with other related genres, and this exercise will shed further light on the centrality and potential social uses of anecdotes.

In terms of the progress of sociability and discourse at ceilis and wakes, quite often conversation beginning with talk about the neighbors or about the deceased leads to breakthroughs into performance in the form of anecdote-telling. In addition, it seems that people often remember and bring up stories from other genres for consideration because of either thematic or formal affinities with anecdotes already told. Of course, legends, jokes, tall tales, and personal experience narratives come to mind for storytellers for various reasons and not always because of affinities with anecdotes. However, because the anecdote shares many aspects with these genres, a given anecdote often sparks associations with stories from other genres.

Conceptually speaking, a link can be drawn from the anecdote to every other common storytelling genre. Contemplative anecdotes have much in common with historical legends. Comic anecdotes overlap considerably with jokes and tall tales. Both contemplative and comic anecdotes have formal affinities with personal experience narratives, some of which share thematic ground with supernatural legends, others with historical legends.

Preliminary as the task of understanding one genre of stories and their potential uses is, more context is necessary to do it justice. Specifically, we need to understand the anecdote's place in the context of other local storytelling genres. That is, anecdotes are grasped as much by accumulating evidence of the internal consistency of stories identifiable as anecdotes, as they are by contrasting them to examples of other identifiable genres. Through comparison and contrast we learn both about the formal interrelationships of genres and about the overlapping, complementing, and contrasting roles they play in the conduct of social interaction and, ultimately, the construction of collective memory and local identity.

6

The Wider Range of
Storytelling Genres

The ubiquity of the local character anecdote suggests its centrality, and yet the anecdote significantly overlaps with jokes, tall tales, personal experience narratives, and legends to the point that the anecdote has the potential to lose its autonomy in the "crowd of neighboring genres" (Stahl 1975:296). This permeability of the boundaries of the anecdote as a genre in fact reiterates its prominence. Storytelling genres appropriate at Aghyaran wakes and ceilis have either direct or indirect thematic, stylistic, organizational, or functional links to the anecdote. Thus, the anecdote is not only quantitatively significant, but also conceptually central in the generic system of Aghyaran storytelling. This chapter identifies genres in addition to the anecdote that are appropriate in the storytelling contexts discussed in chapters 3 and 4. In doing so, it will give special attention to the relationship between each of these genres and anecdotes, and what light these relationships shed on the nature of Aghyaran's central genre, the anecdote.

Although there is much overlap between the genres appropriate at ceilis and wakes, some genres that typically deal with supernatural themes are not as common at wakes for reasons already discussed in chapter 3. Because the range of genres appropriate at ceilis is broader, the ceili will stand in as the default situational context of the generic system of Aghyaran storytelling to be described. In other words, our focus will be on the generic system of ceilis, realizing at the same time that the generic system of wakes is comparable but slightly narrower. Undertaking this descriptive project should inform us sufficiently to further bear down in the next two chapters on specific stories and especially on the common issues raised by and potential social functions of anecdotes about local characters told in Aghyaran.

Defining the entire generic system of local discourse in Aghyaran, in itself an ideal model, is beyond the scope of this project. The system would include smaller conversational genres such as riddles and proverbs (Abrahams 1968, 1976; Yerkovich 1983) and a breathtakingly broad range of recurring, patterned, convention-informed types of verbal exchange familiar from the management of face-to-face interaction in everyday life (Goffman 1971; cf. Hymes 1975:351). Limited but informed, our focus here will remain on genres of "larger" narrative—what Abrahams refers to as fictive genres (1976)—including the legend, personal experience narrative, tall tale, and joke, in order to better understand the anecdote. Many of these narrative genres are more familiar to folklorists than the conversational genres Hymes and Goffman identify, but less familiar than the Märchen, fairy legends, and hero tales that are no longer as central in contemporary oral traditions in Ireland as they seem to have been in the nineteenth century.

These genres to be discussed should be considered paradigmatic ideal types rather than rigid and universal analytical categories for the classification of narrative. Although characterizations of genres are drawn from observations of storytelling events and from subsequent conversations with participants, for the most part I give the genres to be discussed etic names for our convenience.

The closest genre to the contemplative anecdote is the personal legend, a type of historical legend that focuses on the actions and traits of an actual person or persons from a previous historical period. The protagonists in all the personal legends I heard in Aghyaran were locals or near-locals, with the exceptions of St. Patrick, who is said to have visited the area, and of Oliver Cromwell, whose seventeenth-century military campaign through Ireland had a lasting effect on the local political environment. Some folklorists would make a distinction between the personal historical legend and the local historical legend, which details the events that took place at a specific local place. Local legends in Irish tradition may be referred to with the Irish-language term *dinnsenchas,* "place lore." In Aghyaran most examples of place lore involve human actors and what they did at a particular location. In some cases a legend exists simply to explain the significance of a place rather than to memorialize particular people from the past. For the most part, however, location serves as a sort of mnemonic device for recalling events that are the result of actions and reactions of past individuals. Thus, the distinction between personal and local historical legends is relatively unnecessary for our purposes here.

One of the main distinctions between contemplative anecdotes and personal legends in Aghyaran is that of time period. The anecdote memorializes contemporary persons or ones within living memory, whereas the personal legend memorializes those who died before tellers and listeners were born or cognizant of a given personal legend's protagonist. This temporal dimension is relative, hence one reason for overlap between the two genres. One person's experience with a particular character may be narrated in a first-person narrative as an anecdote, and the same narrated events may be recalled as a secondhand personal legend by others in a later generation.

In formal terms, both contemplative anecdotes and personal legends are less constrained textually than comic anecdotes, jokes, and some more recent tall tales—narratives that typically foreground direct discourse, conclude with punch lines, and are thus "organized from the beginning in terms of what will prove to be the outcome" (Goffman 1974:559). Because contemplative anecdotes and personal legends tend to revolve around reportable actions rather than quoted speech, those who tell such stories are allowed relative flexibility in terms of organizational, stylistic, and semantic choices. Contemplative anecdotes and personal legends are thus more susceptible to textual variation from one telling to the next, over time, because they allow tellers to modify their stories to best suit their social and discursive contexts. Both genres provide the building blocks of conversational give and take when the past becomes relevant to people's thoughts about the present. Both genres tend toward the prosaic rather than the poetic because in both genres verbal artistry is subordinate to matters of content and its thematic relevance to a given conversation. What Elliott Oring says of the legend in general is equally applicable to personal legends and most contemplative anecdotes:

> Legends may be artfully told, but their raison d'etre is rarely the creation of an aesthetically satisfying story. . . . Thus, the appear-

ance of a legend in normal conversation may not be readily apparent, for the verbal artistry of the legend may not be distinguished significantly from the artistry of the conversation in which it is embedded. (1986:126)

In addition to overlap in form, there is also some thematic overlap between contemplative anecdotes and personal legends, and this can leave temporal setting and lack of first-person accounting as the only formal elements separating the personal legend from the contemplative anecdote. For example, stories of strong men appeal to many middle-aged and elderly men in Aghyaran. John McElhill often tells an anecdote about Victor Chapman, now elderly and living in Killen. He recalls a time at the corn mill in Speerholme when he witnessed Mr. Chapman as a youth lifting two sixteen-stone bags of grain over the tailboard of a horse cart when others present could hardly lift one the necessary height. This story may or may not survive as a personal legend in future generations, but it could as long as the theme of the strong man remains relevant and Mr. Chapman's feat continues to impress. Other personal legends of strongmen that most likely started as anecdotes have also survived.

One night in mid-January, John McElhill, Barney McGrath, Danny Gallen, and Pat Den Gallagher gathered for a ceili in my house. After a little more than two hours of conversation that inspired several reminiscences and anecdotes, Barney began discussing the topic of men in the not-too-distant past being better fit to carry massive loads of produce and turf to near and far market places. John added to the conversation his anecdote about Mr. Chapman. In response, Danny recalled a short legend about Doney O'Donnell, about whom he had written an article in 1994 for *Aghyaran*. Doney lived locally during mid-1800s, and his name appears in Griffith's Valuation for 1860 as a resident of a Ballymongan farm known as "Hoynes's"—the local Gaelic-inflected pronunciation of Owens's, the family who now own this farm. Danny's story sparked other related ones that join in a larger cycle of legends about Doney.

> DANNY: *Well, did ever you hear about the boy who put his initials on the door of the mill?*
>
> JOHN: *No.*
>
> DANNY: *Did you hear tell of Doney O'Donnell who lived down at Owens's?*

JOHN: *Down at Owens's?*

DANNY: *Aye, Johnny Hoynes. Aye, he was supposed to put his finger through the six and fifty [a metal weight] and carved his initials in the door.*

JOHN: *Was he?*

DANNY: *So Mickey Byrne says.* ◊

JOHN: *I never heard tell of that, now.*

DANNY: *"D. O'D."* ◊

BARNEY: *Aye, that's the boy that used to lift the horse. There was a mare foal down there. And when she foaled he, he lifted the wee foal over his head. Got in under her legs every day, and he lifted her everyday.*

RAY: *Is that right?*

BARNEY: *And when that foal grew to be a big horse he was still fit to lift it.*

PAT: *Aye, he would.*

BARNEY: *Aye, Doney O'Donnell.*

JOHN: *Boys a boys.*

BARNEY: *He was supposed to be unbeatable, you know. There come several men here to fight with him, you know.*

RAY: *Is that right?*

BARNEY: *And he was fit for them all. But then he was coming out of, eh, Castlederg one time with a pony and two creels on it. And I think a pig in every creel. And there was Donegal boys that attacked him, two or three of them. They left him useless. He was never any good after it. Did ever you hear tell of that, Danny?*

DANNY: *Aye, I did surely. I heared he was coming out of Castlefinn, now.*

BARNEY: *Aye . . .*

DANNY: *With his pigs in the creels, and he couldn't sell them in the fair. And these boys followed him out, and they said they wanted to buy the pigs, you see—that's very funny, the*

pigs' d been in the fair and nobody wanted to buy them. But, eh,
they said they wanted to see the pigs, you'd have to take them
down.

So they got the one side to take down a pig from the creel,
and he got down the pig from the creel on the other side.

And then when they seen the pigs they said they wouldn't
buy them, so he says, "You'll have to help me back on with
them," and that's where the difference came from.

They said, "no," said, "put 'em on yourself"—something
you couldn't do, you see, you couldn't . . .

PAT: *No, no, you put on one and the other' d be gone before*
you . . . that's right . . .

DANNY: *So the row broke out and he got a bad beating. I*
think he died six months after that.

John McElhill is a fine storyteller with a clear memory. He also has a
reputation for codding. With this in mind, Danny directs his initial question—"Did you hear tell of Doney O'Donnell"—to John. Danny is about
to launch into a legend about Doney that he does not fully believe, but
perhaps he wants to gauge whether John does or whether John will take
up the story to embellish it further. Notice how Danny dissociates himself
from his story about Doney's carving his initials in the mill door by saying
at the end that he heard it from Mickey Byrne, who also has a reputation for
codding. True to form, Danny laughs, betraying his skepticism that Doney
or any man could carve letters into a door with his finger, much less with a
fifty-six-pound weight hanging from his hand.

Barney, on the other hand, seems to sense the skepticism. Before John
has a chance to respond further and before Doney is dismissed along with
exaggerations about him, he rejoins the discussion. Whether or not Barney believes Danny's story, he adds to Doney's legendary reputation for
strength in a more earnest tone of voice with stories about Doney's lifting
the foal, beating challengers, and eventually being beaten. Moreover, he
brings Danny into accord with him by asking him to verify the story of
Doney's demise. Throughout, Pat Den only speaks when registering his
belief in the plausibility of the narratives—"Aye," "That's right."

Here, Doney's legend is not one person's reporting of a single plot
handed down by word of mouth that can be represented on the page as a

Figure 6.1. Francis McHugh and John McElhill

text, an item of folklore with clear textual boundaries ready for the archive. Other personal legends told in Aghyaran, such as those about highwaymen Black Francis (Proinsias Dubh) and Souple Corrigan, could more readily be printed in a convenient block quote on the page, margin to margin, displaying hallmarks of a discrete text. In this particular conversational setting, however, the legend of Doney is the result of exchange, negotiation, and collective re-authoring using fragments of plots remembered and reassembled from past discussions between these men and their predecessors.

Part of the negotiation is over the issue of belief, and this negotiation aptly illustrates Linda Dégh and Andrew Vázsonyi's critical revision of the previously accepted definition of the legend (1976). Before criticism in the 1970s, the legend was defined as "a story or narrative, set in the recent or historical past, that is believed to be true by those to whom and by whom it is communicated" (Georges 1971:5). Dégh and Vázsonyi demonstrated, however, that tellers and audience members do not always believe the legends they tell and hear. More important than people's strict belief in the events of a legend is the opportunity legends provide for "the expression of opinion on the question of truth and belief" (1976:119). Particular legends may or may not be believed but the issue of belief is implicit in all legends—"any legend, no matter how fragmentary or corrupt, makes its case" (1976:119). In his succinct characterization of legends, Oring states that "The narration of a legend is, in a sense, the negotiation of the truth of these episodes.... In a legend, the question of truth must be *entertained* even if that truth is ultimately rejected" (1986:125).

Whether or not all assembled at the ceili believed every detail of the stories told about Doney, he served as an exemplar of one aspect of ideal masculinity: physical strength. Like contemplative anecdotes, these personal legends about Doney foreground the qualities of a local community member, offer appreciation, and cast him as a heroic type worthy of imitation. Still, Doney is not idealized beyond recognition as a man without human failings and vulnerabilities. When Danny told me again, four months later, about Doney's downfall, he offered a probable explanation for why the Donegal men attacked Doney: "They said he was a man that was inclined to take a drink and would be a fighting man, you know, so he could have enemies in any town." Doney can serve as a concentration in symbolic form of a shared ideal, but his memory still preserves some of his complexity.

Contemplative anecdotes and personal legends share more themes than that of heroic strength. Another personal legend that serves the appreciative role of the contemplative anecdote is that about Peggy "Roe" McGrath and her tragic death in January of 1848, during the depth of the Famine. According to the several people who know versions of the legend, Peggy lived just across the Tyrone border in the Donegal townland of Crilly. She was seventeen when she walked eight miles with her fourteen-year-old brother, Patrick, to the Friday fair in Castlederg. As soon as they reached the fair, the two realized that a storm was coming and decided to return home. As they trekked home through the hills, they were soon caught up in a blizzard. Having lost their way, they eventually succumbed to exposure. Days later, neighbors found their bodies embracing in the snow, one mile from home. A most poignant and widely reported detail was that Peggy had placed her shawl around her younger brother, and her sacrifice has led many to remember her as a heroine. Through the legend, Peggy exemplifies qualities worth contemplating by adults and worth passing on to children.

Another reason the story remains memorable and affecting is that the sense of tragedy is amplified by the theme of star-crossed lovers. Apparently, Peggy and her brother took a less direct, more hazardous route home because her father forbade her to come into contact with a young man of reportedly dubious reputation who had tried and failed to elope with her. As Packy Jim McGrath comments, "He was supposed to say that he'd rather have his daughter dead as married on that boy, and he did see her dead, too." The father, James, was a locally respected stonecutter, and some add to the story that, broken-hearted, he attempted to inscribe a headstone for his children but could not carve more than "In loving memory."

To pigeonhole the story as solely a personal legend that shares thematic features with contemplative anecdotes by offering appreciation of Peggy's heroism would be artificial and constraining. The story's function and affect is as various as the discursive contexts in which it is appropriate to tell. It could serve equally well as a relatively neutral chronicle of past happenings in a particular locale, a moralistic tale offering various warnings to parents, an indictment of societal norms concerning familial and gender relations, a story of desperation during the Famine, or a singer's gloss on similar tragic events in a popular local ballad such as "The Little Penknife."[1] But a conceptual connection between the contemplative anecdote and personal legend is clear in their potential for foregrounding a character's qualities in order to make a point.

The temporal connection between the two genres—with contemplative anecdotes surviving over time in the form of personal legends—is slightly more speculative. Documentary evidence of folklore and oral history recorded in Aghyaran beyond living memory is lacking, so most often the evolution of a particular anecdote from a previous generation into a contemporary personal legend cannot be traced. Judging from thematic overlap between stories from both genres in the present, we can only infer that many personal legends began as contemplative anecdotes.[2] However, looking at the body of Aghyaran personal legends as a whole, it is evident that despite some thematic overlap with contemplative anecdotes, local personal legends place more emphasis on certain themes not as common in contemplative anecdotes.

Whether we name them personal legends, historical legends, or tales of history, the vast majority of stories told in Aghyaran about people in the past, beyond living memory, concern politics and the nature of community in the midst of conflict. Legends of the eighteenth-century outlawed rapparee Proinsias Dubh, or Black Francis, and his redistributions of wealth offer glimpses of brief local—and specifically Catholic—victories over injustice.[3] Legends of the cruelty of nineteenth-century landlord agents and twentieth-century Black and Tans delineate boundaries of right and wrong and assert that nationalist resistance to oppression is justifiable. Yet once the prospect of violence arises, another set of legends becomes relevant. These legends complicate present social reality by revealing that local divisions are not predestined, by asserting that the allegiances that matter are local rather than sectarian. For example, the ill-fated United Irishmen of Aghyaran, poised to take part in the rebellion of 1798, included more Presbyterians than Catholics, with whom they shared a second-class citizenship in a state that privileged Anglicans. Earlier during the Penal Era when Fr. Cornelius O'Mongan was hunted by the yeomanry, it was the miller Kyle, an Anglican, who took the priest in and fired the shots that dispersed his pursuers.

The next largest body of legend concerns tragic, nonpolitical deaths, such as that of Peggy Roe and those of others who drowned, were struck by lightening, were killed in accidents, or took their own lives. A still smaller body of legend concerns sacred origins—St. Patrick's conversion of the local pagan chieftains; his blessing the holy well in Magherakeel; his establishment of the Lough Derg pilgrimage site; his battle with a tyrannical serpent whose blood filled the lough, changed the color of the river, and gave both bodies of water their name: "derg," Irish Gaelic for red. In fact, it is only the smallest body of legend that resembles the contemplative anecdote in its treatment of people remembered for certain personality traits and qualities of character. Interestingly, protagonists of such legends tend to be from the relatively recent past, and this in turn implies that people remembered for personality traits alone must have lived in the recent past in order to survive in collective memory.

If we are interested in a temporal or evolutionary link between the contemplative anecdote and personal legend, the implication we might draw is that some, but not all, contemplative anecdotes will survive as time passes in the form of personal legends. Further exploration of Aghyaran legends would also indicate apocryphal elements being attached to memorable persons. Contemplative anecdotes and personal legends may share formal features such as verb tense and prosaic style, thematic ground such as physical strength and moral fortitude, and persuasive functions such as appreciation of personal qualities and the implication that these qualities should be imitated. Yet only those characters of anecdotes whose actions and personalities remain most memorable, reportable, and in the end relevant to present concerns will stand the test of time in local collective memory.

For instance, Aghyaran's economy may complete a transition from agriculture to service industries. In such a case, daily physical labor may become more of a novelty, and the feats of strong men such as Victor Chapman may no longer capture imagination and make the transition to legend as it seems anecdotes of Doney O'Donnell did. In generations to come the six northern counties may witness genuine political, social, and cultural change. If so, the troops may be gone for good, sectarianism may be undermined, and the miniature, intimate moral victories of Willie Duffy and Paddy O'Donnell may fade from memory. Certain historical situations and people's reactions to them will remain relevant; others will not. Certain anecdotes will become legends because they already exemplify the thematic concerns of currently relevant legends, and others will not.

If a generation can boast an individual of the historical importance or social resonance of a saint, outlaw, or hunted priest, anecdotes about that person will live on in legend. Barring that, those anecdotes that invite reflection on human nature and the human condition, regardless of temporality, stand a good chance of survival. It is precisely people's experiences of the changes peculiar to modernity that may propel into the future anecdotes of Fr. McKeague's common sense in the face of eternal pettiness and Bridie McMenamin's almost unimaginable self-sacrifice, work ethic, and sense of family duty. It is precisely the comparison of past and present in order to evaluate the status quo that gives rise to historical discourse, of which anecdote- and legend-telling are primary forms.

Whereas contemplative anecdotes gesture toward personal legends, the majority of Aghyaran anecdotes are comic and gesture through form, content, and potential function to tall tales and jokes. Through the tall tale and joke we enter the realm of fiction that is nonetheless resonant with the social reality of Aghyaran storytellers and their audiences.

Whether told in third- or first-person, tall tales begin in plausibility but expand through comic exaggeration into entertaining fantasy. Those who tell tall tales depend on the conventions of other genres such as the personal experience narrative and the anecdote to establish the initial plausibility. The first-person point of view and the narrator's claims of veracity, familiar from narratives of personal experience, may prolong the listener's belief in the actuality of events being narrated. The teller's introduction of his tall tale as a story about a known character may lead the listener to expect that the story will end, like any given anecdote, with the protagonist's flash of wit or feat of strength, for instance, that is nonetheless within the realm of possibility. In the end, the teller's exaggeration of reality builds upon itself, and listeners come to realize that the tale is fiction. Yet the artistry of the telling and the clever marshaling of imagination reward the listener's involvement in the performance through his or her willing suspension of disbelief.

The tall tale has been a particularly privileged form in the study of American folklore, yet the American tall tale has its precursors in Europe.[4] In Aghyaran the genre finds a place in ceilis, wakes, and other social situations. However, just as Bauman found in Canton, Texas (1986:18), traditional tall tales of the sort found in the tale type indexes of Thompson (1961) and Baughman (1966) are rarely told in Aghyaran except to outsiders. This may be due, in part, to the fact that they have become too familiar. Packy Jim and Danny both remember that certain local characters of their youth would think up new tall tales during their daily chores for performance at nightly ceilis. However, they believe that now few people bother to compose such yarns, much less tell traditional ones, because television has replaced the tall tale as a primary outlet for fantasy.

Patrick McElhill is an exception to the rule that few tell tall tales. A native of the Drumquin area, Patrick has a wide repertoire of tall tales, jokes, recitations, and songs, and he is widely valued as a chatty character in several neighboring communities, including Ederney in North Fermanagh, Lettercran and Pettigo in Southeast Donegal, and Aghyaran and Castlederg in West Tyrone. One night I hosted a number of local singers, including Patrick, in order to record songs I had heard or heard mentioned but never taped. We sat in a rough circle, and singers took the floor in turns. During a lull between songs, the topic of wakes emerged, and several reminisced about the more raucous wakes they had been to or heard about. With wakes and yarns in mind, Patrick joined in with the following:

> *I was telling a wee story about the time a neighbor man of*
> *mine and me traveled over to County Donegal till a wake.*
>
> *And, eh, the widow had her husband laid out for the wake,*
> *and he had the greatest smile on him ever seen on a corpse in*
> *Ireland before.*

Aye.

I said to her, "What happened to him?"

She says, "The reason he's smiling: he was struck eight
times by lightning, and he thought he was having his
photograph taken." ◊

Though very brief, the story exemplifies a number of common tall tale features. Not all tall tales are told in first-person, but those that are involve the narrator more closely in the action of the story, as Mullen has noted (1988:143). Moreover, Bauman notes that first-person tall tales masquerade, for a while anyway, as a "true" personal experience narrative (1986:20). Using concrete details, Patrick lends his story a sense of plausibility. He introduces the story as one he has told before, and by mentioning the name of the man who accompanied him to the wake, he indicates that there is someone who could substantiate his account. Patrick adds that the wake they attended was in Donegal—close enough to be familiar and feasible, but far enough away that his Tyrone audience cannot readily verify whether the events to be described actually happened. Then comes what Mullen identifies in tall tales as ludicrous imagery, the smile on the corpse, which in turn elicits smiles among Patrick's audience. Exaggeration builds, for this is the greatest smile "ever seen on a corpse in Ireland before." We have a tip-off to the story's true nature as a tall tale. Pleased with the image of the corpse's smile, Patrick as storyteller pauses, satisfied: "Aye." While the audience waits in anticipation, willfully suspending disbelief, Patrick pushes forward through quoted speech. Embracing a persona of innocence, Patrick supposedly quotes himself: "What happened to him?" In appropriating the words of the widow, Patrick pauses his narration at the point of highest suspense, then lets the widow topple his story's plausibility with her absurd response, the story's punch line.

Because this tall tale makes use of quoted speech and a punch line it gestures toward the joke. I have heard the same story told on Highland Radio by Donegal professional comedian Colm Gallen as a joke. He delivered the same plot and punch line as a third-person account in which the setting was not localized and all the characters were anonymous types—a mourner, a widow, a corpse—rather than named neighbors.

Patrick's version may be considered a tall tale because of the first-person voice and stylistic devices intended to disguise the story as a truthful reporting of local events until exaggeration has climaxed in absurdity.

Joke-like and brief, Patrick's story fit its social setting. At the singing session, turns changed quickly between the many speakers when we had switched from songs to humorous chat. Being able to maintain the floor without interruption required brevity. It may also be that people are now more familiar with jokes and no longer as patient with longer tales, and this may condition Patrick's choice of stories.[5]

Today, few tell extended tall tales, and fewer compose their own tall tales. However, tall tales feature with some frequency in people's accounts of the wit of past characters. Remembering a character, people may report his or her best tall tale in a third-person account as an appreciation of his or her imagination and charm. Rather than take ownership of a tall tale—performing it without any attribution or distancing frames—people more often embed tall tales in their portrayals of characters who have come before.

For example, one day I asked Packy Jim to help me trace Peggy Roe's trek over the mountain on my Ordnance Survey map. After he retold the legend while penciling Peggy's route, he stopped to think about the last place he had mentioned, the site of a house lived in by a man known by his nickname as "the Buffer." Brought to mind by location, the Buffer occupied Packy Jim's thoughts, and this is what he had to say about him:

> *The Buffer. He was a character . . . There was a character lived down there—don't know whether there are any remains of a house or not close to Peter Moss's lane—and they called him the Buffer.*
>
> *And he could have told some very tall yarns, and as the saying goes, he was great for telling tall yarns.*
>
> *He was the name of McMenamin but he was termed the Buffer, and he used to tell some very remarkable lies.*
>
> *Aye . . .*

I interrupted the short silence to ask if he remembered any of these yarns or lies.

> *Aye, indeed I do. Oh, indeed I mind some of the Buffer's stories all right, I do, I do.*
>
> *The Buffer told one, one time, he was for Scotland, and he made his way down till Derry City. And when he got the length*

of Derry City, unfortunately the boat had sailed. And there was nothing for it only, only, as the saying goes, to wait for the next day, or the next time the boat was going, perhaps the next day.

So the Buffer was very scarce of money and he had no place to go for his lodging.

So he was wandering about in a frantic state of mind, not knowing, as the saying goes, where to go or what to do. And where did he find himself? On Derry's walls, the walls built by the British, 'round.

And he was wandering around Derry's walls, and he come to one of these cannon that the boys had, a big cannon, on the walls—they're still there I think—and he looked at this cannon, and damn but he says to himself "I found me lodging."

"I'll slip into the mouth of the cannon and I'll sleep until morning and if it happens to rain it won't rain on me. A grand lodging place."

So he got into the mouth of the cannon, and he lay there, and seemingly somebody had some kind of a quare, as the saying goes, trick that they at a certain time, midnight or something like that, this particular cannon was fired, you know? ◊

Ah, an old yarn!

This particular cannon was fired, and begod it was the cannon that the Buffer was lying in. That was the one that was going to be, as the saying goes, fired.

So the Buffer was lying in the, in the cannon. Whether he was asleep or not, I don't know, but suddenly [claps his hands] out the blarge goes. And away, it happened to be pointing toward Scotland, you understand, in that direction, the right direction.

The blarge goes off, out goes the Buffer, and the next thing the Buffer knowed, as the saying goes, he come down with a thud.

> *And, eh, it was on the streets of Glasgow.*
>
> *I suppose he was over before the boat that he missed, I*
> *suppose.*
>
> *He was over before the boat, come down with a thud on the*
> *streets of Glasgow, and he was landed for no money at all.*
>
> *Isn' that a quare yarn? Aye, that was a quare yarn.*

The story is particularly interesting in terms of the management of frames, reported speech, and narrative personas. On some level all stories are quotations of stories, and Packy Jim's story overtly illustrates this notion. The use of a tall tale within a story about its original teller forcefully reminds us of Mikhail Bakhtin's observation that our mouths are full of the words of others (1981:293, 337) and demonstrates again how any given performance "is tied to a number of speech events that precede and succeed it" (Bauman and Briggs 1990:60; cf. Bauman 2004). For our purposes here, the issue of genre is most pressing.

One might characterize Packy Jim's story as a tall tale that is set in third-person and that makes use of quoted speech. However, because it is framed as an appreciation of the Buffer as a "character" capable of telling such a "quare yarn," the story provides another example of overlapping genres. More specifically, by enfolding fantasy within a nonfictional biographical sketch, Packy Jim's story illustrates a conceptual link between the anecdote and the tall tale. Though pregnant with and organized by the plot of a traditional tall tale,[6] Packy Jim's story serves as a complex anecdote about the Buffer. As an anecdote, it is simultaneously comic and contemplative. Its comic thrust is to entertain through preposterous exaggeration, while its contemplative thrust is to appreciate the wit of the man who originally told it.[7]

Aware that tall tales are now rare in ceili and wake conversations, Packy Jim and most others also believe that characters like the Buffer are equally scarce. As Cissie Dolan succinctly put it, "No characters about now like there was then." By embedding tall tales in their anecdotes about such characters, people like Packy Jim not only extend the life of tall tales but in effect beg the patience of contemporary listeners more attentive to the shorter, less involved joke and anecdote. Today, people will listen to a tall tale smuggled through nonfictional narrative in the form of an anecdote, and in the process they may come to better appreciate the artistry and imagination of those who have come before. Such tall tales embedded in anecdotes about those who might otherwise be dismissed as rustic tellers of long-winded lies offer a chance for reflection on change and an evaluation of gains and losses over time. Stories like Packy Jim's not only remember a now-rare form of sociability—people entertaining each other with tall tales—they also offer appreciation of individual creativity and verbal skill felt to be dulled or lacking today. Having told me a string of anecdotes about past pranksters and their most creative tricks, Danny considered for a moment the role of wit in the past. "Aye, it was by wit you lived. Whether it's smuggling or playing a trick or telling a yarn, that's how you got by."

A much more common humorous genre in Aghyaran is the joke, which overlaps considerably with the comic anecdote in formal terms. The most obvious features shared by many jokes and comic anecdotes are reported speech and punch lines. Like comic anecdotes, jokes are highly end-oriented narratives. Joke tellers must organize their stories in a way that offers listeners exactly what they need to know in order for the coming punch line to have an impact. Often the buildup for the punch line in both jokes and comic anecdotes is established through dialogue. As with comic anecdotes, punch lines and end-oriented organization in jokes contribute to their textual stability over time. Moreover, what Bauman has observed about the role of direct discourse in anecdotes also applies to jokes: "[W]hen quoted speech is the focus of the narrative and a particular utterance is the very point of it, the text is formally more constrained and less susceptible to change from one telling to the next" (1986:75).

In part, the emergence of quoted speech and the expectation it produces are shared generic markers of the joke and comic anecdote. They are also conventions for communication, shared by tellers and listeners, that help generate anticipation and guide interpretation. Once the teller of a joke or anecdote switches from exposition to dialogue, the listener expects that some form of climax or resolution, probably a punch line, is on its way. The listener may or may not be able to predict how the punch line will subvert or rekey the previous representation of narrated events and reported speech, but the anticipation itself produces an engaging tension soon to be abruptly resolved. Shared anticipation of subversion brings the audience and teller closer together in their involvement in the performance, and the punch line's subversion itself accounts for much of the pleasure taken by those who tell and listen to both jokes and comic anecdotes.[8] During the same singing session in which Patrick McElhill told the joke-like tall tale of the smiling corpse, he told a relatively popular joke I heard four other people tell:

> *There was a story about the ... told about the Yank over on a visit to this country, like, you know, probably staying with the wife's relatives or stopping off in a hotel, you see.*
>
> *But, eh, he went out for a morning's walk, like, up the road, you see, you know. So, of course, Paddy he was leaning over the gate looking down the fields, smoking the pipe. And when they come within talking distance, a bit of conversation arose then about, eh ...*
>
> *The Yank says, "I guess," he says, "Paddy, you own a bit of a ranch 'round here."*
>
> *Aye.*
>
> *And Paddy says, "Oh," he says, "we call it farms," he says, "in this country," he says. "It goes down over there," he says, "from the road on down till the tree and on down to the river and up the side of the river to thon old barn and back up to the road again."*
>
> *Aye.*
>
> *So the Yank, he pushed back the big brimmed hat on him. He says, "I guess," he says, "if you were out in Texas to see the ranches," he says, "I've got out there," he says, "it takes me two whole days to go 'round it in my car."*
>
> *Aye.* ◊
>
> *Paddy took another pull of the pipe, and he says, "I'd an old car like that one time, too, but I got rid of her."* ◊

Likewise, Tommy Mongan has a repertoire of at least a dozen "Paddy and the Yank" jokes, in which the American is brash and boastful but Paddy, lesser in wealth and education, bests the Yank through superior wit or in some way deflates the Yank's sense of self-importance. The following from Tommy is a variation on the Paddy and the Yank joke in which the two Irish protagonists are given the common, iconic surnames Murphy and Casey:

Figure 6.2. Tommy Mongan

*There were one about Murphy and Casey, you know,
having a restaurant. And Murphy was doing the cooking, and
Casey, he took the orders, you know, he was the waiter.*

*And they were wild busy, you see, but this Yank came in
anyway. And he wanted a steak, you see, a sirloin steak. But he
didn't want it rare or he didn't want it medium, he wanted it
right in between.*

*So Casey goes up to Murphy and he says, "That Yank's in
again, and he wants a steak," he says, "and he doesn't want it
rare or he doesn't want it medium, he wants it right in between."*

*Well ◊—you see, Murphy was wild busy, you'd've seen the
sweat running off him, you see.*

*And he says, "Well you can tell that fucking Yank," he says,
"to come up here and kiss my, not the right cheek, nor the left
cheek, but right in between." ◊*

In formal terms, both Patrick's and Tommy's stories demonstrate how
many jokes build up through dialogue, and crescendo in an utterance—the

punch line that reframes what has come before (cf. Sherzer 1985). If humor depends upon the discernment of incongruity, then the punch line is the trigger that allows for its discernment in jokes (cf. Oring 1989; 1992:1–15, 81–93; 2003:1–12). The same dynamic was also at work in Danny's comic anecdote about Willie Duffy at the checkpoint and, in the last chapter, in John Collins's comic anecdote about John McHugh caught in the ladies' lavatory. Like jokes, Aghyaran comic anecdotes achieve humor through abrupt cognitive reorganizations accomplished by punch lines.

One of the major features separating jokes from comic anecdotes, however, is their status as fiction. Whereas jokes are told and received as fictions, anecdotes are told and received as nonfictional accounts. If an anecdote is not believed to be an accurate reporting of events and utterances, at least the issue of truth is entertained by performers and listeners, as in legend-telling (Oring 1986:125 after Dégh and Vázsonyi 1976). Thus, the comic anecdote—not just the contemplative anecdote—is a genre of historical narrative despite its structural, thematic, and functional similarities to the fictional joke.

Our first clue that Patrick's and Tommy's jokes are jokes and therefore fictions is the fact that the characters are not named locals but character types. "The Yank" stands in as a label for the idea of the arrogant, ugly American abroad, and "Paddy," "Murphy," or "Casey" stand in as labels for the idea of the unpretentious, wily Irishman at home. Although Patrick's and Tommy's jokes might be plausible as anecdotes if the dialogue was attributed to specific locals and specific Yanks, there remains a sense that the setups and punch lines are just a little too ideal to be true. As fictions, jokes enjoy more latitude than anecdotes for the sort of exaggeration, idealization, and generalization they share with the tall tale.

Without strict localization, Patrick's and Tommy's jokes are free to travel by word of mouth or mass media and to be told in all the places and contexts where they are found to be humorous as entertainment and relevant as commentary. Paddy and the Yank jokes may be told as glosses on the behavior of specific locals and visitors in a given place. However, they are not tied to a specific community, but rather to Ireland as a society where the scenarios depicted are feasible and pertinent. Bauman makes similar observations in identifying a major difference between comic anecdotes and jokes in the extent to which these narratives are grounded in specific communities. In the process, he raises the possibility that the joke as a genre grew out of the punch line–driven anecdote in the midst of the personal mobility, rise of mass media, and resulting permeability of small local communities that characterize modernity:

> Unlike our anecdotes, however, jokes are not at all rooted in community; they are anonymous, impersonal, and generalized. Indeed, if one were inclined toward speculation, one might suggest that the modern punch line joke, which emerged as a recognized form only in the nineteenth century (Röhrich 1977:4,8), might have evolved out of the punch line anecdote under the social conditions of the modern industrial era. Anecdotes of the kind we have been examining thrive in the intimate social environment of the small local community, whereas jokes belong preeminently to the impersonal milieu of urban industrial society (Röhrich 1977:9). As imaginative products ungrounded in a known community or real individuals, jokes can only be metaphorical and speculative in their relationship to actual experience. (1986:77)

Jokes are common today in Aghyaran, whether at ceilis, at talent shows and concerts in Killeter Hall, on the radio, or on television. But this appears to be a relatively recent development effected in part by the mass media and in part by the experiences of locals working in Irish cities or farther abroad. I asked Danny if he and others in Aghyaran would call Paddy and the Yank stories "jokes" or "yarns" or both, and he said they would be known as "jokes." According to him, the distinction had much to do with their origin: "A yarn would be something more local, you know, that had been put together." I then pressed him on the issue of jokes and their provenance and popularity. He recalled that although jokes were common in his youth in the fifties and sixties, they were brought into local storytelling mostly by men who had traveled:

> *Oh aye, there was loads of them [jokes]. James McLaughlin*
> *and these boys that would have been in public houses and*
> *that and heard a lot of that stuff would have told them, you*
> *know. And Frank McLaughlin, he would have spent a lot of*
> *time about Dublin and other places. They came from places*
> *like that, you know. People that had been away, worked away,*
> *would have told them.*

Tommy Mongan spent the majority of his adult life working in England and returned to Ballymongan relatively recently to retire. He recalls that it was in England that he first heard the majority of the "Paddy and the Yank," "Pat and Mike," "Murphy the Irishman," and "The Irishman, the Scotsman, and the Englishman" jokes that comprise a large portion of the repertoire of fictional humorous narratives from which he draws during ceilis and other social gatherings. Charlie Lunney confirms the same pattern: such jokes were more a part of his experience working in London than they had been in Aghyaran before he left. While in England, jokes that featured stereotypical Irishmen provided Tommy and Charlie common ground with other Irish ex-pats from very different communities north and south of the border. Although jokes became more important for men like Tommy and Charlie in the "impersonal milieu of urban industrial society," they also had their place back in Aghyaran in the relatively "intimate social environment of the small local community" (Bauman 1986:77).

Once jokes such as Tommy's traveled back to Ireland, many continued to have resonance with daily experience at home. Billy McGrath tells a joke similar in effect to "Paddy and the Yank" jokes. Its popularity probably owes much to real-life situations in which relatives return to Aghyaran from living abroad and are seen to be putting on airs of sophistication:

> *Two Irishmen were living at home but had a brother out in America. Used to come home now and again, but they hated to see him coming for he'd very big words, he had every thing blew up out of proportion, you see, according to this country. Big words like "coincidence," "limousine," stuff like that.*
>
> *They were up around the fire one night, anyway. Johnny says to him, "There's a word you raised, that you use very often, Mickey, is 'coincidence.' What's the meaning of that word?"*
>
> *"Well," he says, "I guess I'll tell ye," he says. "If your cat and my cat kittled [gave birth] on the same day, that'd be coincidence."*
>
> *Johnny took out the pipe in his mouth and spits in the fire, "Jeez'," he says, "it would not, would be a miracle for our cat's a buck [male]."* ◊

Although "ungrounded in a known community of real individuals," Billy's joke is perhaps more than "metaphorical and speculative" in its "relationship to actual experience" (Bauman 1986:77). Billy's story provides direct commentary on the annoying behavior of those who have left Aghyaran and returned to show off how they have "bettered" themselves. Although a fiction, Billy's joke dovetails with nonfictional accounts. For instance, Danny tells an anecdote about Harry McDonnagh set in the 1940s. Charlie Gillespie owned the Blacktown pub at the time, and when Harry would "go on the tear," drinking all day in the pub, Charlie would allow him to sleep it off in his hay shed. One day Harry came into the pub from a night in the shed "and him all covered with hay and dog's hair." In the pub he found a couple of returned Yanks "bumming and blowing" about their political connections in America. Harry just stared at them and listened. When the Yanks had finished boasting about their trip to the White House, Harry made himself known. "Oh boys, you're lucky," he said, "for I'm just coming from the Dog House."

The connection between Billy's joke and Danny's anecdote reminds us that in addition to shared formal features, jokes and comic anecdotes share thematic issues. The jokes just discussed serve to sum up a personality type labeled "Paddy." Paddy's subversive retorts not only highlight and deflate pretensions of the self-important, they also paint him as the sort of iconoclast much appreciated in anecdotes about local characters such as John McHugh, Willie Duffy, Paddy O'Donnell, and Harry McDonnagh.

These four Aghyaran characters happen to be Catholic bachelors, but it is important to note that the personality type they exemplify through anecdotes need not be defined by religion or marital status. The type is defined more by underdog status, as in Paddy and the Yank jokes. Thus, a Protestant, even a relatively prosperous one, can fill the same role of the underdog wit in narrative when sparring with outsiders. For example, Charlie Lunney, a Catholic, tells an anecdote about Willie Hunter, a relatively wealthy Protestant. In this anecdote, Hunter takes exception to the complaints of women sent to the country from Belfast during the German bombing raids of World War II.

> *Oh, he was a wild man, Hunter was. A wild character. Sure, the evacuees the time of the war, you know, there were evacuees coming out from Belfast.*
>
> *And sure, in the country places there were no toilets or hot water, damn all. It didn't matter if it was white blowing with snow, you did your business behind the ditch.*

> *And these ladies started to ask Hunter where the toilet was.*
> *They were complaining about the "amenities" and wondering*
> *how anyone could live in the country at all.*
>
> *He didn't want them at all, you see, but he had to take*
> *them. He couldn't do nothing about it.*
>
> *He says, "I've seventy acres of land out there. You can piss*
> *and shite wherever you like, over the whole thing. And if that's*
> *not enough, cross the water, I've got fields on up to Laght."*

Like Paddy in jokes and like Catholic bachelors in anecdotes, Mr. Hunter is appreciated for highlighting a contempt for affectation that people in Aghyaran tend to share. In a place where many consider themselves to be underprivileged and looked down upon by the wider world, a Protestant is briefly exalted by a Catholic storyteller as a local hero, and it is this hero's local rather than denominational affiliation that is significant. His retort is pointed and extraordinary, transgressing as it does the usual norms for politeness and hospitality. Yet his bluntness also provides vicarious enjoyment for those who share his self-image as marginal in the greater scheme of things but nonetheless undeserving of condescension.

Jokes and anecdotes serve to sum up other personality types that resonate with local concerns. There is a cycle of jokes about Murphy, another stereotype of the Irishman, in which Murphy is overly literal-minded or blithely unconcerned with the complexity surrounding him. Despite his dimness, however, he is unwittingly comical in his rejoinders that serve as punch lines. Most often, his conclusions about a given situation would be logically sound were they not founded on mistaken presuppositions made out of ignorance. Murphy's common sense is that of the country bumpkin who does not realize he is out of his depth in a changing, urban, and supposedly more sophisticated world. Patrick McElhill tells a Murphy joke:

> *Murphy got a job one time in a museum of archaeology, or*
> *something, in Dublin. And his job was to stand beside a thirty-*
> *foot-high, eh, skeleton of a dinosaur.*
>
> *Aye.*
>
> *And he explained all about it to the visitors who came in.*
>
> *One day, this woman come in, and she says to Murphy,*
> *"What age is this skeleton?"*

And he says, "It's three million years old and seven months."

She says, "That's amazing," she says, "how you can
pinpoint its age so accurately," you know. ◊

"Well," he says, "when I came here, that skeleton," he says,
"was three million years old. I'm here seven months." ◊

Earlier during the same evening, Patrick told three anecdotes about a pair of older bachelors in Ederney, real people. These two were portrayed as very similar in personality type to the fictional Murphy. Patrick tells his third anecdote about them:

Another problem they had one day in Omagh after they,
after the one-way streets come into operation. It was Castle
Street was one-way, then, could only go down it.

And they were used always to going up round to the chapel
every time they went into Omagh, and of course they went up
the street.

And every other motorist that was coming down was all
waving and flashing lights and then the people on the footpath
was doing this at them [waving] to stop, stop.

Aye.

And, again, Francie says to Paddy, "Isn't it surprising how
many people knows you when you're out?"

Before the laughter died down, Danny remembered a very similar story involving John McHugh:

That's like John McHugh, the time they changed the system
in the town, you see. John wasn't out a wild lot. He was starting
to dote anyway.

But this day he went the wrong way in the one-way thing in
the town, you see. And they started blowing horns at him. He
was sitting here telling it one time, and he says, "I thought they
got wild friendly about Garrig [Castlederg] altogether!"

Regardless of social and historical context, comical stories have probably always poked fun at the foolishness of others. In this social and historical context, however, the foolishness identified is inflected. The fools are identified with the old-fashioned and provincial. Paddy and Murphy are ostensibly the same people, but serve as two sides of the same coin in different joke cycles. Likewise, John McHugh and other bachelors feature in anecdotes that exalt them at home in their contests with local authority but portray them as rubes in the wider world. The jokes and anecdotes that feature foolish character types allow people to reflect on the changes that surround them and assess their own worldliness. People may recognize themselves in these stories, and with greater self-consciousness they may wish to present themselves as unlike the personality types involved. With jokes about the fictional Murphy and anecdotes about actual local bachelors, we see examples of narratives in two genres that allow people to have a laugh at the expense of the hapless and to pity their ignorance. Implied criticism may serve not only to define wit by illustrating its opposite, but also to engender a sense of superiority for those in a position to laugh.

Being in a position to laugh, however, can be a sensitive matter, and this is a point at which the joke can part company with the comic anecdote in Aghyaran. The characters portrayed in jokes are fictional. Unless a joke is offered as a pointed gloss on the foibles of a particular individual (cf. Oring 2003:85–96) or unless it crosses some line of accepted taste or decency, there is little room for people to take offense. In contrast, as we saw in the ceili at Jamie's, some anecdotes may be funny but can nonetheless insult listeners, for the characters in anecdotes are actual individuals with friends and relatives willing to come to their defense. Several times I was asked to turn off my recorder or not repeat an anecdote because either the characters involved were still alive or their friends and relations would not find it amusing. Of course, I complied.

The fact that the majority of protagonists in comic anecdotes are older bachelors owes much to the freedom of bachelors to remain undomesticated. Their transgression of societal norms is good material for narrative because it not only pinpoints these norms but also allows people to question or reaffirm the authority of these norms. It is equally true, however, that given storytellers' aversion to offending their audiences, the safest targets for anecdotes that imply criticism or pity are older bachelors and especially deceased bachelors who have the fewest remaining family ties.

Classed as fiction, jokes have more latitude than anecdotes to characterize people as fools, make more pointed statements, and deal with issues too sensitive for portrayals of actual individuals. During the singing session already introduced, Sally Kelly McHugh sang a humorous song, "Nineteen Years Old," which portrays a young man tricked into marrying a prosthetically enhanced ninety-year-old masquerading as a teenager. Patrick responded with a joke brought to mind by this situation:

> *That's like the old story I used to tell about, eh, see,*
> *Finnegan courted the widow Quinn for over eleven years. A*
> *wild woman from the Mourne Mountains. With, eh, a face like*
> *a disused quarry ... and a figure like six mile of bad road ...*
> *and long red hair down her back, and none on her head.* ◊
>
> *So that's the picture of the widow.*
>
> *Finnegan decided to bring her home to visit to his ninety-*
> *year-old father who lived in a wee thatched cottage out on the*
> *side of the mountain. And when the old man saw the widow he*
> *took a turn and went in till a weakness.*
>
> *Aye.*
>
> *That's what my grandmother used to say if somebody*
> *fainted in chapel, she said they "took a turn and went in till a*
> *weakness."*
>
> *Aye.*
>
> *But when he came to, anyway, the old man took Finnegan*
> *to the one side and he says to him, he says, "In the name of God,*
> *where did you pick her up? No teeth, cross-eyed, knock-kneed,"*
> *he says, "she's a write-off."*
>
> *Finnegan says, "Father," he says, "there's no need to*
> *whisper," he says, "for she's deaf as well."* ◊

Clearly, the characters are fictional. Finnegan and Quinn are common, stock Irish names like Paddy and Murphy, and as such the choices gesture toward character typification. Further portrayal tells us that we are dealing with a typical elderly bachelor, his rustic female counterpart, and a savvy old man, who will serve as a mouthpiece for the audience's horror at the bachelor's choice for a bride. Yet working against the aura of fictionality in the story are the facts that the characters are referred to as if real people and that the story is set in an actual area of Co. Down.

Figure 6.3. Sally Kelly McHugh with grandchildren Clara and Shannon McHugh

Patrick names his characters in part to ease narration. However, by naming his characters and localizing his story, Patrick also grants the joke some of the flavor of an anecdote. Although we know the story is a joke, it begins with named characters whose actions and words we expect to entertain or enlighten us, as in an anecdote. It being framed *as if* a true story, portraying known people and places, we may enjoy the outcome of the narrative *as if* it were a piece of anecdotal gossip about locals, but without the expense of offending anyone in particular. Everyone knows a bachelor Finnegan and a widow Quinn, the type of them anyway. Since the characters involved are types, the audience may fill their roles with people from their own experience, but this is left up to the imagination of the audience.

Because jokes are fictions and their characters virtually anonymous, they may treat issues too delicate for anecdotes about actual people. A large number of jokes popular in Aghyaran deal with relationships between men and women. Some anecdotes, mostly comic ones, do so as well, but no anecdotes in Aghyaran deal with, for example, adultery. John McElhill tells a joke that does:

Did ever you hear, eh, what do you call him, Aussie Bryson, there, telling the one about the fellah that was going with a lassie?

He said that this son was going to get married to this girl. And the father says, "Alright," he says, "who would she be now," he says.

"Ah, she's wee Lizzie Mitchell," or something, you know.

"Ah," he says, the father says, "sure, you wouldn't marry that'n," he says, "for that'n would be a sister of your own, or half-sister of your own."

Well, the fellah was in a bad way about it, anyway.

Anyway, he started to go with another one, and he went with her for a couple of years. Says he, "I'm thinking of getting married this time, alright." She was from Derry or some road.

"Ah, that's such a one. See, she's another half-sister of yours, too," the father says, do you see.

So then he took it very bad. So he said to the mother that he was getting married and his father told him this and he couldn't marry.

"Ah," she says, "will you hold your tongue," she says, "never let on you heard all that from that old eejit, for he's not your father at all." ◊

As we have seen, the comic anecdote and joke in Aghyaran share several formal features, thematic issues, and potential functions in social contexts. There may even be an evolutionary link between the two genres. Where there are differences between the genres—in terms of their status as fiction or nonfiction, the naming or anonymity of characters, or the sensitivity of issues addressed—jokes and anecdotes may draw on each other's generic features for certain persuasive ends. Despite the conceptual connections between joke cycles about stereotypical Irishmen and comic anecdotes about Aghyaran locals, John's joke above reminds us that not all Aghyaran jokes necessarily deal with issues of local or group identity. Furthermore, unlike John's joke, not all Aghyaran jokes are potential commentary on social problems, tensions, or anxieties. Some are told simply for their entertainment value and the humorous shock of incongruity. Yet even in these cases where jokes seem to deviate from anecdotes by portraying unknown people for no particular persuasive end, jokes may gesture back to the comic anecdote. Danny tells one of his favorite jokes:

> *There was a boy going away to England for a holiday, and he had this cat. And he asked the brother, he says, "Would you keep this cat, look after it till I come back in a week?" And he says, "Make sure nothing happens to the cat," and he says, "I'll be ringing, anyway, to ask about me mother and that, see how you're getting on."*
>
> *Well after a couple days he rang and first thing he says to your man, "What about the cat?"*
>
> *"Oh, begod," your man says, "the cat's dead." He says nothing else.*
>
> *"God, that's a wild way to tell a story," he says. "You could have broke it to me gently." ◊ He says, "You could have said the cat was playing with a ball of wool and she went up on the roof and the fire brigade come and she fell down and died peacefully."*
>
> *So after being annoyed about that, anyway, he rung again, another couple of days. He says, "Did you bury the cat?"*
>
> *"Aye."*
>
> *"And what about my mother?"*
>
> *"Ah," he says, "she was playing with a ball of wool . . . " ◊*

After the laughter subsided, Danny attributed the joke to John McCracken, who is now deceased. McCracken was known as a sort of regional celebrity from his appearances on radio and his emceeing talent shows and concerts in western Ulster. (Colm Gallen, who told the smiling corpse tall tale as a joke on radio, and Aussie Bryson, to whom John McElhill attributed his adultery joke, play similar roles now.) Between those gathered to listen to Danny's version of McCracken's joke—Patrick McElhill, Sally Kelly McHugh, Danny Gormley, James Hugh O'Neill, and Mickey Hegarty— they recalled a sort of social biography of McCracken, memorializing him as "a mighty teller," "powerful craic." McCracken became the topic of conversation, and those who knew him recalled meetings with him and embedded their favorite McCracken jokes in their reminiscences of this character. Like tall tales embedded within anecdotes appreciating tall tale raconteurs, these jokes became instrumental in anecdote-telling—the process through which past local characters find a place in collective memory. The joke may stand alone as a joke, but through storytellers' attributing jokes to original tellers the joke may become co-opted by and find another conceptual link to the anecdote.

When anecdotes about local characters are told in first-person, we are to assume that the narrator is describing events he or she has witnessed, but the focus of these anecdotes is on the behavior and words of other people. Such an anecdote is a narrator's testimonial of someone else's character, and at issue are the ideas that person may be made to exemplify. The direction of attention is outward. However, one may also tell a story in first-person singular that reflects on the narrator as a persona. The direction of attention is inward. Such a story fits Stahl's (now Dolby's) definition of the personal experience narrative (1983:268), a genre she has done the most to bring to the attention of folklorists (see also Stahl 1977a, 1977b, and 1989). In effect, many personal experience narratives are anecdotes of the self, serving to present a certain image of the narrator's persona through autobiographical narrative. Despite differences concerning the inward or outward direction of focus, anecdotes and personal experience narratives have much in common. Stories in both genres typify individuals, represent those individuals' personal values or ethics, and offer these up for listeners' appreciation or evaluation.

In the late 1970s and early '80s, debate over whether personal experience narratives could be considered folklore exercised some and centered on the issue of whether their contents were traditional. Memorates, described by Carl Wilhelm von Sydow as firsthand accounts of supernatural events, were easily accepted; their contents involve traditional beliefs and serve as "personal testimonials either supporting or denying the validity of established elements of culture" (Stahl 1983:270). Yet personal experience narratives recall secular, everyday experiences—embarrassing faux pas, tragedies avoided, lessons learned, minor victories and defeats in the social realm. Personal experience narratives were saved from neglect by folklorists with the argument that although their contents may be idiosyncratic and nontraditional, elements of their narrative form, style, organization, and function may be understood as traditional. In other words, the consistent generic features of personal experience narratives rather than their contents qualify them as traditional; narratives characteristic of this genre conform to communicative conventions understood and shared over time within given speech communities. Moreover, idiosyncratic values and attitudes reflected in personal experience narratives may provide contrast and further definition to attitudes and values collectively shared.

The personal experience narrative may be worthy of the folklorists' attention, but the genre is more common in some societies and speech communities, namely those in which one's self is appropriate subject matter for storytelling (cf. Glassie 1982:59). People do give first-person accounts of their experiences when exchanging stories at wakes and ceilis in Aghyaran. Even more so than narratives in other genres, personal experience narratives are appropriate and common in just about every conversational context. Moreover, personal experience narratives are not the preserve of those with the special qualifications or performative competencies for legends and jokes, for example. Nevertheless, personal experience narratives are not as common in Aghyaran as they are in the social circles I am familiar with in the United States. Glassie made a similar observation about the relative scarcity of "experiences" or "true tales of the self" in Ballymenone of the 1970s and '80s. As Glassie notes: "When they do appear they come cautiously, apologetically, carefully shaded so they will not reflect on the brightness of the narrator" (1982:59). Caution is necessary in Aghyaran because although self-presentation through narrative is not in itself frowned upon, personal modesty is expected. Otherwise the immodest self-promoter is labeled a "bum" or "a bit of a blow," and may become the subject of anecdotes critical of self-absorption, egotism, or other infractions of the local ethic of equalitarianism.

This point was brought home to me one cold and rainy afternoon on the street in Castlederg. Two Aghyaran men and I were huddled in the doorway of Charlie Lynch's pub when a third Aghyaran man drove past. One of my companions began but then abandoned a gossipy story about the man in the car. My other companion filled the silence with a question, "He's a bit of blow, isn't he?" The first man shot back, "A bit of a blow? God help us, he's the full blast!" Given a man willing to talk himself up, exceptions are made to the general unspoken rule that overt criticism of neighbors is to be avoided. Personal experience narratives, then, are dangerous territory and require narrators to closely monitor the narrative personas they create for themselves. Otherwise, narrators risk general disapproval, even becoming the subjects of derogatory gossip and anecdotes told behind their backs.

When a personal experience narrative reflects values and attitudes that are both personal and extrapersonal, we find a point of convergence between the individual and the group, and a story worth telling. Consider one of John Glackin's personal experience narratives. Born in Segronan townland in 1917, John became involved in registering Catholic voters for the old Nationalist Party after World War II and later became involved in monitoring local election procedures. At the time of his story, local voting took place in Orange Halls, a fact that irritated many nationalists. Although a Catholic and a nationalist, John had developed a good working relationship with the Ulster Unionist Party officials in Killen Orange Hall, where Aghyaran residents traveled to vote.

> JOHN: *The more Killen was supposed to be a very bad place, and I was in it for years. And, eh, none of them ever said very much to me in it, but, eh . . . I mind Tommy George Sproule—he was a Unionist—and he was telling me about this man Speer—he was a Unionist agent.*
>
> *And he said Speer told them all, "If John raises an argument about somebody don't follow it up, for he'll be right."*
>
> *So I think they believed that anything I brought up was pretty near right.*
>
> RAY: *So they got to trust you.*
>
> JOHN: *They did.*
>
> RAY: *That's not so bad.*
>
> JOHN: *They trusted me. Aye. For I mind I was away in England working and there were a Sinn Fein election. And they used to have the Orange flag, you see, flying over the door of the, eh, hall.*
>
> *So Mickey McSorley and a few of them from Ballymongan come over and they rose a row about the flag. And, eh, they didn't get it taken down either.*

> *But I come back out of England then, about five or six*
> *weeks after it. This Tommy George Sproule says to me, he says,*
> *"You were over about Killen more nor anybody else, and I never*
> *heared you complaining about the flag."*
>
> *I says, "Oh no, I wouldn't be complaining about the flag*
> *for," I says, "any of our side was coming down the street and see*
> *that rag hanging up there, that would rise the blood in them*
> *and they'd be sure to vote right." ◊*
>
> *He says, "We never took, we, we never thought of that."*
> *Never put up the flag after it. So I got the flag down*
> *without any bother.*

As a sort of autobiographical anecdote, this personal experience narrative serves in part to characterize John as clever. Given local disapproval of "bumming and blowing," the story may at first seem immodest, but John's victory is not his alone. In righting a wrong, from a nationalist perspective, John stands in for all northern Catholics who see themselves as burdened with second-class citizenship. John's values and those of his fellow nationalists overlap in this story, which potentially allows for vicarious enjoyment on a collective level of a personal victory. Moreover, being over ninety years old, John may be granted more latitude than a younger narrator to recall his personal successes. It is not coincidence that the only personal experience narratives printed in *Aghyaran* are reminiscences of elderly men and women. Not only are older community members allowed more latitude in discussing their experiences, they are generally encouraged to do so because their stories are understood to be more than personal possessions. Their stories are valued as collective property, links with the past that allow for contrast to and reflection on the present.

Stahl distinguishes between "self-oriented" and "other-oriented" impulses in telling personal experience narratives (1983). While John's story may hover somewhere in between self- and other-orientation, the vast majority of personal experience narratives told in Aghyaran are decidedly other-oriented. In other words, the majority of personal experience narratives de-emphasize the persona of the narrator in order to focus on that which is story-worthy and of collective interest.

For example, Tommy Mongan and Danny Gallen, among others, tell stories about their time working in England, but these personal experience

Figure 6.4. Alec Byrne with Maggie Cashman

narratives serve more to allow reflection on shared experiences of emigration and socioeconomic change than to characterize Tommy and Danny as heroic or exemplary figures. They don the role of protagonists in their own stories primarily to characterize shared experience through personal memories. Having done well for himself and his family in Scotland, Alec Byrne, too, has plenty of narrative material with which to construct a virtuous personal origin myth of the self. Alec Byrne as self-made man may be a subtext in his personal experience narratives, but overt statements to this effect would typically meet with some form of censure. In my presence his stories about work in Scotland were appropriately modest by local standards and consistently led to stories about his experience of contrast and change when returning home. This allowed general reflection and direct statements about socioeconomic trends that have both benefited and burdened people in Aghyaran.

If the majority of personal experience narratives told in Agharan are other-oriented—justifiable when connecting with collective concerns—they most frequently survey the very themes common in local historical legends: human tragedy, politics, and the dynamics of community in the face of sectarian division. Alec Byrne's upsetting account of his attempts to save his daughter's life after a car wreck just yards from home connects in theme with legends of tragic deaths such as those of Peggy Roe and of John "Caper" O'Donnell. Danny Gallen's firsthand recalling of the IRA robbing the dole from Killeter Hall in the early '70s connects with legends of the exploits of locally born rapparee Proinsias Dubh. Johnny Corry's personal experience narrative of being physically intimidated into singing "The Sash" at a Protestant-owned forge connects with legends of local sectarian tensions such as those of nineteenth-century Ribbonmen and Orangemen engaged in faction fights and of Protestants smashing Drumawark cross to spite Lough Derg pilgrims. Cissie (née Monteith) McCay's account of slipping out of her Protestant childhood home on the Twelfth of July to marry a Catholic connects with legends of Catholics and Protestants joined in common cause despite sectarian division, such as those of the miller Kyle and Fr. O'Mongan and of the Aghyaran United Irishmen. Although these personal experience narratives each describe events of autobiographical relevance and propose an image of the narrator/protagonist as a type of person, a significant thrust of these stories is bearing witness to events of wider and continuing relevance, events that propose for their audiences images of the environment in which the individual operates.

This potential for first-person narratives to be other-oriented and speak to collective concerns is equally clear in stories of personal experiences of the supernatural. Folklorists have referred to such stories as memorates and noted their thematic connection with supernatural legends. From an emic perspective as well, personal experience narratives of mysterious events tend to be understood as belonging in a genre separate from personal experience narratives of secular events, actions within the social realm. Many formal and stylistic features of the two genres are identical, yet the subject matter of memorates ensures that they emerge at very different points in ceili conversation than personal *secular* experience narratives. In addition, stories of ghosts, wraiths, banshees, and fairies are not as frequently heard at Aghyaran wakes today. As we have seen, the commemorative mood of the wake is more conducive to acts of declarative commemoration and celebration through narrative. Acting as a symbolic reconstitution of community, the wake depends in part upon shared belief and leaves pronouncements about the afterlife to the funeral mass. Talk of the supernatural at a wake may leave open too much room for reexamination of belief. Thus, mystery and the supernatural are not usually appropriate topics for those at a wake who are invested in reaffirmation of both the individual and the group, gathered to concentrate on the social realm.

Because of shared thematic concerns, there seems to be little emic distinction made between first-person stories of supernatural experience that folklorists would call memorates and third-person accounts of such experiences in the past that folklorists would call supernatural legends. Stories about ghosts are "stories about ghosts," regardless of what person the stories are told in or whether they are set in the near or distant past. In first-person accounts, as with anecdotes and personal experience narratives, the narrator makes claims to veracity by taking responsibility for the story: "I witnessed this." In third-person accounts, claims to veracity are realized by attribution to reliable sources or by appeals to the reliability of tradition. "Oh there's something about it, now, for he wasn't one for telling lies," says Packy Jim about his neighbor's story of a ghost. "The old people wouldn't have told lies; they were more truthful than the young people going now, you know," John Glackin says, referring to a legend about locals hearing fairy music. Accounts of mysterious encounters are, like historical legends, subject to laws of reliable evidence. Stories of mystery may or may not be believed, but both stories of personal experience and those of others' experiences are marshaled to consider the limits of belief, the shape of reality.[9]

During a recorded ceili with Danny Gallen, Barney McGrath, John McElhill, and Pat Den Gallagher on January 12, 1999, Barney was reminded by previous local character anecdotes of a woman who dreamed that her son died in America and the next day received a letter confirming this. With mystery raised as a topic, conversational storytelling during the following hour and twenty minutes ranged over wraiths, the banshee, witch hares, fairy sweepings, and fairy retributions for farmers disturbing fairy thorn trees and fairy forts. Toward the end of this run of dialogue, I recounted a ghost story Packy Jim had told me that mentioned a local Ribbonman. Perhaps with the location of Packy Jim's story and the Ribbonman in mind, Barney recalled that political tensions were high when his family moved away from the area where the ghost story took place. Conversation then shifted to politics for the remainder of the night and allowed for a few stories, nominally legends, of the Black and Tans and the IRA. Some of the previous supernatural stories were debunked and dismissed, others were accepted as authentic or at least unexplainable, and still others piqued discussion of past politics felt to be relevant in the present. Those stories told in first-person were subjected to the least interrogation when authenticity might have been questioned, probably out of deference to the narrator.

At most social gatherings, in my experience, stories of personal experience with the supernatural are rare, and most stories of mystery offered as true are secondhand, coming from known and credible sources. During this ceili, in over an hour of conversation about mystery, only two stories were firsthand accounts, both from John McElhill. In the first, he recalled walking Shanaghy Road as a boy on a summer night with Maggie Moss, and they saw a man enter a bush but couldn't find him. Both were shaken by the idea that it could have been a ghost. Danny added that the very spot John described is where a poteen-maker known as Shannion was shot and buried by the "redcoats" in the 1820s. Later, John responded to the turn in conversation to mysterious lights, also known as Willy the Wisp, by offering a plausible, rational explanation for many sightings: running hares, wet with dew, reflecting moonlight. Danny seconded the explanation. Then John proceeded with the following memorate:

> JOHN: *But I can tell you a story, now, about a light. I mind it well. Old William James Hamilton died, up at the burn [stream], you know.*
>
> DANNY: *I know who you're chatting about.*
>
> JOHN: *But anyway, William James died. And John Sproule come to the burn. John Sproule come to the burn.*
>
> PAT: *That man, ah, that's right.*
>
> JOHN: *John come then to his aunt's, she was the wife of William James Hamilton.*
>
> DANNY: *[to me] That's the house that James Hegarty was flooded out of.*
>
> RAY: *I see. I see*
>
> JOHN: *But anyway, this light showed about it in the field. And the light would have left, and it went a certain distance away, miles from it, and come back again.*
>
> DANNY: *Mmm.*

JOHN: *So anyway, I seen us watching now from our house, at home—that's where Neil's living, you know [to me].*

RAY: *Yeah.*

JOHN: *But the light would have come out over McLaughlin's hill, and it would have lit out in the front of you, this light. And we watched the light. We watched the light often. So I'll tell you, Humphrey was there, at the time.*

DANNY: *Jack Humphrey, aye.*

JOHN: *And John Sproule was living with the old aunt at the time. And anyway we told him about it. We told John about it, and Humphrey, about this light in this wee field above Hamilton's house and the way it worked.*

So begod, we allowed anyway that we would go to see it anyway one night. And we went to the light, the whole lot of us, the whole lot of us—Owen McCrory I think was in it. I don't know whether Joe was in it or not—but we went to the light.

And the light, we had the light surrounded.

And it ris', and it nearly blew us down!

PAT: *Boys.*

DANNY: *[chuckles]*

JOHN: *That's true. It did. Boys, that's as true as I'm sitting here. The light, it ris', and it went a way out miles beyond us.*

DANNY: *Mmm.*

JOHN: *And I'll tell you, sir,*

PAT: *[interrupting] The light's a strange thing altogether.*

JOHN: *[to Danny] Your father was leaving our house one night, sir. Used to come up and rake our house, for my father and him was very good and they chatted. So they went out, I mind—and I was out, I was a young boy—and this light, sir, come. It was the same light. It come. And do you know where it lit? It lit in that wee three-cornered bit belonging to you [Danny], there.*

DANNY: *The Diamond.*

> JOHN: *I mind them as well watching that light, sir. And that's where it lit, sir, down there [pointing in the direction of Danny's field]. And it left that again, and it went back to the same place it was in. That's right. That's right, so it was. I mind that well. That's true.*

From the beginning John asserts the genuineness of his testimonial with concrete details of the setting and the individuals involved. He lists as many potential corroborating witnesses as he can remember. Most of them are dead, but they and their reputations are known to John's audience. Notice how John turns his attention to Danny after the climax of his story. Danny chuckles, perhaps betraying his incredulity, and John moves quickly to establish a connection with Danny, to soften his skepticism, to involve him in the story. Danny's father and John's father were good friends, John tells us. Danny's father saw that light as well, and more than that, the light landed in what is now Danny's field. Note also how John begins to use "sir," politely but somewhat pointedly, to amplify his statements of fact. The added layer of formality seems to express his sincerity, his willingness to go on record vouching for these events. Then, of course, there are his direct statements throughout, "Boys, that's as true as I'm sitting here," "That's right, so it was," and "I mind that well."

Compared to stories of secular personal experience, first-person stories of supernatural experience, memorates, include more overt statements intended either to guide audience interpretation of narrated events or, in other cases, to highlight the difficulty of assigning a clear interpretation. Such statements signal the narrator's belief, disbelief, or interested but agnostic stance. Thus, on some level, memorates present an image of the self as a type of person and connect with anecdotes and personal experience narratives invested in characterization.

Embedded belief statements also offer invitations to further discuss the issues of perception vs. truth and the nature of reality, and herein lies the other-orientation of supernatural experience stories. Like other-oriented personal narratives of secular experience, memorates "use the self to record a segment of everyone's external reality" (Glassie 1982:741). Because of the thematic content, the issue of character in stories of mystery is not often foremost except in deliberations over the trustworthiness of the source of a given narrative. Moreover, because memorates are few but related legends are numerous, secondhand accounts are often added in support of a narrator's claims.

As soon as John finished his story, Barney joined in with a secondhand account of the same phenomenon. His conclusion reiterates the implication that the light is otherworldly. As a whole, the rhetorical intent of Barney's story is to leave open the possibility that what John witnessed is not a figment of imagination. Others have seen it as well.

> BARNEY: *I heared my father on about the same thing up about his country.*
>
> RAY: *Is that right?*
>
> BARNEY: *He said on a summer's night you would have seen it. It came from one house to another.*
>
> JOHN: *Aye, surely.*
>
> BARNEY: *And then, I often heard my father saying, then, that they started saying a prayer, a prayer then when the mass was finished. They started, the priest started saying a pra yer after mass. They started saying that prayer. And from after they started saying that prayer, there never was no light seen after.*

Summarizing intergeneric relationships thus far, we have seen that in terms of thematic and formal features comic anecdotes directly connect with tall tales and jokes, and contemplative anecdotes directly connect with personal experience narratives and historical legends—themselves thematically linked. The connection from anecdotes to supernatural legends and memorates discussed here is the most indirect, and this is the result of a difference in topic.

True, stories of mystery in first-person are similar to personal experience narratives in terms of form, and stories of mystery in third-person are like historical legends in that they describe local events in the past and are subject to negotiations over the truth-value of their depictions. However, comic and contemplative anecdotes, personal experience narratives, historical legends, jokes, and tall tales employ both fiction and nonfiction, both comedy and drama, to investigate aspects of the social world. They explore, and in part constitute, interrelationships between the individual and the group. Stories of mystery—whether those of personal experience shared or those of others' experiences remembered—may be part of the same processes of sociability as stories in other genres, but they belong to a separate realm of contemplation: cosmology and teleology. As such, despite their potential for investigations of worldview (cf. Santino 1988), stories of mystery lead us away from our main concerns with how people use stories—especially anecdotes—to imagine and enact community, forging individual and collective identities. As we will see, central in these concerns is the issue of character—the characters of particular individuals and the character of the community these individuals are used to symbolize.

Figure 6.5. Barney McGrath

7

Anecdotes and the Literary Character

If Aghyaran anecdotes are uniquely suited for contemplating the characters of those people depicted in them, then we need to know more about the issue of character. Of course, the term "character" has several meanings. "Character" may have an evaluative connotation when defined as a person's relative moral excellence. "Character" may also have the more neutral connotation of an individual's disposition or essential nature. In this chapter, I am concerned with "character" in the sense of an individual portrayed in narrative. In local character anecdotes these portrayals are established through various strategies for displaying psychological and ethical traits. These traits distinguish one character from another, perhaps assigning a character to a recognizable type and allowing that character to embody a given ideological stance. Put another way, my task in this chapter is to discuss character in literary terms. At issue here is what narrative strategies are employed in local character anecdotes in Aghyaran to depict personality.

We have learned that at wakes people tell anecdotes about the deceased that reconstruct or imagine otherwise ephemeral conversations and actions. Taken together, these narratives illustrate the deceased's most marked personality traits or characteristics and thereby epitomize him or her from the perspective of those who remain. This form of commemoration is most often celebratory and appreciative. With the issue of personality raised, thematic associations lead mourners to recall anecdotes of other local characters, some living but more not, and to branch out into other genres of narrative, such as jokes and legends, that allow a broader range of rhetorical resources for sociability. The same issues, genres, and motivations are found in the ceili, which, like the wake, allows for reflection on human nature and the nature of community through discussion of past and present neighbors. The differences between wakes and ceilis lie most importantly for our interests in the wider breadth of genres appropriate at ceilis, the smaller scale of attendance, the different temporal trajectories of sociability, and the freer play of conversational focus, given that there is no centripetal force at a ceili repeatedly redirecting attention to the memory of one individual. In either situational context, however, the ongoing process of characterizing individuals through anecdotes—on the surface an effort to locate individuality—can also have a depersonalizing effect, from a biographical perspective, over time.

Complex individuals are often rendered in already meaningful tropes. So although the personality of an individual is located or epitomized in an anecdote, that individuality may be seen in non-unique, typological terms. Rather than establishing a collection of psychologically realistic portrayals of unique individuals, Aghyaran character anecdotes gesture toward categories of character traits and types. This flexible taxonomy of characters and personality traits is eloquent of local interests and concerns, and significant in terms of ethnography. Our goal now, however, is to understand something of why this typological gesture emerges and how it is established.

That our memories and narrated remembrances of others would become simplified over time seems natural, perhaps even obvious. One truism about memory is that it is not an experience storage system that provides true recall, but a project of re-creation mediated by the concerns of the present. One truism about historical discourse is that the past is gone and only those traces of the past that are relevant to a given present will be enlisted for narrative in that present. The passage of time plays a role in the narrative process that sees a complex individual become a less complex assemblage of noteworthy personality traits or become an even simpler, more compressed character type. Equally fundamental to this transition are the exigencies of narrative construction in general and of specific generic conventions in particular.

Let us consider different versions of one story as an illustration of how a person may become typified long after narrated events have occurred, even to the extent of remaining named but becoming virtually anonymous. Three versions of a story from three narrators will demonstrate how, through narrative and over time, a person may become less an individual and more an assemblage of traits, or simply a narrative persona with little sign of individual personality beyond what can be inferred from his actions. The story is about a priest who curses a B man during a checkpoint interrogation. Mickey Byrne's version was mentioned in my description of the ceili at Jamie Barclay's in chapter 3. Due to thematic content, temporal setting, and the various rhetorical uses made of the story, it lies in terms of genre in the muddy borderlands between local character anecdote, historical legend, and supernatural legend.

I first heard the story from Mickey, who identified the priest as Fr. James McCrory, Aghyaran curate from 1940 to 1950, and later I heard Cissie Dolan tell the story during a ceili at her home. My first opportunity to record the story came in an interview with Cissie, but I had Mickey's version of the story in mind when I asked her about it.

> RAY: *Well, there was a story you told me once about a Father McCrory who had been stopped one night by the B men.*
>
> CISSIE: *Aye.*
>
> RAY: *But I couldn't, I couldn't quite get all that story written down. What was the story behind that?*
>
> CISSIE: *Wouldn't . . . it was Father Floyd, wasn't it, they called the priest?*
>
> RAY: *Was it? Okay.*
>
> CISSIE: *Hmm. But anyway. They stopped him when he was going out on a sick call or something, and the B men held him up, do you know. And of course they held him back for a good while, you know. Just the ordinary B men, the locals, Protestants, with a uniform and all. They searched him and everything, you know.*
>
> RAY: *Mm-hmm.*
>
> CISSIE: *And one of them says, "Will you be at, in the fair tomorrow, McCrory"—or eh, aye, "Will you be at the fair tomorrow Floyd?" And he says "Aye, I will, but you'll not."*
>
> RAY: *Is that right?*
>
> CISSIE: *And he was dead before the next morning. Died suddenly. Well, that was the story anyway.*

RAY: *Would that have happened long ago?*

CISSIE: *Well, just in the twenties, I suppose, the time of the Troubles and the IRA got formed up and round about the time the boys was lifted for the Argenta and all.*

RAY: *Right.*

Cissie's version is succinct, even sparse. One difference from Mickey's recollection of the priest and B man incident is that the priest Cissie identifies is Fr. Michael Floyd, Aghyaran curate from 1907 to 1922, and therefore Cissie's version of the story is set twenty-odd years earlier.

In 1922, Cissie would have been twelve years old. Although she remembers well the Black and Tans coming for her brother, she would not have known Fr. Floyd on a more personal level, and we can see that her version of the story is not primarily intended as a testimonial of the priest's character. Here, Fr. Floyd is an actor—a vehicle for plot functions, in Vladimir Propp's terminology (1968). Cissie makes no direct mention of a curse, but we are led to believe or at least consider the possibility that the B man dies because Fr. Floyd's words are more than a prediction and have their own illocutionary force. As an actor in a drama about power relations in a politically tense environment, Fr. Floyd is portrayed not as a personality but as the sort of figure one would find in an historical legend, such as Proinsias Dubh who stole from the rich to give to the poor or St. Patrick who converted the fierce pagan chieftains. The priest's character is not developed in terms of psychology or subjectivity; rather he serves like Proinsias Dubh or St. Patrick as a representation of the possibility of power, perhaps even moral force or divine justice, emanating from a position of marginality.

Categorizing the story as an anecdote or a legend is not of primary importance, but a consideration of genre is instructive. Forced to categorize Cissie's version of the story, we might note its similarity to anecdotes due to the importance of quoted speech. In addition, consider temporal setting in relation to the narrator. Taking place within Cissie's memory but depending on the narrated memories of her elders, the story is suspended in generic terms between anecdote and legend. However, the way in which personality is deemphasized in favor of the symbolic import of the actions of dramatis personae reminds us more of legends than of anecdotes, with the exception of some contemplative anecdotes. Moreover, the thematic content overlaps considerably with that of both local historical and supernatural legends, treating as it does both politics and mysterious power, both the social and sacred realms of experience. It is the sort of story that was likely repeated, shortly after the narrated events occurred, as an anecdote. Because of thematic content it is the sort of story most suited to survival over time as a legend.

Three weeks after I asked Cissie about this incident, John Glackin, seven years younger than Cissie, had occasion to bring up the story during a recorded ceili with me and Charlie Lunney. Charlie had been discussing the mysterious bad luck experienced by certain neighbors after disturbing sites associated with the fairies and sites of early Christian devotion. John was certain that bad fortune was the result of lack of proper respect, and he supported his claim with the following:

> JOHN: *It doesn't do, it doesn't do, now. Look at the Sproule boy that tackled Father Floyd. He was on the B men.*
>
> CHARLIE: *Sproule?*
>
> JOHN: *Sproule of Legatonagon. There's not a Sproule in it now.*
>
> CHARLIE: *Aye.*
>
> JOHN: *But eh, he was, he stopped Father Floyd, and Father Floyd was a very stubborn man anyway, you know.*
>
> CHARLIE: *I think so.*
>
> JOHN: *He give him a lot of old chat and Father Floyd says "I'll be on the road tomorrow, but you'll not be on it." And when he went over and went till his bed and some of them went to waken him in the morning, he was dead.*
>
> RAY: *The B man was dead.*
>
> JOHN: *Aye, he was dead. For I heared old Charles Brown telling it, you see. Charles, eh, he used to ceili in the priests' house, so eh, he was in whenever Father Floyd come in. He was very cross looking when he come in. And he reached for a book from some pocket and started reading it, and old Father McConalogue says, "What are you doing?" "I'm going to make sure there'll be nobody holding me up on the road the morrow." And he took the book from him, but he had the harm done. Sproule was dead. Aye. Aye, he was very stubborn, Father Floyd.*

Conversation had been revolving around the need for respect when dealing with that which is mysterious or holy, for whether or not we understand such things they have power. Recognizing this train of thought and giving it further definition, John seized the opportunity to tell how Sproule the B man paid dearly for his lack of respect for a man of the cloth. On the one hand, his story invites contemplation of the priest's power and of what implications this power has in both political and theological terms. In this case, the priest can be understood as a catalyst of events. Like Cissie, John foregrounds plot and action rather than what we might call character development. On the other hand, John and Charlie are also drawn toward characterizing Fr. Floyd as an individual, specifically as a proud and stubborn man, in an anecdotal style. Charlie continues this line of thought:

> CHARLIE: *They say he was a tough man.*
>
> JOHN: *He was.*
>
> CHARLIE: *He was a good age before he was made a priest.*
>
> JOHN: *He was.*
>
> CHARLIE: *I heared my father on about him. They used to have them making roads in the bog about Meenreagh, in that country, that's where he come from. And eh, the boys, the Protestant men come with their horse and carts and they were going to go on anyway and drag their turf when the weather was good, no odds about them on the road, putting up the road. And they say he had been out the night before drinking poteen somewhere and dancing, you know.*
>
> JOHN: *Aye.* ◊
>
> CHARLIE: *Young fella.* ◊ *He reached for the shovel and he just broke the shaft like that across his knee and he went down the road and he chased the whole lot, they had to go. Nearly killed 'em.*
>
> JOHN: *He was coming up, eh . . .*
>
> CHARLIE: *And that's, then he got to be a priest, after that.*

Charlie has added to the picture of Fr. Floyd as volatile and unwilling to bow down to Protestants, as a man of passions with a sense of justice in a social environment he understands to be unjust. First there is a telling: "Aye, he was very stubborn Father Floyd" and "They say he was a tough man." Then there is a showing, with the anecdote of his reaction to the Protestants tearing through his work crew on the bog road. Charlie explores Fr. Floyd's youth, making a bid to locate the man's true nature before he became a priest. John takes the conversation a step further with a story that marries the anecdotal image of Fr. Floyd the uncompromising man and the legendary image of Fr. Floyd the priest with extra-normal powers.

> JOHN: *Jamie Sproule was driving him up in a horse and car from Castlederg one night, and the Hamiltons where Crawfords shop is now, the Hamiltons was very prominent.*
>
> CHARLIE: *Aye.*
>
> JOHN: *And, eh, they were calling after them, and Jamie he says to the priest, "Hold you that horse there. I'll go back to them." "No," he says, "don't bother going back for," he says, "it'll not be long till the grass'll be growing at their door." And Hamiltons went out like snow off a ditch. Oh, he was a tough man.*

From there, the conversation could have gone in a number of directions: Protestant-Catholic relations, Fr. Floyd's temper, an evaluation of Charles Brown and others as reliable sources for these stories. Before changing topic entirely, however, John and Charlie wound down this strand of conversation by discussing whether priests still have this sort of power. Charlie seemed to have some doubts but, seeking to agree with John, he recalled one priest who performed a successful exorcism in the parish. John maintained that priests still have such powers but that the bishops have forced priests to keep them in check.

Although eventually John presses the stories about Fr. Floyd back into service for contemplating mystery and supernatural power, the original line of inquiry, we see in the exchange both John and especially Charlie willing to discuss Fr. Floyd as a type of person. Charlie depends on what he has heard rather than personal experience, as does John, but John also draws on personal dealings with the priest after Fr. Floyd transferred from Aghyaran to Gortin parish. Although John was born in 1917 and Fr. Floyd left Aghyaran in 1922, John nonetheless had more opportunity later, living in Drumquin, to get to know the priest than did Cissie or Mickey.

Having characterized the priest in psychological terms as a type of man—volatile, proud, stubborn—John and Charlie also bring to mind another, less psychologically defined type: the magically endowed priest, familiar not only from Aghyaran folklore but also from Irish folklore in general. In his *Occasions of Faith* (1995), Lawrence Taylor investigates representations of powerful priests in Donegal folklore. Fr. Floyd shares elements with both the social activist Fr. Magroarty (chapter 4), who fought against oppression of Catholics by Protestant authorities, and with drunken Frs. McGinley and McShane (chapter 5), who had healing powers and the ability to effect curses. Although Charlie attributes youthful drinking to Fr. Floyd, he does not portray him as an alcoholic. However, conceptually Fr. Floyd is like the type of the powerful drunken priest because of his difficulties with self-control. Taylor notes that if magically endowed priests are not drunks they are somehow deviant, errant, or eccentric. One possibility is that their marginality or liminality makes them symbolically suited for such power and that their lack of control accounts for their sometimes reckless wielding of it. Stories of Fr. Floyd are bound to be understood in the context of other Aghyaran stories of named and unnamed, past and present, priests who heal parishioners or exorcise malignant ghosts and spirits. Therefore, Fr. Floyd's depictions may lose some personal specificity while appealing to a known and already meaningful type of character. This gesture away from strict biographical fidelity toward preexisting typology becomes more explicit in Mickey's version of the story.

Having heard Mickey tell the story once, I had my first opportunity to record his version during a ceili with Danny Gallen, later joined by Barney McGrath and John McElhill. A couple of days earlier Danny and I had been to a ceremony held by a group from Pettigo who erected a stone cross on Drumawark Hill overlooking Lough Derg. The original, ancient cross on the site had been destroyed by Protestants in the 1890s, and I asked Mickey if he could tell me anything about that incident or add to the scant story I had heard that each of the men involved in smashing the cross met with debilitating accidents or early deaths. Mickey responded, "There wasn't a man involved but came to some harm later. I heared them go down the list of what happened to each man, but I just wouldn't mind it now." He deferred to others who might know more. The common theme of magical or divine retribution reminded me of the priest and the B man story, and since the story was not too far off topic I hoped Mickey would commit his version to tape.

RAY: *Well now, you told me a story once about some B men here in Aghyaran who, eh, who stopped a priest.*

MICKEY: *Aye, Danny could tell you that one, too, now. Aye, remember Father McCrory who was in Aghyaran, and Bobby Hamilton was on the B men, him and Sam Hemphill?*

DANNY: *Aye.*

MICKEY: *You might have heared that'n Danny.*

DANNY: *I heard you telling it and that's the only time I heared it.*

MICKEY: *But, eh, this Sam Hemphill, now—by the way, he's only, he's just dead there, buried a short time ago.*

RAY: *Is that right?*

MICKEY: *This Sam Hemphill I'm on about, and he was married on a sister of this man, Bobby Hamilton.*

RAY: *I see.*

MICKEY: *Anyhow, Sam was on the B men, too, and they were at Aghyaran crossroads there. You know up at the chapel. And, eh, they were standing there anyhow and Father McCrory, he came along. I think he was on a sick call or coming from a sick call.*

DANNY: *Aye.*

MICKEY: *But Father McCrory was a great priest, a great curing priest and all.*

RAY: *Yeah?*

MICKEY: *Well, I know that for a fact because I used to have a spot of ringworm on my hand, on my wrist, and I went to him on a Sunday morning, and it was gone on the following Sunday.*

RAY: *Right.*

MICKEY: *He was a great curing priest, like, but anyhow Father McCrory, um—what was I going to say about him now?—aye, came along, he came along and they stopped him, you see. So um . . . the fair was the next day or so, and that be*

down there in Castlederg. We used to call it "the fair" in them
days. There were the fair in Castlederg always, one a month or
something, and Friday was coming up, the fair was coming up,
and Fr. McCrory, they bid Fr. McCrory good night anyhow.
They didn't hold him very long. And this Hamilton man said to
Father McCrory, he says, um, he says, eh, "I'll see you in the fair
on Friday, Father"—Hamilton set down "I'll see you in the fair
on Friday"—"No," he says, "Bobby," he says, "I'll be in the fair,"
he says, "but you won't."

RAY: *Hmm.*

MICKEY: *And Bobby I think was, he died off the next day*
or something.

RAY: *Is that right?*

MICKEY: *Very short time after it anyway.*

RAY: *Right.*

MICKEY: *But it was Sam Hemphill who told that.*
Wouldn't you wonder at him telling it, like?

DANNY: *Aye, but there was something . . .*

MICKEY: *Eh?*

DANNY: *There was more to it than that, Mickey. I don't*
think they were too nice to the priest.

MICKEY: *They what?*

DANNY: *They weren't that nice to the priest. There were*
something happened that annoyed them.

MICKEY: *Aye, I thought they weren't too nice maybe.*

DANNY: *No, that's the way I got the story first time*
around.

MICKEY: *Aye, I wouldn't have it right, now, because I*
don't . . . I think I would have been away at that time.

Unlike Charlie's Fr. Floyd, Mickey's Fr. McCrory is not a portrayal of personality, but we do know what sort of priest he is in typological terms. He
can both cure and curse; he is a powerful priest. With this character type in
mind, Danny continued with two versions of a story he had heard in which

horses pulling a hearse came to a dead stop, frothing at the mouth and refusing to budge, until a priest whispered a few words in their ears and laid his hands on their backs. The first version was set in Aghyaran townland and the second in Shanaghy. Barney arrived in the midst of Danny's telling and added another version of this story that he had heard from his father, this one set in Pettigo. Such priests seem to harness a sort of chthonic power, and it is significant that in one version of the story of the priest and the horses a Protestant minister had first been called to the task and failed. If different denominations provide different conduits to the sacred, this story of the priest and horses can imply that the mediators in one faith have a more direct link to supernatural power.

Like many of his generation, Mickey is well aware of social categories and boundaries, but he is not prejudiced against the other side of the house. Throughout his life in Aghyaran and in England he has worked for and alongside Protestants, maintaining close friendly and neighborly relationships. He is not invested in possible political overtones of his story about the power of Fr. McCrory and, indeed, initially played down the likelihood that the priest was provoked by the B men. (Still, Danny's addition that the B men "weren't that nice" is not necessarily motivated by political beliefs; provocation is necessary in an orderly narrative for Fr. McCrory to have plausible motivation for his curse.) In the four times I heard Mickey tell this story without my asking for it, he did not offer the story as commentary on politics or local history. He was responding to turns of conversation that involved either remembering Fr. McCrory, discussing curses and cures, or expressing wonder at mystery and the extra-normal power of others.

If Mickey is no bigot, he is also, of his own admission, no historian. Notice how in the above telling and at Jamie's ceili he defers to others, taking responsibility for telling the story only when others will not. Mickey does not see himself as one with a great memory for stories once told to him, but among the stories in his repertoire are those about a priest who could cure and curse. For him the story of Fr. McCrory and the B man is not primarily a tale illustrative of political history or an anecdote illustrative of an individual's personality. Mickey's interests, reflected in his repertoire of repeated stories, are in his own and others' personal experiences of recent events and in stories of mystery that challenge or affirm belief.

When requested to tell stories of history, Mickey often elides people and groups of people who fulfill similar narrative functions from a contemporary perspective. Asked about local men involved in 1798 agitation, he tends either to refer to them as being in the IRA of the past or to speak of them as if they were the IRA, despite a very different eighteenth-century political landscape in which the majority of Aghyaran United Irishmen were Presbyterians. Asked about men who were members of the old RIC (Royal Irish Constabulary) in Aghyaran, he has referred to them as B men despite the fact that the B Specials did not exist until after Partition and the disbanding of the RIC. For him, in his memory and in his stories, character typology is more important than exact chronology when re-creating, through narrative, events to which he was not a witness or when relating others' stories that he does not feel he has mastered.

For a number of reasons it is more than likely that Cissie and John are correct to identify the subject of the original story as Fr. Floyd. Cissie and John are valued locally as reliable sources for stories of past events; they are known for keeping the facts straight. Cissie and John are respectively twelve and five years older than Mickey, have spent more time at home in the parish, and would have had more exposure to Fr. Floyd and stories about him. Moreover, Fr. Floyd was curate in Aghyaran during the time of Partition, when political tensions where high and the B men were more frequently patrolling the roads, so Cissie's and John's temporal setting for the story is more convincing.

My best guess is that because Mickey knew Fr. McCrory before intermittently leaving to work in England and because Fr. McCrory cured him of ringworm, Mickey has elided Fr. McCrory and Fr. Floyd after being told a story by Sam Hemphill about a powerful priest. Mickey knows from personal experience that Fr. McCrory was a powerful priest, so it would be easy for him to add other stories of powerful priests to his own mental biography of Fr. McCrory. Whatever the case may be, we have a story that over time no longer depends on biographical fidelity to remain worth telling, one that involves a protagonist who, although named, is virtually anonymous. Any feasible name will do because locating the individuality of a person known to teller and audience is not the point of the story. Fr. McCrory becomes a type serving in the narrative as a vehicle for plot functions.

~๏~

My aim has not been to demonstrate that Mickey is an unreliable historian—something he himself proclaims in response to requests for certain stories, especially those about the more distant past. Mickey's story provides us a good example of the fact that in terms of dramatis personae, typology often takes precedence over individual uniqueness or biographical fidelity as stories about actual individuals make a transition from anecdote to legend. Past events may be stored in memory, understood, and represented in orderly chronological narratives like those informing the majority of written histories. Or the past may be catalogued in memory in spatial terms, with sites on the landscape providing mnemonic devices for past events that remain relevant to present concerns. Or understandings of past events may be governed by understandings of the actors involved. In this case, the past is mediated in typological terms, with character types and traits representing the range of human responses to shared conditions and providing ready-made rhetorical resources for narrative. This last possibility seems to be driving Mickey's construction of a probably chronologically and biographically incorrect story that is nonetheless resonant for his audience, providing as it does commentary on the present by referring to the relevant past.

Even Packy Jim McGrath, who is valued for his very keen memory for names and dates, is driven by thematic and typological concerns when discoursing on the local past. When challenged, Packy Jim's knowledge of chronology, location, and actors involved in a given story is usually flawless, but in normal conversation his concentration is on significance more than sequence or setting. Coming upon the notion of political resistance by Catholics and left uninterrupted, Packy Jim will skip back and forth between the centuries to offer you, systematically, every story he knows of Proinsias Dubh the rapparee, Sean McHugh the Ribbonman, known republicans of the 1920s, and those of the present generation—rebels all, with different names and adversaries but sharing the same narrative function. Among Packy Jim's many verbal gifts is his mastery of the legend—a genre in which character type is foremost because thematic concerns and plot dominate over character development.

Having investigated three versions of the priest and B man story, we see that the protagonist is treated as a character, in the literary sense, in two modes. The first is a character as a type of personality who in anecdote-like narrative embodies certain collectively recognized psychological or behavioral qualities. The second is a character as a type of actor who in more legend-like narrative enables certain plot possibilities. Charlie and John grant Fr. Floyd a certain psychological depth by discussing his character traits. These traits are shared by other local characters that reoccur in local folklore, so they serve to locate Fr. Floyd's individuality in already meaningful terms.

Sharing traits with others known for volatility, such as Dennis Corry or John McHugh, the Fr. Floyd of anecdotes becomes slightly less than unique but nonetheless exemplary of certain remarkable human qualities. Some of Fr. Floyd's individuality is preserved, and some is bound to be elided, compressed, or co-opted for rhetorical purposes. This gesture toward typology in anecdotal stories is partial; delineation of human nature and a certain amount of psychological realism are the goals. The gesture toward typology in legendary material is more thorough. Cissie's and some of John's portrayals of the priest evoke the legendary type of the powerful priest whose significance lies in his capabilities more than his individual personality. Mickey's portrayal goes so far as to effectively negate individuality through elision, leaving mostly type. What we may safely assume to be Mickey's mistake in identifying the priest does not matter when a character is less a mimetic device than a function of plot. Telling the story about Fr. McCrory rather than Fr. Floyd does not matter given the second mode of characterization, which revolves around the symbolic significance of people portrayed in narrative more than around individuality, personality, and psychological realism. These two modes parallel conceptions in literary studies of what a character is.

As Roland Barthes points out in his investigation of Balzac's *Sarrasine*, characters are not people but linguistic constructs, rhetorical entities, or simplified identities entirely complicit with and acting as agents of the discourse of which they are a part (1970:178–181). However, the extent of this complicity through simplification or typification varies. Formulated to describe different types of character in the novel, E. M. Forster's delineation of "round" and "flat" characters (1927) provides useful vocabulary for considering the portrayal of actual individuals, transformed into characters, in purportedly factual oral biographical accounts. The distinction between round and flat is a matter of textual complexity and rhetorical intent. Whereas flat characters are referential, round characters are mimetic. Flat characters receive little development and serve mostly to reference particular issues or notions and to help further plot. Chaucer's Parson in *The Canterbury Tales* or any of the fabliau-like and allegorical characters in the framed pilgrims' stories would be examples. Round characters, however, are granted enough treatment by an author to reflect a subjectivity or "secret inner life," in Forster's terms, that appears realistic enough to endure on its own outside of the text. Joyce's Gabriel Conroy in "The Dead" and many other characters from *Dubliners* would be examples. As Gerald Mead summarizes the concepts of flat and round characters in literature, "'Flat' characters are understood by a single concept, 'round' characters call for more concepts to account for their total presence, and the 'roundest' require even contradictory concepts to describe their role" (1990:96).

Cissie's Fr. Floyd and Mickey's Fr. McCrory are fairly flat characters whose inner life or psychological complexity are not suggested because their narrative function as a type—the powerful priest—predominates. Charlie's anecdotal Fr. Floyd is a fairly round character given traits and motivations that make his reaction to the Protestants who disrupt his road building and his pastoral rounds seem plausible, even predictable. In this case, Fr. Floyd seems to be a coherent personality existing independent of narrative; the supporting story seems to be an illustrative glimpse into this integrated, pre- and post-existing self. As we will see, certain individuals such as John McHugh who attract numerous anecdotes can be seen as even rounder characters. Seemingly contradictory attributes found in the cycle of stories about McHugh and others discourage our developing a sense of rigid personality coherence. Seemingly contradictory attributes appeal through complexity to what some literary scholars might define as a more contemporary sense of verisimilitude that assumes the incoherence of the subject. Still, such a round character may be seen in typological rather than individualistic terms as an eccentric, a type defined by complexity, unpredictability, and resistance to convention.

The fact that more than five centuries separate Chaucer's and Joyce's very different conceptions of what a literary character is and does reminds us that the literary character is a culturally and temporally situated construct. As Uri Margolin asserts, "The history of modern Western narrative reveals an ever-increasing concentration on individuals' interiority: their verbal and mental aspects, a process referred to by Erich Kahler as 'the inward turn of narrative'" (1990:117). In Forster's terms, Western literature has made a general transition from emphasis on flat characters to a focus on round ones over time in an effort to convey verisimilitude through psychological realism.

Local character anecdotes often share with novels the capacity for rounder characters and at least an implicit interest in what Margolin calls the interiority of subjects. As seen in stories about the priest and B man, however, Aghyaran folklore can reverse or perhaps retrace the temporal trajectory found in the history of characterization in Western literature. That is, an actual person, known by and contemporary with the tellers and audience of anecdotes about him, may be portrayed as a relatively round character, as in a novel. Whereas, over time, the same person becomes more typified as a flatter character, becoming flattest if this character reemerges even later in legend.

Although this trajectory from round to flat characterization in Aghyaran folklore is in part a temporal one, it is equally and simultaneously a generic one. There may be instances of a temporal, evolutionary connection between certain anecdotes and legends. In such cases, greater character typification seems to be the result of time passing. When we take into consideration other genres of Aghyaran folklore, however, the flatness or roundness of characters utilized seems mostly a matter of generic convention—more on this soon.

A story told by one narrator as an anecdote resembles the modernist novel in its portrayal of characters, and the same story told by another as a legend resembles early modern literature in its portrayal of characters. As we have seen, whether an individual appears as a character in a narrative from one genre rather than as a character in a narrative from another genre can be a function of the passage of time. That is, the choice of genre and characterization style can be a matter of the narrator's relative experience of or temporal relationship to the characters portrayed. Time and genre are interrelated, and both affect choices for flat vs. round characterization in Aghyaran folklore. In the end, these choices are up to a narrator who necessarily stands in some temporal relationship to the characters to be portrayed and the events to be narrated. Moreover, the competent narrator has at his or her command the rhetorical resources of different genres.

Before becoming too committed to speaking of characters in Aghyaran anecdotes as flat or round, we should consider emendations and expansions of these notions in literary studies. Clearly the local character anecdote and the novel are very different forms of discourse, yet scholarly attention paid to strategies of characterization in the novel provide us greater purchase on parallel strategies in oral narrative. Concerned with modern literature, David Fishelov attends to "the complex process of determining whether, to what extent, and in what sense we perceive a character as a 'type' or as an 'individual'":

> The tension between the individuality of a character and the fact that this very individual is an "intersection" of abstract typical traits is evident in every character of literature. In every one of them, this basic tension manifests itself in a different way. If an author chooses to stress the typical aspect(s) of a character, the character's individuality will be overshadowed by its typical properties—and vice versa. (1990:74)

The same tension may be found in the portrayal of characters in Aghyaran anecdotes, much more than in other genres such as the legend, joke, and tall tale.

At first Fishelov appears simply to have replaced Forster's opposition of flat and round characters with an opposition of type and individual. However, Fishelov uses insights consonant with reader-response theory (though not identified as such) to distinguish between how a character is portrayed within a text and how it is perceived by those who receive the text. This distinction allows for both flat and round treatment of a character at the textual level by an author, and flat and round reception of a character at what he calls the constructed level, where the reader's experience and conceptual makeup inform perception and interpretation. Combining the distinctions of flat and round with textual and constructed levels of meaning anticipates four possible, though potentially overlapping, categories of character: 1) pure type, a character that receives both flat textual treatment and flat reception, 2) individual-like type, a character that receives round textual treatment but flat reception, 3) type-like individual, a character that receives flat textual treatment and round reception, and 4) pure individual, a character that receives both round textual treatment and reception.

Pure types and type-like individuals are the most common characters in the genres of Aghyaran folklore under consideration. The saint, the powerful priest, the faithful sister, the tyrannical landlord, the rebel—these are types of characters found in local historical legends. They are not portrayed in psychologically realistic terms, but they are full of potential as embodiments of ideas. Granted, the characters in legends are representations of actual people. Nevertheless, type dominates over individuality. Given flat textual treatment and reception, they are pure types serving the rhetorical needs of narrators within performance contexts. The joke is also home to pure types—the deceptive lawyer, the boastful Yank, both the wily Paddy and the dense Murphy. "The Widow Quinn" may be named in Patrick McElhill's joke about the desperate bachelor seeking his father's blessing in marriage, but she stands in not as a specific person but as a stock character, the embodiment of rural homeliness and backwardness, "a wild woman from the Mourne Mountains."

The majority of Aghyaran anecdotes portray characters as type-like individuals. Observing at a ceili or wake that an anecdote about Johnny Owens pulling a prank on John McHugh leads to an anecdote about Tommy Hilley pulling one on Willie McLaughlin, and so on, indicates the existence of the trickster as a locally appreciated type. However, no matter how typical or inevitable the characterization of known tricksters becomes on the textual level, such typification is not enough to turn Johnny Owens or Tommy Hilley into a flat pure type on the constructed level for those who tell and receive these anecdotes. Johnny and Tommy may be deceased, but those who commemorate them through anecdotes bring to their understanding of these stories an appreciation of the complexity and psychological depth of these men as they knew them in life.

If anecdote characters cannot become pure types, neither can they become pure individuals. Whereas novels are often invested in the development of character and character change (or lack thereof) over longer stretches of time and circumstances, the local character anecdote allows only for single episodes that offer defining moments rather than extended considerations and reconsiderations of a given character.

The tension between type and individual, flat and round, in local character anecdotes becomes clear, and the balance struck is effected by a number of factors: temporal, generic, and social. As time passes, those who remember deceased individuals through anecdotes may appeal to already meaningful tropes, to be discussed, that increase a character's typological rather than individualistic aspects. However, even without a significant passage of time, the project of constructing narrative itself is inevitably a process of selection and thereby simplification in terms of action, dialogue, and characterization. Moreover, genres as rhetorical frames invite particular patterns of selection and simplification.

Regarding the anecdote, generic conventions such as quoted repartee climaxing in witty punch lines may overpower strictly faithful accounting of events. A protagonist may be portrayed in terms that are ideal from the standpoint of what makes a good anecdote character and what corresponds with an individual's social profile or reputation already established through similar anecdotes. Therefore, along with the brevity of anecdotes, the resonance and rhetorical value of personality types and traits preclude anecdotes from offering more comprehensive representations of an individual's complexity. In fact the imperatives of genre may result in an actual fabrication of narrated events in order to underscore how well a given individual exemplifies a certain character type.

Finally, given the pull toward simplification and typology in anecdotal characterization, those who tell anecdotes must always be aware of audience and social context to avoid offending friends or relatives of the person under discussion with implied criticism or perceived misrepresentation. In order to construct a well-received and entertaining anecdote, a storyteller may be tempted to idealize an individual as a character type or as a relatively flat assemblage of traits. In certain social contexts, however, a storyteller may either have to avoid unflattering anecdotes altogether or strike a different balance in the tension between type and individual by offering a rounder, more complex, and perhaps more charitable portrayal of the character in question. The latter is often the case at wakes, where even people not often discussed during life become characters in anecdotes told in the presence of their closest friends and family.

Whether at wakes, ceilis, or other social occasions, it is safer to speak of the dead and safest to speak of those, such as elderly bachelors, who not only are easily characterized in typological terms but also have few living allies monitoring what is being said about them and how. Unless a person in life is particularly eccentric and therefore unconcerned with how others speak of him or her, or unless a person is unequivocally to be commended, he or she is unlikely to be the subject of many anecdotes while alive. Talking even slightly negatively behind backs, referred to as "scandalizing" or "passing remarks," can be dangerous. Henry Glassie touches upon many of the same temporal and social factors that influence how a person, after death, may become characterized in anecdotes as a type:

> To connect themselves and discover their minds, people must talk. Other people provide the most obvious, useful, interesting topic. So people enjoy speaking in celebration of others, but investigation into human nature cannot be confined by affirmation, and negativity cannot be allowed to escape through the community. The

solution is to speak of the dead, making history the way to discuss the present. People from the past are made black holes of gossip, sucking energy into them. I was able to watch this as men died. One never mentioned in life became after death the very type of greed. Another became the model of the solid farmer. (1982:41)

Our concern now is what makes for a story-worthy character in Aghyaran. Who may be considered a "character" in the local rather than literary sense of the word? Whereas the pure type and the type-like individual are character types in the sense of literary-like strategies for characterization, there are also character types in the sense of locally recognized types of humanity. Our concern now is with specific examples of this latter sort of character type—the rough bachelor, the trickster, the fool, etc. Everyone who is waked in Aghyaran lives on at least for a brief while as a character in anecdotes. But some anecdotes about certain characters circulate longer and more widely than others. What types and traits continually reemerge in a wide corpus of Aghyaran character anecdotes? What can they tell us about collective concerns? How do they shape collective memory and inform local identity?

8

Anecdotes and the Local Character

To say, as has often been said, that "John McHugh was a great character" reveals something about what a character is in local rather than literary terms. If one man is considered a character then others are not. In emic terms, "characters" are not the narrative representations of all dramatis personae appearing in folklore; they are types of individuals distinguished most often by uncommon wit, effusiveness, gullibility, volatility, backwardness, or some other marked trait of excellence or eccentricity. True, the deceased at a wake is treated as if a character, in the local sense, through anecdotes seeking to identify the essence of the deceased. Therefore, eventually all are afforded the opportunity of being celebrated for individuality while also being characterized in terms of traits and types. However, those like John McHugh who are consistently referred to as "characters" are treated and portrayed as such usually during life, definitely at their wakes, and indefinitely after death at ceilis and the wakes of others. Simply put, in local terms, characters are those people who offer the most entertaining material for anecdotes and are therefore most often discussed. Having earned a reputation, they attract attention from storytellers who are eager for more material and who are not above using traveling motifs or apocryphal elements when adding to the social biographies of local characters.

The attributes that qualify one as a character, in local terms, are usually behavioral or psychological rather than physical. So, for instance, being exceptionally strong or ugly does not make one a character, but behavioral and psychological attributes may be demonstrated by actions portrayed in narrative, as well as through quoted speech. While some may share personality traits with those spoken of as characters, the character qualifies as such because he or she embodies certain attributes, perhaps in excess, even to the point of transgressing lines between socially appropriate and inappropriate behavior. Often these transgressions are exactly what make stories of characters entertaining, set social norms in relief, and allow for either a challenge to or reaffirmation of these norms.

Until now, I have used the term "character" mostly in the literary sense of a narrative representation of a persona. The broad and permeable genre I have identified as the local character anecdote serves to characterize—to discern and represent the personality of—actual individuals, whether or not they would be considered characters in the local sense of the word. Like legends, contemplative anecdotes in particular feature people who are appreciated for virtues such as bravery, patience, or consideration of others. The individual portrayed in a contemplative anecdote may be labeled a "hero," "saint," or "modest wee man," but that individual is not called a character in local parlance.

The telling of contemplative anecdotes provides a clear example of people identifying qualities worth emulating. Contemplative anecdotes, like legends, act as windows into the shared values that any ethnographer seeks to identify and illustrate. Glassie's consideration of "exploits," more of which seem to have been told in Ballymenone than in Aghyaran, would parallel a lengthier consideration here of local contemplative anecdotes. I wish to focus, however, on comic anecdotes and the people identified, labeled, and portrayed as characters in order to reiterate that serious social work is being accomplished in Aghyaran as much through humor as through more clearly contemplative commemorative discourse.

All characterizations of individuals in anecdotes serve as models through which people may consider human nature and behavior. Therefore the objection might be raised that focusing only on characters, in the local sense, skews our understanding of the full range of individuals deemed worthy of narrative portrayal in Aghyaran. Granted, the decision to investigate characters necessarily narrows our focus. However, the fact that the majority of anecdotes told at Aghyaran ceilis and wakes are intended as comic and revolve around characters persuades me that this portion of local discourse is significant and worthy of closer analysis.

The nineteenth-century novelist and amateur folklorist Patrick Kennedy may be applauded for his collection *The Book of Modern Irish Anecdotes: Humour, Wit and Wisdom*, but he sells his subject short: "This Irish medley has no higher ambition than that of agreeably occupying a leisure hour during quiet evenings at home, or periods of forced inaction in steamboat or railway carriage" (1872:iii). When considered in social context, the very sort of stories that fill Kennedy's collection cannot be dismissed as light entertainment. When appreciated as a form of sociability, telling and listening to comic anecdotes about local characters may be understood as an entertaining though concerted effort to survey at least some range of the types of humanity that not only comprise but symbolize one's community. The larger body of Aghyaran anecdotes serves as a community study initiated by locals long before any ethnographer arrived on the scene.

Beginning with the types of characters most often discussed in Aghyaran, we can investigate what messages the regular portrayal of these types may be used to communicate. However, the notion of character types must eventually give way to other meaningful constructs when attention is turned to a specific individual who features in numerous anecdotes that together portray that individual's idiosyncratic complexity.

Some character types that emerge in Aghyaran anecdotes offer commentary on proper ways of living in a changing social and economic environment. Although aware and sometimes accepting of the urban stereotype of country dwellers as lackadaisical, people in Aghyaran also take note of a new type of neighbor in their anecdotes: the ambitious and highly competitive farmer-capitalist.

Given economies of scale and the fact that there is more productive land suitable for mechanized agriculture elsewhere in Ireland, Britain, and Europe, widespread commercial tillage is mostly a thing of the past in Aghyaran. Today the majority of Aghyaran farmers are really part-time pastoralists who supplement their incomes with other part-time and seasonal jobs. Still, a handful of ambitious farmers have bought up or leased the farming rights to several small hill farms in an effort to patch together full-time agrarian enterprises that, despite poor-quality land, are at least marginally viable in a developing economy.

Rather than being applauded for clever husbandry, this type is often regarded with ambivalence. Seeking to better himself through an emerging pan-European and increasingly global market economy, the farmer-capitalist is seen to have rejected an older lifestyle considered, perhaps, less effectual, but more communal and cooperative. Through anecdotes, the capitalist drone is conceived as a type and made fun of for always being on the go, having adopted the "time equals money" creed identified as American, modern, and/or urban. One anecdote about a certain man who fits this type concludes with the observation, "He's racing all the time, just. Never lays a tooth on his spuds, just swallows 'em whole."

Generally this type is portrayed as an eccentric with no regard for norms of politeness and sociability. He is often described as "ignorant," meaning in the colloquial curt and brash, rather than uninformed. Another anecdote portrays a known individual cast as a farmer-capitalist rushing into a local shop about dinnertime. Needing to feed his workers, he grabs up four loaves of bread, throws down his money on the counter by the till, and makes for the door without any of the customary polite chat. The shopkeeper points out that one of the loaves he has selected is not sliced. The farmer throws down the loaf in disgust, saying, "Och, I haven't time to be slicing bread!"

Sometimes character types such as this one are balanced by opposite types, allowing for illustration of the range of appropriate behavior from one extreme to the other. Opposite the new farmer-capitalist is the old-fashioned hopeless one. Danny remembers an anecdote told during a ceili at Johnny Owens's about some farmers of this type.

> *We were talkin' about it [changing ownership of a particular farm over the previous few decades] one night in Owens's, you see, to this man who's from over there, you see, and he knew all about the Dalys.*
>
> *But he said they were awful bad farmers, and they went out of it. They weren't fit to keep it.*
>
> *And Johnny says, "How bad were they?"*
>
> *"Well," he says, "they were this bad," he said, "I heard my father saying that there used to be hens about the street and," he said, "when the cock went to crow, he had to prop himself against the wall."* ◊
>
> *So the hens weren't too well fed.* ◊

In Danny's telling, we are led to believe these were incompetent, perhaps lazy farmers. It is equally likely that other farmers met similar fates, losing their farms through economic hardship and no fault of their own. Still, the meditation on what constitutes a proper balance of industry and leisure continues in another anecdote about a local blacksmith, entrusted with keeping the farming community productive yet distracted by his own artistic temperament. Crediting a relative, Josie McSorley, Danny remembered this anecdote about Eddie Hillard during a recorded ceili with Jim and Sarah Falls.

> DANNY: *You see, he lived on, really on Josie's farm at the roadside.*
>
> JIM: *That's right. He did. He did.*
>
> DANNY: *And he said, in the spring, he said it was wild handy. You could get anything done, the forge right beside you.*
>
> *And Josie went out to plow one morning, and the horse had pulled a shoe. So he thought he'd slip over to the forge to get one on.*
>
> *But when he landed there, your man McMenamin—lived below the road—was there already to get a set of shoes on. And Josie said, "That was bad enough," but he said, "Worse still, Hillard didn't seem to be in great form of working."*
>
> *He said, "He was working at McMenamin's horse, but he was lilting wee bits."*
>
> *And Josie says, "He was working sometimes, and sometimes he was studying, but," he said, "He just suddenly dropped the horse's foot, and he says, 'I have it!'"*
>
> *And he says he ran into the house and left the two of them standing there, and they couldn't know what was wrong with him. And the next thing they heard was the fiddle.*
>
> SARAH: *Uh huh.*
>
> JIM: *Aye. His tune.*
>
> DANNY: *His tune. Your man had been some road the night before, and he heard a tune, and he was lilting it and trying to get it in his head, and as soon as it clicked with him, he had to get it on the fiddle.*
>
> SARAH: *That's right.*

JIM: *Yeah. Aye.*

DANNY: *And meanwhile, more customers waiting, all these farmers waiting on him, losing daylight.* ◊

We have seen Bridie McMenamin celebrated at her wake as a tireless worker—the sort, we are told, that is hard to find today. She and others of her type are considered heroes rather than characters in emic terms, struggling bravely and without complaint to get by. But there were others in the past, like Hillard and the Dalys, who are considered characters for not being "too fussed" about work. Anecdotes about them attract laughter—an appreciation of comic incongruity and the transgression of norms but also, in the end, a form of rejection. The contrast of these two types familiar from the past identifies some, like Hillard and the Dalys, as characters operating outside convention and others, like Mrs. McMenamin, as exemplars of ideal or praiseworthy behavior. This comparison, though rooted in the past, is relevant to the present.

Now most people work enough, not attracting much comment, except when the eldest generation point out that the young ones today are spoiled by never having experienced the unrelenting exertions of yesteryear. At the same time, some in the present are workaholics, toiling compulsively not just to get by but to get ahead. Many see this as part of a shift toward competition and individualism, a shift that invites ambivalence, skepticism, and again the simultaneous bemusement and rejection signaled by laughter. In comparing the farmer-capitalist of the present and the free and easy type of the past we see a contrast of past and present ways of being, which affords critical perspectives on the contemporary conditions. In contrasting the two character types we may perceive an inherent commentary on both behavior and change.

Between the capitalist drone and the free and easy type lies proper behavior. More entertaining for those at leisure tonight who will wake tomorrow to work another day are the eccentricities of those types who either "kill themselves working" or "wouldn't shift a finger on fire." Because the farmer-capitalists mentioned are still on the go, enslaved to the clock, they and those who tell stories about them remain nameless here so as not to give offense or betray confidentiality. The farmer-capitalist character type serves as a symbol of a contemporary trend, complicating the stereotype of staid country living. Hillard the smith is no longer alive, and although the Dalys—one of the pseudonyms I am asked to use—remain, the generation who lost their farm have passed away. The type Hillard and the Dalys illustrate serves as a symbol of a nonchalant attitude toward work that is perhaps more untenable today.

Although the farmer-capitalist shares the markers of excess common to all local characters, this is a unique character type in that it is identified specifically with present-day trends and entirely illustrated by living individuals cast as characters. However, the majority of Aghyaran anecdote characters either are based on deceased individuals, literally of the past, or portray characters that may be living but are in some way emblematic of a past or passing era. Characters are seen to be in short supply. As Cissie Dolan expresses the common attitude, "No characters about now like there was then." Even though people perceive characters to have been more prevalent in the past, there are still characters to be found. Most often, to say of a contemporary, "Ah, he's a character, now," is not only to appreciate that he or she is "good value" in terms of entertainment but also to claim for him or her a certain rare authenticity rooted in past-ness. With the exception of the farmer-capitalist character type, to be considered a character now is usually to be seen as carrying on older ways of being, both positive and negative. Like the past/present comparisons anecdotes establish, the perception of the rarity of characters is an acknowledgment of change—from the ways people make a living and socialize to the ways they behave and treat one another. Although reoccurring character types may change over time, I suspect there will always be characters as long as they provide material for narrative that invites meditation on behavior and change.

If anecdotes of the contemporary farmer-capitalist betray ambivalence, so do many about that majority of character types squarely identified with the past. In an era of electricity and indoor plumbing, a number of characters discussed in Aghyaran are classified as "rough," considering how they lived. The most popular type of the old-fashioned rough person is the lone bachelor indifferent to cleanliness and other concerns of a modern society in which we have been raised in the fear of germs. In fact, a lack of hygiene reemerges again and again in anecdotes, but also in jokes and comic songs, as a stock sign evoking outmoded ways.

Danny tells an often-repeated anecdote about Paddy Alec McSorley, a man born in the 1880s, that he heard from Jamie Hegarty, a man also known as a character for his clever turn of phrase and inclination toward exaggeration.

Jamie Hegarty said that they were putting in spuds in the spring, so they went down for the manure out of the doughal [dung hill], you see. And they were graiping it into the carts [lifting the manure into the carts with farmyard forks], but he said somebody stuck the graip in a calf, this big rotting calf that died and had been buried in the doughal.

And Hegarty says to Paddy, "What's this?"

And Paddy went over, "Ah," he says, "an old calf."

And Hegarty says he picks it up with his two hands and fired it into the ditch, and then, he says, he turned 'round and he rubbed his two hands on his hips and says, "I must go in and make yous boys a drop of tea!"

A number of people relate favorite personal experiences of encountering this rough bachelor type. Jim Falls remembers having to find a way to decline a meal from one old bachelor who boiled tea in the same water that he used to boil unwashed potatoes and eggs straight out of the hen. John McElhill remembers working as a boy for an old bachelor who kept bullocks and hens in the house. John says he moved on to another employer after the farmer's bitch pupped in his bed. Jim quips, "There were houses you weren't safe to yawn in." His wife Sarah marvels, "People were really dirty, like. They seemed to have built up a resistance."

For the most part, the rough bachelor is portrayed as unaware of any other way to live. While others may label him "miserable," to his own way of thinking the rough bachelor is merely being frugal and practical. Keeping food in the fertilizer bag hung from the loft simply keeps the vermin away. Wringing milk from the kitten that drowned in the milking basin or buttermilk from the rat in the churn just saves a little money, for "what the customers don't know won't hurt 'em."

Not bathing is a trait particularly identified with the rough bachelor type. A few contemporary bachelors are jokingly said to have never bathed since the day they were born, and such codding is meant to liken bachelors of today with those of the past. Some tell stories of elderly countrymen being taken to hospital and dying of shock from being bathed. Usually the victims in these stories are either long deceased or unnamed. Especially when the bachelor is anonymous, we see character portrayed more in terms of the pure type than the type-like individual.

The rough bachelor makes a full transition into pure type in jokes, which may in turn travel and become attached to actual bachelors in apocryphal anecdotes. During a recorded ceili with Danny Gallen, Mickey Byrne, Barney McGrath, and John McElhill, John recalled a local rough man, which caused me to prompt Danny for a joke about two bachelor brothers I had heard him tell a few months before. At first, Danny had difficulty recreating the joke, which he had heard comedian Francie Brolly tell on Donegal's Highland Radio. He begins ostensibly quoting Brolly, repeatedly saying "he said" instead of taking personal responsibility for the joke. Remembering the detail of the brothers being black with soot, Danny begins to break into a more performative mode, shifting to the literary present and quickening his pace. Note how he switches the deictic references of personal pronouns from Brolly, the original teller, to the dramatis personae of the joke, letting them speak for themselves.

> *Two old boys lived together. Had a farm, he said. And I think he said they were wild lazy, didn't work too much. Didn't win turf right and never had a good fire. He said they used to pull in sticks and burn them, and the whole place was black— wasn't that it?*
>
> *Aye.*
>
> *And they were black themselves . . .*
>
> *Aye, this is it, aye. I'm getting it now.*
>
> *Aye, he said they used, they used to throw paraffin oil on these old sticks, said, everything in the house was black.*
>
> *But where they lived, the house was level with the road, you know, the roof of the house. Bad bend in the road and the house was down below it. Thatched roof.*
>
> *So some one of the neighbors, this young lassie got a new Minor car, you see, Mini Minor.*
>
> *And she was out driving anyway, and at the bend in the road she went off the road. Straight through the thatched roof and just landed the car on the table. ◊*
>
> *So the ambulance arrived anyway, the doctor and all. They took the girl away to hospital. The two boys didn't seem to be too bad, but they thought the life was scared out of them, took*

'em anyway. And they said they'd keep 'em in overnight for observation.

They had to clean them up, you see. And they both got a bed in the same ward, big long ward. One of them over at the top and the other boy over at the bottom.

So the next morning the two boys was out early—there was nothing wrong with them—and pulled on hospital dressing gowns and they were walking about. And one boy met the other fellah coming up the ward and says, "How're you doing?"

"Ah not too bad."

And he says, "What are you in here for?"

"Well," he says, "You'd hardly believe it." He says, "A car came into the house and nearly killed me and my brother."

And the other boy says, "That's very funny, the same thing happened in our house." ◊

They didn't know each other from the washing up!

In response to Danny's joke, John recalled an anecdote of a named bachelor from Killyclogher in shock from his first bath in hospital, again reinforcing the notion of a rough bachelor type, at home in more than one genre.

Closely allied to this rustic bachelor type is another sort of rough person who consistently violates norms of polite society by using direct, uncensored "rough" talk, usually involving cursing. Jim Falls remembers such a coarse talker, Micks McGlinchey, sitting up with a few others to watch over a dying neighbor.

He was in his bed and, you know, on his last bit, going from one day to the other, and Micks was in it this night, and Johnny took him down, and some of the neighbors that were in ceiliing, to see him.

So, eh, Micks—he always cursed anyhow apparently— and, eh, somebody—he was just lying there, you know, looking up at the ceiling—and somebody said, "God, he's not too well. He's in a stupor."

And Micks says, "Ah, that's right, that's right. The bastard is stupid."

Most often the offended party is an authority figure of some sort. For example, there are anecdotes in several versions about a rough talker cursing to a priest and being oblivious of any offense. Talk of a Fr. Doherty, his curing powers, and his chronically swollen feet led John McElhill to tell one such anecdote. Francie Malloy, "a wild curser," met the priest at his mailbox, and looking at his feet, exclaimed, "Jesus Christ, Father, you going out and your shoes not tied." Micks McGlinchey, again, is remembered by many for his chance meeting, in some versions, with the Prior of Lough Derg, or, in other versions, with the Bishop of Derry. The clergyman politely asks Micks how the people are in Ballymongan, and Micks replies, "Nothing only a pack of bastards, whores, and gits" (and worse, in some versions). Again, such characters are identified with unrefined country ways of the past. Like the rough bachelor, the coarse talker is an eccentric and a social deviant who is both implicitly criticized and appreciated for a lack of domestication.

In addition to roughness of words and deeds, lack of education is a third major trait associated with past, unsophisticated ways that are embodied in a character type attracting both interest and ambivalence. Several local characters are portrayed as using malapropisms or unschooled assumptions, especially when conversing with authority figures. Because anecdotes about such characters tend to emerge as a group in conversation, it seems safe to cluster these characters into a type. Certainly there exists the type of the fool, which we will examine later, but the characters of this uneducated type are not so much unintelligent as ignorant, perhaps through no fault of their own. Consider an anecdote about Cicily Alec McSorley, a teacher in Crigh school during the 1920s. The narrator had been a pupil of hers and prefers to remain nameless.

> *Master Kane was looking at the role books one day, had the names of the children and their parents in it, you see. Dan McAleer, he had been taken out of an institution [orphanage], and he was fostered by McAleer, Tommy McAleer—would have been a friend of Mrs. McAleer's husband, now.*
>
> *Anyway he went down to the lower division of the school and he asked this assistant teacher who was Cicily McSorley and had only been in the sixth class and got in to teach without going any road.*

She never went away anywhere.
  She never trained.
    She was a junior assistant mistress.
  But looking at the role books and parents' names he asked
her "Is Dan McAleer illegitimate?"
    And she studied a wee minute ...
      "Ah ... no ... I think he's healthy enough." ◊

The anecdote itself can serve several functions depending on conversational context. The narrator told this version of the story after I asked her about her experience of going to school in Ballymongan. Her impressions were similar to those of many of her contemporaries: corporal punishment was common and severe, conditions were poor, and as this story illustrates, not all teachers were qualified by today's standards.

After our laughter at the teacher's malapropism died down, the woman who told the anecdote seemed to feel the need to soften criticism of Cicily Alec: "But that's the way it was then. No odds about her. She did her bit." This refocused the point of her story on depicting the past, rather than finding fault with one individual. In the end, we do not smirk so much at the memory of Cicily Alec but at the type of person, familiar from the past, that she is used to represent.

Reactions to these character types of the rough bachelor, the coarse talker, and the uneducated blunderer can range from mild bemusement and pity to disgust and renunciation. In laughing at these types, people in Aghyaran on one level reject them as models for behavior in the present. People distance themselves by identifying these types with a local past characterized by poverty, disadvantage, and lack of refinement. All three types may be seen as unpolished rustics—"rednecks" in the vernacular of the southern United States or "culchees" in the vernacular of the south of Ireland. One statement being made by laughing at anecdotes about them is that "we are better than that now" or perhaps "my neighbor is still this way but I know better." Proud of their local identity, many people in Aghyaran see themselves as the equals of the city-dwellers, British tourists and authority figures, and boastful returned Yanks, all of whom are thought—for good reason—to look down upon them. Through anecdotes about these unrefined character types, people in Aghyaran are to some extent joining in a long tradition of representing poor Paddy, and in so doing they impose self-criticism perhaps to preempt criticism perceived from outsiders.

At the same time, there is potential appreciation of these character types, and not just for the entertaining comic relief they provide during sociability. In terms of time, perhaps these characters are out of step in an era of self-conscious modernity. They may be seen as misfits or even social deviants. But in terms of the notions of place, community, and local identity, they are "our" social deviants who play a significant role in defining who "we" are.

Being rough and unrepentant can have its own virtues. The lone bachelor was only dirty from the perspective of others, and his lack of hygiene, as we now term it, never did himself any harm. Perhaps we should question our own fastidious, modern standards. There is something to be said for freedom from conformity. The cursing eccentric spoke his mind, the unvarnished truth, regardless of the social standing of his audience. Perhaps our modern notion of polite conversation can reduce us to kowtowing, restraining us from treating everyone as equals. There is something to be said for straight talk and contempt for deference. The unschooled blunderer may be indicted for grasping beyond his or her reach, but ignorance is not the same as a lack of intelligence. Perhaps we should look to the social causes of disadvantage and unequal education. There is something to be said for the attempt if not the execution.

All three character types may be less than domesticated or less than sophisticated. Nevertheless, backwardness may also be worn as a badge of honor, even authenticity, in contrast to the alienating, dehumanizing, and antagonistic elements of modernity embodied, in part, by the new farmer-capitalist character type. These three unrefined character types may be rejected from a contemporary perspective as eccentric or old fashioned. At the same time, they may be appreciated for their transgressions. They embody the autonomy from outside authority and general nonconformity that many in present-day Aghyaran, Catholics and Protestants alike, value as part of their locally inflected personal identities.

Patrick Mullen observes a similar phenomenon in the local character anecdotes of an out-of-the-way fishing community on the Texas Gulf Coast (1988:113–129). The rough-living Taylor brothers, for example, are stigmatized for their appearance and behavior, yet admired for their independence of spirit, which locals imagine to be a distinguishing characteristic of their community as a whole. To explain this ambivalence, Mullen employs Erving Goffman's notion of the "in-group deviant": an eccentric in a close-knit community who "comes to play a special role, becoming a symbol of the group and a performer of certain clownish functions, even while he is denied the respect accorded full-fledged members" (Goffman 1963:141). As Mullen observes, such characters are often humbled in stories of their encounters with other community insiders, but they are often the victors in battles of wit with outsiders (1988:126–129, cf. Glassie 1982:48–49). In certain circumstances, these in-group deviants become the mascots of their peers, who see themselves as a community of virtuous underdogs.

One example of this phenomenon in Aghyaran is an anecdote told by former smuggler John McShane about an unlikely fellow smuggler, David Logue. Short of stature, sporting a funny moustache, Logue is a comical physical specimen. Add to this his weakness for drink and his being past his prime, and Logue would appear to fit the profile of an easily dismissed sort of person. Still, John tells us, he was a "droll sort of a character." When Logue is caught vouching for and trying to sell a cow on behalf of his neighbors, who have smuggled her in from Donegal, he must face Crown justice. Hapless as Logue may seem to those in the courtroom, he slyly plays the fool, subverting insiders' and outsiders' expectations and stereotypes about his kind to score a point for the common countryman against external authority.

> JOHN: *Remember, Ray, there was, eh, the McMenamins.*
> RAY: *Uh-huh.*
> JOHN: *They were, eh, there near Castlederg. And they had eight heifers between them. But they were great men, very intelligent in the ways of the law.*
> RAY: *I see.*
> JOHN: *They had eight heifers and a cow, smuggled.*
> *And there was a wee man, David Logue. He was a wee small man, but he was a droll sort of a character. And he was an old man to them. Then he was a man between seventy, 'round about seventy-five.*
> *So he was a great man, and he was very fond of the drink, this wee man. And he was down the road on this side of Castlederg with the cow. And I don't know if he was informed on, but they lifted eight heifers, they lifted the cow. The police surrounded them and took 'em away.*

But the case went on anyway. The McMenamins were very intelligent in court and they got the solicitor on it and, eh, they got the cattle back.

RAY: *Is that right?*

JOHN: *Aye, they said they reared the cattle.*

But this wee man he was very . . . he got a pound for taking the cow, and—down to Castlederg—and no sooner David would have the pound but it was gone. He just drunk it, you see?

RAY: *Yeah?*

JOHN: *So eh, anyway, he was put up in court, too. David was called in to tell the way it was with this cow. And this cow, she was a cow with one horn.*

And eh, Simms . . . Murnaghan was for them, and Simms, he was for the Crown, for the government, that lifted the cattle.

RAY: *Uh-huh.*

JOHN: *And eh, anyway, David was sworn, and, "Mr. Logue," Simms says, "you had one cow here."*

"Yes, your lordship."

"And what color is this cow?"

"A red cow, your lordship."

"Well, you say, Mr. Logue, this cow's a polly [hornless] cow?"

"No, your lordship, she has one horn."

"Well, Mr. Logue, on your evidence here you say this cow, she's a red cow with one horn."

"Yes, your lordship."

"And can I ask you, Mr. Logue, can you tell me which side of the head was this horn on?"

"The outside, your lordship." ◊

The whole—I was there that day—and the whole crowd in the courtroom went into a fit of laughing. And David never smiled. He had a wee old moustache, and he was about four foot and a half high.

"Your lordship, I can't know what they're laughing at."

And the "lordship" was laughing himself. ◊ *He kept laughing . . .*

Aye, that's what he said, sorry:

"I'm sorry, your lordship, maybe it's an insult to you, these boys laughing."

It was no insult at all, for the way he was laughing away himself.

Those from the past who inform present collective identity may be defined by wit as much as by a lack of sophistication. We have seen this sort of subversion and "playing the Paddy" before in the anecdote of Paddy O'Donnell's explaining Comhaltas to the Cockney checkpoint soldier. Both Logue and O'Donnell, potentially marginal characters in other narrative contexts, are appreciated for manipulating an assumed or imposed character type to prove to outsiders that these folks in Aghyaran are "not so slack" after all.

We have seen that many local character anecdotes provide commentary on contemporary conditions by contrasting past and present ways of being. Such commentary also allows for meditation on the nature of a community, over time, that can boast such characters. Perhaps there were more rustics, deviants, and droll characters in the past, but those who remain and the memories of those deceased provide both a sense of continuity and some critical leverage on the range of behavior that serves in part to define a sense of community, locality, collectivity. This range of behavior embodied in a loose taxonomy of character is certainly wider still than what we have seen so far. Let us turn now to a group of character types that illustrate a chief preoccupation in local character anecdotes: wit.

Like most local character types, those that help define local genius are on some level associated with the past. "No characters about now like there was then." As Arjun Appadurai (1996) and Regina Bendix (1997) have noted, one characteristic of modernity is a continually reemerging belief that authenticity existed in the past but has been lost or severely compromised today. Perhaps this belief in the wane of authenticity is even more firmly held in a place like Aghyaran, where people have experienced such monumental transition in as short a period as a century. Characters may embody both what was wrong with the past—that which seems embarrassing from a present perspective—and what was right with it—an authenticity that seems threatened today.

That having been said, I have observed in various performance contexts that anecdotes about character types focusing attention on wit are not always used to comment directly upon the past, present, and change. Take for example the fact that contemporary individuals are represented as witty characters in equal numbers to past ones. This supports my general impression that people in Aghyaran see their place in the world as "a territory of wits," in Hugh Nolan's apt phrase that Glassie highlights in his *Passing the Time in Ballymenone*. One aspect of local identity is that, in contrast to relative disadvantage and marginality in terms of power and location, Aghyaran is, always has been, and always will be home to sly, droll, and quick-thinking characters. Such acuteness is perceived as something essential and timeless, a quality valued in common by locals and best illustrated by the examples of exceptional characters.

Wit enjoys several manifestations in local folklore. Portrayed in legend is the wit of the outlaw who employs all manner of trickery and bluff to rob from the rich and supply the poor, to challenge Crown authority, and to escape capture. Portrayed in personal experience narratives and anecdotes is the similar form of wit embodied by the smuggler who either outsmarts the police and customs officials or slips away to exploit the artificial border, marginality itself, another day.

In anecdotes of local characters, wit is usually recognized in the form of verbal skill. One of the more celebrated local character types is what we might call the "man of words," borrowing a term from Roger Abrahams (1983). In Aghyaran being quick with a comeback is one of his most marked characteristics. At a recorded singing session at my house, Patrick McElhill told an anecdote of one such character listening to the efforts of a middling fiddler. The fiddler concludes his tune, saying, "Aye, that's 'St. Patrick's Day,'" but the man of words trumps this performance by replying, "Well now, it may be the day before or the day after, but it's not 'St. Patrick's Day.'" Later during the same session, Billy McGrath recalled a story framed as a personal experience but serving to characterize another man of the same quick-witted type.

This is a true story. We were working down in Killybegs, 1973, and the fellah working along with me was the name of Joe Byrne, great working man, wild hard worker.

And, eh, he met his wife about England. And he came home and they settled down in Ardara . . . with his sister-in-law. She was the owner of the farm apparently.

They used to come into Killybegs every Friday evening to do their shopping, and Joe would have been working till going home, you see. But Joe was a great man to go to the pub on a Friday evening for a drink—that was the only evening that he went out.

We were in with him, anyway—whole load of us boys from Aghyaran.

And, eh, the sister-in-law, she came in, anyway, this evening, and she says—she had a wee bit of a roast—she says, "Joe Byrne, are you going home?"

"Aye," he says, "I'll be out in a minute. Go you on and sit down, I'll be out in a minute."

Minute passed.

   Five minutes passed.

      Half an hour passed.

She came in again.

"Joe Byrne," she says, "We're not waiting no longer on you."

He says, "I'll be out in one minute."

He had a wee drop of whiskey in the glass, and he put it up to his head. And the sister-in-law says to him, "You know this, Joe Byrne," she says, "If I was married to you I would give you poison."

And he put up the glass again, put it down, and he looked at her. "You know this, Susan, if I was married to you I would take it." ◊

That definitely happened. That happened.

Victorious, Joe Byrne wins his peace and fortifies his reputation as a character. Still, his comeback seems too good to be true. Some might be eager to discover whether this really happened as Billy claims. Note the following anecdote told about Winston Churchill:

> Lady Astor is reported to have said to Churchill, "Winston, if you were my husband, I would poison your coffee." "If you were my wife, Nancy," replied Churchill, "I would take it." (Barrick 1976:42)

The same anecdote has also been attached to Samuel Johnson and George Bernard Shaw. It is possible that Joe Byrne heard some version of this anecdote and waited all his life for the chance to use the punch line. More likely, though, Billy McGrath or another storyteller from whom Billy heard the story reused this traditional, migratory anecdote and attached it to Joe Byrne. Billy's object in telling his story is not deception but establishing that this is the sort of thing Joe Byrne would say. The truth-value of the story is that this is the type of man Joe Byrne is. Characters of this type not only entertain but also provide audiences vicarious enjoyment of clever things "we" as a community, comprised in part of Joe Byrnes, are apt to say.

With a talent for comic timing and oratorical display, this man of words character type is fully in control as a verbal competitor, ready for any contest of wits. He is similar to what Roger Abrahams refers to, in his ethnography of West Indian men of words, as the "good arguer," the man who can turn any conversation into a show (1983:xvi). Another subtype of the man of words appreciated in Aghyaran parallels to some extent Abrahams's "good talker," a master of clever or fanciful expression. Whereas the West Indian "good talker" earns his reputation more through set pieces such as toasts and recitations, the Aghyaran "good talker" is appreciated mostly for his creative, improvisational expression. For example, Billy McGrath during the aforementioned singing session recalled Hughie Kerr's imaginative talk, mimicking his distinctive, rapid-fire delivery in a short anecdote:

> *He went to bog one Saturday morning.*
> *And he says, "It was wet in the morning. I didn't bother*
> *going out till after dinner time," he says. "I got my dinner and I*
> *jumped on the turf spade and I never got off her till I landed in*
> *the back of Meenafergus."* ◊

The townland of Meenafergus being some distance from where he would have started, Hughie is appreciated as a character not only for his exaggeration but also for his colorful imagery of nonstop work with which audiences may identify. Exaggeration is a key element characterizing this type's way with words. This type is apt to get caught up in the fun of language, embellishing beyond credibility but putting on display the act of narration itself.

Another example of the "good talker" is Jamie Hegarty, who was mentioned before as the original author of Danny's anecdote about Paddy Alec McSorley, the rough bachelor offering to make tea after handling a dung-covered carcass. Being well known for colorful exaggeration, Jamie figures in another of Danny's anecdotes typifying the old man, now dead, as a character who never let the truth get in the way of a good story. The Francie mentioned below is Francie McHugh, who was briefly jailed during the reintroduction of internment for suspected republicans in August of 1971.

> *Francie was in the bog with Neil McElhill, you see. Jamie*
> *was there. We were there. And we were taking the dinner—*
> *Francie was only just out of jail. And Jamie was quizzing*
> *Francie what it was like, see.*
>
> *And he says, "I'm sure there was some bad boys in there*
> *when you were in, Francie."*
>
> *"Oh, aye," Francie says, "The boy that was in the cell with*
> *me wasn't good."*
>
> *"And what was he in for, Francie?"*
>
> *"Oh, he was in for murder, Jamie." You see, and this chat*
> *went on.*
>
> *But anyway, that night it seems that, eh, there was a crowd*
> *in Hegarty's, and Francie had come in. And Jamie didn't know*
> *he was in—there was a crowd in—but he was telling the boys*
> *that come in the kind of nights Francie McHugh had in jail.*
>
> *He says, "Francis was telling me today that he was in with*
> *a bad boy in jail."*
>
> *And somebody says, "What was the boy in for, anyway?"*
>
> *And he says, "Murder ... He stuck a knife in a boy's belly,*
> *and he give it a big durrr, and he let the puddings out of him!"* ◊

> *That was typical of Hegarty, now. Aye.*
> *"He stuck a knife in the boy's belly." And he said, "He*
> *give it a big durrr, and he let the puddings out of him." ◊ The*
> *puddings! ◊*

With a reputation as a colorful exaggerator, a man such as Jamie Hegarty would not be classified as a liar, for no one would take his stories at face value. As a type, the good talker's goal is not to mislead or to test people's gullibility, but rather to revel in and be appreciated for imaginative hyperbole.

Similar to this good talker is the codder—a man of words also known for exaggeration, but one whose goal is deception of a generally good-natured sort. This character type displays verbal wit through his management of information and manipulation of others' perceptions rather than through poetic expression or oratorical skill. The codder, in fact, depends on a certain more gullible type of character who, because he or she is "wild fond of news," invites a great deal of codding at his or her expense. Of this inquisitive and gullible type, Danny tells us, "They got what happens in this country—if you ask questions or quiz people about anything, you're going to hear nothing only lies, you know." (Being in the habit of asking questions, I am familiar with this phenomenon.)

John McElhill, for example, has earned a certain reputation for codding and could not miss an opportunity to "wind up" Sarah Jane McGlynn. Sarah Jane may be deceased, but she is remembered with a smile as the quintessential community gossip. One anecdote told by many involves Patsy Connolly, who had been dating the same young woman for many years. This annoyed Sarah Jane, who thought they ought to be married. One night ceiliing with Sarah Jane, John wonders out loud about the diapers he saw on Patsy's clothesline. Soon after, John employs a confederate to wonder in Sarah Jane's presence whether the girlfriend is living with Patsy. This becomes too much for Sarah Jane, who marches off to see the new P.P. She asks, "Tell me, Father, is Patsy Connolly married?" He replies, "Well now, Sarah Jane, there are just some things that parishioners don't want talked about." Although new to the parish, the priest knows well enough the type of Sarah Jane and how not to spoil someone's perfectly good round of codology.

Involving confederates and stretched out over several days, John's codding is not typical in its elaborateness. Most often verbal codding is accomplished in isolated events during ceilis and sometimes wakes. As seen in the account of Tommy Mongan and Mickey Byrne codding each other at Jamie Barclay's ceili, codding involves one person sharing a bit of altered or fabricated news that establishes a contest. If anyone believes this news that is too good to be true, then the gullible party becomes the new source of entertainment and may have to endure a certain amount of ribbing for having been fooled. The contest may then become the basis of a new anecdote. Danny tells a very popular anecdote that as a narrative is somewhat complicated but illustrates a few possibilities for identifying character types.

> *I mind Patrick Hilley told this at a wake one time. It seems Willie Laughlin took sick, and the ambulance arrived up. Probably a doctor had been there and sent the ambulance up. And they took him down to the hospital in Castlederg—that's what they did with all old people at that time, like, you know.*
>
> *And Patrick Hilley told that when they landed in the hospital—it would have been common—everybody would've been put into a bath. An old man from a thatched house, he'd have been really dirty, you know. The house would've been anything only tidy. The hens roosted in the house, you see, and I think there could have been cattle in it at a time.*
>
> *So Hilley said the girls in the hospital told him they put him into this big bath. The bath would be situated in the middle of the floor in a washhouse, you see, and there'd be maybe three or four nurses around him washing him.*
>
> *So they stripped him off, sat him in the bath, and they were scrubbing and brushing on him with several different things, and they're having a lot of difficulty getting the dirt off him, you see. And somebody come up with this idea if they got spoons and scraped him. ◊*
>
> *And Hilley says "They were scraping probably fifteen minutes," he says, "when they come on another shirt." ◊*
>
> *And the people he told that to really believed it. He told that at a wake, you know, and there was a lot of young girls in*

the company, and he sees them sitting with their eyes wide open. ◊
They really believed it.

Danny's narrative is an account of Patrick Hilley's codding at a wake, an
account that serves to characterize Hilley as a man of words, specifically a
masterful codder. In this way it qualifies as a local character anecdote. In
addition, the story within the story—the yarn Hilley spins—is itself a sort
of local character anecdote serving to portray Willie "Laughlin" McHugh,
who died in the early 1950s, as a rough bachelor. While Hilley's original
codding, the narrated event, is an exaggeration of actual news used to test
an audience's gullibility, it accrues a certain initial credibility and coherence by resonating with other stock stories of rough bachelors. In Danny's
retelling, Hilley's codding is so successful as a coherent narrative that it
overlaps with the tall tale. Regarding character types, Patrick Hilley exemplifies the codder, a paragon of wit; the young girls fit the role of the gullible
types the codder depends on; and Willie Laughlin reprises the role of the
rough bachelor, a laughable icon of old ways.

Also embodying a much-esteemed form of wit, the trickster is a character type who is similar to the codder but who depends on manipulating
situations more than words. For those in Ballymongan and surrounding
townlands, the star tricksters include living characters such as Mickey
Byrne, John McElhill, and Tommy Mongan and those who have passed
away such as Jim McKelvey, Tommy Hilley, James Gallagher, Tom McSorley, and Johnny Owens.

Verbal codding as elaborate as John McElhill's enlisting confederates
to wind up Sarah Jane McGlynn begins to overlap with what we might call
pranking or practical joking, which involves more physical action designed
for the same purpose of fooling others about the true nature of a given situation. In Aghyaran the custom is known more often as "playing a trick" or
"pulling a smart one," and the trickster is appreciated specifically for his
intelligence, especially the capacity to think several steps ahead in anticipation of his victims' reactions.

Pulling a smart one is putting to recreational use the same sort of apti-
tude it takes to buy or sell cattle for the best price at a mart, to take fullest
advantage of government schemes and subsidies, or even to smuggle for a
profit without being caught. Like most actions associated with characters,
practical joking is considered something that occurred more often in the
past. Danny may be correct in saying that nowadays people do not have to

invent their own entertainment and that the sort of work people undertake today does not leave them as much time to think up tricks. Still, during my fieldwork I was witness to, confederate in, and both victim and instigator of several pranks and counter-pranks. Practical joking usually requires a relationship between tricksters and victims that is stable enough for all involved to understand that no true offense is intended.

In addition to tricks, stories of tricks played are legion in Aghyaran. In his investigation of point of view in personal narratives of practical jokes, Bauman refers to the observations of folklorists Richard Tallman (1974) and Kay Cothran (1974) that practical jokes and the stories told about them are essentially complementary parts of the same expressive tradition (1986:35). These contests of wit, the stories told about them, and the relationships they establish and sometimes threaten could easily support another book-length project. For our purposes here, I must focus more narrowly on the character types established by and appreciated in stories of tricks that serve in part as local character anecdotes.

To draw too strict a distinction between the codder and the trickster would be artificial. Often the same person is adept at both verbal and practical joking, and often one type of deception may lead into the other. Such is the case in an anecdote of Myles McGlinchey fooling his perhaps overly inquisitive neighbors. As one storyteller who prefers to remain anonymous recalls, anyone can cod the gullible, but it takes a character like Myles to orchestrate an elaborate trick.

> *The people up about Crigh were telling Tom Byrne and Paddy Byrne—two old men, you see—that Myles McGlinchey had got very fond of whiskey. And Myles had a big farm, a well-to-do man, you know. And Tom and Paddy were being led to believe that Myles was going to drink the place out of it, you know. And they were concerned about him, you know. And they used to advise him, but . . . .*
>
> *He had a lot of corn to thresh in the springtime, and he invited the two boys down to help with the thresher.*
>
> *So before they came, he got all the whiskey bottles he could find, and he filled them with tea, and he pushed one in here and there to different stacks of corn.*

> *So when Tom and Paddy arrived at the thresher, he says to*
> *Tom, "You get up on that stack there, Tom." And the opposite*
> *side of the thresher, he says to Paddy, "Maybe you'd fork this*
> *one."*
>
> *The two boys started forking the corn, and every wee bit*
> *they'd go down, they'd come on a bottle.* ◊
>
> *And they'd call to somebody, and they'd say, "Here, for*
> *God's sake, take that away and hide it."* ◊
>
> *And then they counted up between them how many bottles*
> *of whiskey that they found.* ◊

A trickster like McGlinchey may target more than one type of person for a "smart one." Targets portrayed in anecdotes usually have the reputation as some sort of character, either a gullible type or a witty type. Characters known for gullibility are easy targets. Stories of tricks played on the gullible reinforce their reputations as fools, and individuals are pressed into service as a type that defines wit by displaying its opposite. When witty characters are the target of tricks a challenge to their reputations is implied, but one their reputations will likely weather. Mickey Byrne, for example, was often the target of Johnny Owens's tricks. However, even when Mickey is "beat" in anecdotes about these tricks, he loses no status as a witty character. Mickey and Johnny had a close enough relationship that all understand that Johnny's tricks were more expressions of camaraderie than actual aggression. Given the equal number of stories of Mickey's tricks on others, Mickey's reputation does not suffer.

A man like Tommy Hilley, who some say "would've raised a fight in Heaven," is appreciated, at least by those who are not his targets, precisely for his transgressive, provocative behavior. All tricksters falsify some bit of reality, violating expectations, and thereby eliciting a reaction (cf. Goffman 1974:83 and Bauman 1986:39–40). Usually such manipulation causes only a brief suspension of the sort of trust and balance a sense of community is founded on. All tricksters are in the business of what Ilana Harlow, after her informant Brian Foley, identifies as "creating a situation": intentionally shattering the monotony of everyday interaction through violations of expectations. Focusing on stories of tricks to reanimate corpses at wakes—of which I recorded six versions in Aghyaran—Harlow is convincing in identifying the impulse to create situations as an aesthetic, even an ethic, much prized in Irish social contexts (1997).

Yet there is also a sort of trickster who when creating situations routinely crosses a line by being indiscriminate with his choice of targets. He would "have a hand" at anyone, whether or not there was an already established joking relationship and whether or not the target had already been recognized as fair game. Some targets are fair game as established scapegoats and others as fellow tricksters, both recognized types of character. Having a hand at those who do not fit into either of these two categories—non-characters, if you will—is a potentially serious and offensive statement. At stake for the target is social status and respect. Troublemaking for its own sake may be seen as unlicensed behavior and the troublemaker as displaying "bad form." Still, the trickster is always an ambivalent character, and in the retrospective narrative of his troublemaking, a bit of appreciation may creep into a storyteller's coloring of events. For example, Danny describes in the midst of a long string of anecdotes about Johnny Owens a tense situation Johnny created:

> He'd a great wit. But I tell you, Ray, in fact, he was dangerous to be out with. See, he would play a trick, and then that could get you into trouble, you know.
>
> Like, the one he did on Tommy O'Donnell at the wake over at Essan, over there. The wake, it was Paddy McGlinchey's father who'd been dead. And I remember going on Sunday afternoon —had to take my father and mother over there, you see.
>
> So I went in the early Sunday afternoon. And it was a wee small kitchen, and there wasn't a lot of furniture about. There'd been a chair up here and one down here and two planks in between. So there'd have been a row of people setting on planks and behind them, the same again. Small house, packed with people.
>
> So there was an odd bloke lived over there by the name of Mickey Corry, and he was a very rare bloke now, you know. Had a very bad temper, and he wouldn't have been the full shilling, just, you know.

So he was sitting on the row in front of Tommy O'Donnell, Johnny Owens, and myself. But Tommy was sitting directly behind Mickey Corry. Johnny was farther up, and I was farther down.

So Johnny reached down, and he clicked Mickey's ear with his finger.

And now Johnny—you'd need to get clicked by Johnny to feel this. He was really good at it. You'd think somebody had cut the ear off you. It just could sting the point of your ear, you know. I remember at school, same thing, he was really good at it.

And Mickey Corry turned round, and he just hit Tommy O'Donnell up the face with his hand and the house full of people.

And you could hear a pin drop, everybody went quiet, there wasn't a word, you know.

And Tommy's face got as red as the fire. People were waiting to see was there going to be a fight or what was going to happen. ◊

And that stillness stayed for over ten minutes, and people started talking again, and people started moving out. We went home.

I would say Johnny got some telling off from Tommy. Tommy had taken him over to the wake and all. Johnny never had a car, you see. But it really backfired. ◊

And the same thing, if you're in the town with Johnny, and he'd be in the passenger seat, as usual, you'd be driving. You'd be walking up the street, or you'd be driving up the street, and if some man was near the curb with a hat on him, Johnny would reach out and clip the hat off him as he passed him. Something like that, you know, things like that. That was typical.

The trickster is by nature a competitor in an economy of reputation, for all pranking can be seen as a contest of wits with an implied winner and loser. Stories of tricks played on those who are not fair game—those who cannot afford to be portrayed as losers—do not circulate with any regularity. Without established reputations as witty or gullible types, such targets would be considered victims, and the trickster would not be celebrated. Such an event could be narrated, however, if it makes some statement about the otherwise unspoken rules of pranking, as does Danny's account of Johnny's trick backfiring at the McGlinchey wake. A prank that goes too far could also be narrated if the troublemaker is himself beaten.

Danny's account of his trickster great-uncle, Tom McSorley, illustrates some of these observations about tricksters and their targets. In this anecdote, we see Tom targeting certain more gullible types and another great trickster intervening, perhaps on behalf of these innocents, to trump Tom's original trick.

> Well Tom and his brothers were contractors. They went
> 'round the country building houses. A lot of the work then
> would have been a way back at the end of the last century,
> hundred years ago, you know. There'd have a lot of houses
> with a thatched roof, and people might have been that wee bit
> wealthier and they'd often get a job of taking off the thatched
> roof, maybe raising a single-storey house to a two-storey,
> putting on a slate roof, windows, doors—a lot of that sort of
> work they did.
>
> But they were up about Fermanagh, anyway, doing a
> contract similar to that, building a two-storey house which
> had been a one-storey house. And, eh, Tom was a jokey boy,
> anyway.
>
> But the house they were working on, there were some old
> people about it. And Tom would put on shows. Everyday he did
> something unusual.
>
> But one day there were a couple of old women about the
> street and they looked up and Tom was standing on his head,
> on a scaffold, up beside the chimney. A place where most people
> would have bother standing on their feet, you know, and he was
> standing on his head and his feet up against the wall.

So they inquired of some of the laborers there—I think it was Paddy Doherty of Pullykean who generally labored for them, you know, he'd have mixed the mortar and that—what kind of boy was Tom?

"Oh," he says, "he's a funny boy that." He says, "In fact, I think he even goes so far as to practice black magic."

So there was no more word about it for a few days.

But the old woman had milked the cows everyday and had the milk, had the churn of milk sitting there ready for churning. And they started churning one day, but they failed to get any butter on the milk.

And they wondered what had happened, so they thought on this Tom McSorley and the black magic. So they thought that he might have cast a spell on the milk.

So they went to Paddy Doherty, and they told him the story. And they says, "Do you think would he have cast a spell on it or done something wrong?"

"Oh," he says, "I wouldn't be a bit surprised. If you can't get butter on your milk and Tom McSorley about it, he'll have done something wrong. There's something."

And they said, "What could we do about it? We'd hate to throw it out."

He says, "You mightn't have to throw it out." He says, "If you could get his jacket when he's not watching and burn his jacket underneath the cow, you'd probably get butter on your milk."

And they got Tom's jacket and burned his jacket, but the milk still didn't go to butter. ◊

I think what he had done, he had put two pound of sugar into the churn, you know. And if you're trying to get milk sour, to get butter on it, that's what you usually do to sour the milk, keep it sitting for three or four days. And he put in a dose of

sugar, which sweetened it, done the opposite thing. So the milk
was useless. ◊

   But anyway, Tom lost his jacket out of the craic.

Danny and others who relate Tom's pranking grant the women anonymity, saving any named individuals the label of gullibility and transforming the women, in literary terms, into pure types. The focus is on Tom, and because he flirts with cruelty, his portrayal requires slightly different handling.

   In social terms the older Fermanagh women are not fair game. They are not part of Tom's community and have no joking relationship with him. Considering their age and their superstition, the women are portrayed as gullible country folk too easy to target. Usually tricks were and are played among men, so the targets' gender, as well, reiterates their status as victimized innocents. Moreover, destroying a woman's butter may be interpreted from a broader social perspective as more than a slightly mean-spirited trick, perhaps even as an attack on that woman's economic autonomy. At the time, men sold stock and produce on an occasional and seasonal basis, spending that cash as they saw fit. Women's steady incomes for running a household and whatever extra funds they controlled would have depended on selling butter, eggs, and handicrafts such as sprigging. Had the story concluded without Paddy Doherty's counter-prank, it is unlikely the story would have been repeated in any sort of celebratory way, as an example of a trickster's wit. For a successful, repeatable narrative, Tom must be humbled.

   We can only speculate to what extent, if any, Paddy considered Tom's trick to be going too far at the time and whether this motivated him to strike back on behalf of the women. Note that Paddy had already had some fun codding the women about Tom's dabbling in black magic. Danny identifies Paddy's motivation as seizing the opportunity to get "one up" on Tom, having been a target, though a fair one, of Tom's for years. At the end of Danny's story, I commented that Paddy was really thinking. Danny replied:

   Oh he was, aye. Paddy would have been used to Tom's tricks,
   you know. And Tom would be playing tricks on Paddy all the
   time, so he was one up on him there, you know. And at that
   time it would be a serious thing to burn a man's jacket. He
   mightn't have too many jackets.

Given that it would have been serious to burn a man's jacket, we might conclude that Paddy chose an equally excessive counter-prank that could even the score on behalf of the women. It is also one that allows him to continue having an appropriate or at least admissible amount of fun at their expense, fooling them about Tom's ability to cast spells. Regardless of what actually happened, from a narrative perspective Paddy's counter-prank is necessary to humble Tom the transgressor, and the story as a whole is all the more memorable for resonating with other much-appreciated stories of two great tricksters pitted against one another in competition.

Many anecdotes about tricksters, especially troublemakers, cannot be told without proper consideration of one's audience. The trickster is easy enough to celebrate for his wit, but there are those who might be offended by portrayals of certain individuals as losers in a contest of wits (hence more pseudonyms in this chapter than in any other). As mentioned, those with a reputation for wit can afford the challenge implied in anecdotes in which they are the targets of tricks. They have wit to spare. No serious or long-lasting offense is intended in the original trick or the story that circulates about it. This is not to say that tricks are not played on occasion in order to get a rise out of a character known for volatility. However, the end result of such a trick and stories told about it is not a decrease in respect or appreciation for the target in question, as it might be for the average person, but simply a reiteration of his celebrated character status. Storytellers must be more circumspect with and usually avoid anecdotes involving targets who are not classed as characters and may be seen merely as dupes.

Witty characters are few, and stories of both tricks and competitive repartee require dupes or less articulate types. So it seems that one last character type, the fool or community scapegoat, fills both the social and the narrative role of an arguably safe target for all manner of trickery and codology. He may be mimicked behind his back, fooled into believing a certain woman fancies him, or given a humiliating haircut. The scapegoat is arguably a safe target because "having a hand" at him has become acceptable in the eyes of many, but there are limits to the sort of abuse that may be directed at scapegoats without censure.

Parallel to Goffman's "in-group" deviant, the scapegoat is an ambivalent character. On the one hand he is not afforded the respect of other, less marginal community members, and on the other, he is granted an extraordinary local celebrity status as a character and may occasionally feature in folklore as a hero in, for instance, contests with outsiders. A merely dull or occasionally foolish person will not do. As with all characters, an eccentric, someone extreme in some respect, is required for the role.

Although regularly done, portraying the scapegoat through anecdotes can be a very tricky prospect. In the social circles most available to me during fieldwork, truly significant wealth and more widespread class differentiation has only recently been a possibility. An ethic of equalitarianism is firmly ingrained, at least as an ideal. In a place, age group, and stratum of society where relative marginality and disadvantage is, if not present reality, at least remembered as shared common experience, ideally one's neighbors were not and are not to be judged in terms of economic success. Mettle, quality, character—these are judged in terms of wit. The enervation, even emasculation caused by poverty is countered or nullified in social interaction, in folklore, by the prospect that intelligence, in its many forms, is all that matters. Still, the metaphor of competition is difficult to avoid when wit is so often defined through narratives structured as contests of words and deeds. In many cases, if one embodies wit, narrative structure dictates the need for one who embodies its opposite. Given a social context in which a reputation for wit ensures not only celebrity but a form of transcendence of the more humbling associations with that very context, being classed a fool becomes a double burden. Further, it is not entirely compensated for by character status or by rejoinders to anecdotes such as "Sure, he was harmless though" or "Ah, no odds about him, a decent sort anyway."

On the one hand, people may rationalize having a hand at a recognized fool, saying that he was never happy unless he had someone "digging at him" or that he soon forgot a given incident and looked for more attention. On the other hand, people will express disapproval when codding or pranking crosses a line and when people seem to take too much delight in chat about those cast as fools. One, more introspective man in particular has given considerable thought to this phenomenon he terms "scapegoating": the tendency for one's words and actions to be exaggerated by others trying to best illustrate in their storytelling the type of the fool much appreciated for comic value.

> *I'd be a shy person by nature. I'd be a shy person by nature, and like, that old remarks or drawing attention at people, you can be made shyer, you understand. And if you're foolish you can be made foolisher.*

It's like what a man said—about the road down there— that had a son. He used to frequent the neighbor's house, and then he used to work for another man periodically on the land. And they were discussing the son going to this neighbor's house and back again.

"Well," he says—he had been about the house, too, and half reared about the house when he was a young lad, eighty years ago or more.

He says, "If you went to that house with little wit, you left it with a bit less," do you understand?

The Irish personality is, if you're a wee bit simple, they'll try and make you worse. Or a bit foolish, they'll try to make you foolisher. They play on what they think would be your weak point. That's the Irish, do you understand. And the Irish, even though you're not a fool, in every locality there's somebody and they're a scapegoat, do you understand.

That's, as far as I know, one of the tricks of the Irish. It's not nice, but it's something that's ingrained in our personality.

Every Irishman's not like that, now. But there's a quantity of them that's mostly like that.

The printed page accessible to all is not an appropriate place to use any sort of biographical detail about Aghyaran characters classed as fools or the people who tell the stories. At the end of the day, pseudonyms are not completely adequate; they can be decoded. No matter how much mitigating context I offer, the friends and relatives of characters portrayed could be offended. Moreover, narrators could be too quickly judged cruel by those unfamiliar with the social practice of identifying certain high-profile community members in terms of type on a continuum between wit and its lack. For now, this is enough.

Not all the possible types of local character have been sketched. Still, enough have been illustrated to identify what sorts of people are considered most story-worthy in Aghyaran. Common themes and preoccupations in comic local character anecdotes are clearer, even if their implications are not yet fully expounded. A character's words and deeds may provide some diachronic statement, establishing a comparison of past and present types of humanity. A character's words and deeds may provide some synchronic statement, establishing a representation of wit or its lack by which people may be judged. More importantly for now, enough examples of character types have accumulated to push beyond the serviceable but limited descriptive and analytical power of the notion of character type.

9

Anecdote Cycles and Personality Traits

When engaged in conversational storytelling about local characters, people's memory for anecdotes works in at least two ways. If the topic happens to be Willie Laughlin, people may remember and make bids to tell every relevant anecdote involving him. The individual becomes the centripetal force of mental association, as is often the case at wakes. However, with Willie Laughlin raised for discussion, people may also remember and make bids to tell stories of other rough bachelors. Character type and perhaps narrative plot similarity become the centripetal force of mental association. These two ways are by no means mutually exclusive; people's associations often oscillate between the unique and the shared, individual and type, and may easily be steered in entirely new directions with the ebb and flow of subjects commanding their attention.

I have focused thus far on the second mode of association—through character type—in order to delineate a range of models of human nature and behavior that seem significant due to their continual reiteration in Aghyaran folklore. The fact remains, however, that an individual remembered may fit more than one type, especially when multiple stories about him or her are taken into consideration. For example, Dennis Corry's primary reputation is for having been a sometimes volatile tough man, rather than a jovial man of words. Still, his identification as a type is complicated by his verbal genius, occasionally portrayed in anecdotes. One of the most widely circulated anecdotes about this veteran smuggler involves a man asking him what his wife's maiden name was. Dennis responds, "It was *Wilson,* and if I had it to do over, it would *still* be Wilson." In another anecdote, Dennis and his wife are not speaking after an argument, and during a visit from Tommy Hilley, Dennis turns to him to say, "Tell me, Tommy, how long does a woman live after she's gone speechless?" Although any one anecdote about a given individual does not offer much insight into his psychological complexity, numerous stories about that individual taken as a body of biographical description may suggest a character's singular rather than typical nature.

Of the thirty characters discussed in the last chapter, almost half of them are people remembered by only one anecdote in the social circles I was most familiar with. So an Eddie Hillard or a Francie Malloy appears, in David Fishelov's literary terms, as a type-like individual reaching more toward pure type than pure individual. This is not to say that cycles about Eddie Hillard, Francie Malloy, and other "one-off" characters do not exist or have not existed. Many in this category, such as Joe Byrne, live far away from Ballymongan, the center of most of my socializing. Many, such as David Logue, are long dead. Those who knew them better, having interacted daily with them, may have more stories about them, but the passage of time and geographical and social distance ensures that only one story or a few stories about them circulate among the people I have come to know best. These flatter one-off characters in anecdotes, as well as the pure types familiar from jokes and comic songs, contribute to the recognition and perpetuation of character types that individuals well known in a particular social circle are often made to depict in any one given anecdote.

In social circles around Ballymongan, however, characters such as Johnny Owens and Jamie Hegarty feature in cycles of anecdotes told about them. These cycles continually re-establish both the types of characters they are appreciated for embodying and their individual personalities, which cannot entirely be contained by character types. Characters who attract cycles of anecdotes are portrayed as relatively flat type-like individuals in any given anecdote, but their portrayals may gesture toward Fishelov's pure individual (round treatment and reception) when we take into account the cycles of anecdotes told about them. When featuring in a cycle of anecdote, a person may be seen as an amalgamation of varied and even contradictory characteristics and traits. As a narrative persona featured in many texts this individual is similar to but not quite as round as literary characters of the modern novel. Unlike novelists, Aghyaran anecdote tellers do not have the luxury of developing the psychological realism of their characters over an extended period. Nevertheless, these storytellers' type-like individuals may take on more complexity and approach Fishelov's pure individuals through the amalgamation of brief anecdotes.

Put another way, storytellers in this oral tradition of composing and swapping local character anecdotes achieve roundness of character by stitching together a series of flat portrayals. The idea of flat vs. round is a visual analogy used to elucidate a verbal phenomenon, and we can extend the usefulness of this analogy with a consideration of perspective in graphic arts. A visual image perceived as round has been rendered in perspective, usually through some system of foreshortening. However, the one- or two-point perspective developed in Western art is not the only possible way to create a sense of depth. The axonometric perspective of traditional Chinese and Japanese art and of later Persian miniatures produces depth by layering and overlapping flat images. The same dynamic is at work in local character anecdotes. A character in the text of any given anecdote may not be as round as a character in a novel, but the anecdote can be novelistic in impact. A novelistic sensation of roundness may be achieved through accumulation by telling a longer cycle of relatively flat but layered and overlapping anecdotes about an individual, most likely at his or her wake.

Moreover, even in the absence of an uninterrupted cycle of anecdotes about a given character—such as in a ceili, where chat more often floats from one individual and proposition to another—a given anecdote may be novelistic in impact given the contextual information audiences bring with them to the storytelling event. If a character is well known, audiences will already have in mind a more complicated impression of that character shaped by previous narrative. Thus, on the level of reception, one brings this contextual information to a new, relatively flat portrayal and it snaps into place among all previous, remembered portrayals. Flat textual treatment meets round reception, and the type-like individual, in Fishelov's terms, enjoys much the same affect as the pure individual.

⁓ঌ

As we have seen, rehearsing, expanding, or in some cases creating a cycle of anecdotes about a certain individual is precisely the aim of commemorative verbal exchange at wakes. Also popular at ceilis and other

Figure 9.1. John McHugh,
self-portrait

social gatherings, cycles about the most extravagant characters not only
predate but will also survive well beyond the wakes of those individuals.
The best example in my experience of a character featured in an extensive, enduring cycle of anecdotes is John McHugh, who died in 1995. His
prominence in collective memory is due not only to the relative recentness
of his death but also to how well his words and deeds suited local conceptions of the character. Larger than life, John cannot be contained by one
type of character but fits several, making him a favorite and virtually end-
less subject for entertaining reminiscence.

Fragmentary bits of information mentioned to me over time provide
us a little biographical background. Having been born in Essan townland,
across the Derg from Ballymongan, John had two brothers, Pat and Eddie, but now all three are deceased. None of the three ever got married,
but John threw his hat in the ring a few times only to become moderately
bitter toward the successful suitors. Pat is better known on the northern
side of the Derg as a character in his own right, having been a fiddler, pub-
goer, and occasional actor in local dramatic productions. John and Pat were

somewhat competitive as brothers, and more so when drinking. Several remember them arguing over who was the better mummer. Apparently they really "went at each other" with wooden swords when they played opposite each other as Prince George and Prince Patrick.

Whereas neither Pat nor John could be described as mild-mannered, Eddie is widely considered to have been the most "sensible" of the lot. Being remembered like John Mongan as the very type of patience and consideration, Eddie is not fully a character in the local sense of being a celebrated eccentric. During ceilis, memories of a "modest wee man" add little to the entertaining give-and-take of stories about more competitive codders and tricksters. Still, especially after moving in with John in the latter part of his life, Eddie served in life and in anecdotes as an obvious and well-suited foil to John and his excesses.

According to John's good friend, PJ Gallen, the common knowledge is that "John wouldn't have had a wild hard life." Although born in Essan, John lived with his Aunt Hannah in Ballymongan, where he went to school. After inheriting a "legacy" from a relative in America, John and his brothers had little use for hard work. In addition, John greatly benefited from another aunt, who had done well for herself in America, when she came home to retire in Aghyaran. Finally John inherited the modest Ballymongan farm after Hannah's death, but it was not long until he needed to find a job in order to continue drinking freely in pubs and keeping a fancy car. When he found employment in Killeter Forest, he rarely showed up on time, having become accustomed to rising as late as he pleased.

Despite all this seeming privilege, sloth, and squander, John was widely appreciated for being the best of craic and regularly invited out to pubs, weddings, and funeral dinners. The Ballymongan-Shanaghy mummers never assembled without commandeering John to play Jack Straw and serve as a sort of group mascot. Winner of the coveted "Mummer of the Year" award—invented by the mummers especially for John—he could not be beat as the epitome of the revelry and leisure in which other, hardworking men can only afford to indulge once annually at the dark time of the year. Some envied and even criticized John for his year-long Huck Finn–like existence, but his ability to live outside the usual restrictions of societal norms also transformed him in collective memory into a celebrity. He remains an embodiment of freedom from responsibility that others can at least vicariously enjoy.

Although John was infamously tight with his money, he was always "the big man" in the pub, freely buying rounds for all "the good boys" who gathered around him. Despite the fact that Eddie was forced to buy most of the groceries and household supplies, when Eddie died many commented that John was at least "wild decent" about supplying the wake with drink. This was in some contrast to Pat's being more miserly at John's wake not long afterwards. Because John was the essence of the weekend pub session, the craic of the mummer's van, and the merrymaking of the old-fashioned wake, his friends and neighbors could not allow his last send-off to slip away without a proper celebration of his life as a character. During a ceili at Danny's house with PJ Gallen—Danny's second cousin—and later his neighbor John Gerald O'Donnell, I asked Danny what John's wake was like. He paused, smiling, and replied:

DANNY: *Like a weekend at Lisdoonvarna.* ◊ [*a town famed for music and drink in County Clare*]

The wake was lively, now, you know. There wasn't much nonsense, you know, but it was a good wake. You know, there was a lot of chat about John. There was nobody to control the place, but still everything would have been in order, you know.

I went over the first night. We'd have been there all day I suppose. And I thought I'd go for the first night and stay maybe a wee while, then maybe sit the second night. But the first night I went over, I was going to leave at twelve o'clock or one, after the rosary was over. But the craic was good and I stayed till the morning, you know. And I think I stayed the most of the next night as well. ◊

The house was full of people, you know. And there were stories being told in the kitchen and stories being told in the room. You could have changed about. And all these boys that had worked with John in the Forestry, Willie McLaughlin and them. The thing went all night. The house was full of people, you know.

And there wasn't much to drink the first night. Pat had left no drink. Mind the second night, yous went and got a case of . . .

PJ: *Aye, we went up the road.*

DANNY: *And there was a wild lot of drink the second night. A lot of the same people back again. And there was bottles lined up over all the windows. There was bottles every road the next morning. Pat would have had some shock when he seen it.* ◊

And the only thing that happened that night, John Rodgey went to sleep and they come over here for a razor and shaved the two eyebrows off him, or one was it?

PJ: *One, aye. Oh, you wouldn't want to sleep at a wake, now.*

Setting aside for the moment the notion of character types, let us consider the personality traits most often associated with John by reviewing some of the stories that would have been told about him at his wake and that remain in circulation today. Quite a few anecdotes about John establish the general impression of haplessness. His haplessness as a driver, homemaker, brother, farmer, etc., is not in itself as funny as his indifference to the consequences of his slackness, something most people cannot afford. Already we have seen him in chapter 6 driving the wrong way through Castlederg, wondering about all those waving at him and how friendly the people about town must have become. Having hit Lilly McKelvey's car for the second time, John rolled down his window to say, "Ah, you've done it again, Lilly." In general John was to be avoided when driving, for he drove fast and often "took his half out of the middle of the road."

Haplessness as a farmer started early for John, who, being spoiled, lacked industry. Danny recalls,

> *Oh, I heared Maggie Byrne saying that she seen Hannah up in the fields lumping corn and John in his bed, you know.*
> *And when she did call him, that she didn't call him till she had a big fire on and his bread toasted and all that, you know,*

and the egg and all ready for John. *Everything had to be right for* John, *you know.*

Earlier at a ceili with Jim and Sarah Falls, Danny remembered a cousin of John's who had been at Eddie's wake and slipped off about five o'clock in the morning to survey the farm. The cousin best summed up what everyone in Ballymongan already knew about John and Eddie as farmers.

> *He says, "I was up around the farm there," and he says, "You know this?" he says, "It was a right wee place if anybody any good had had it."*
> *He says, "Them two boys must have been useless."*
> *He says, "There's a field up there, and I was up there thirty years ago, and that drain was open." And he says, "The drain's still open, never was piped."*
> *He was dead right. John was no farmer.*

In addition to being a "holy terror" on the roads and "no farmer" in the fields, John at home was no model of domesticity, nor did he see much need to improve. Pat Den Gallagher remembers that John rarely washed his hands, and when he did he never dried them on a towel, just shook them on the floor or wiped them off while petting his dog, Rover. Tommy Mongan, Mary Alice Mongan, and several others remember his infamous turkey fiasco. Apparently one Christmas John had to race to town at the last minute for a turkey. As PJ remembers the event,

> *John McHugh, he heads to the town Christmas Eve, and all he could get was a wild big brute of a turkey.*
> *And he come home and the turkey couldn't be fit into the oven. And John, he cut it. Cut the turkey.*
> *And the old side was away in the cooker. The oven and the firebox was all the one. It was all ashes.*
> *But the turkey, one side was as black as coal and the other side wasn't even cooked at all. Raw. And the sandwiches after, well, we chewed a bit, but. . . .*

Apparently Eddie did most of the cooking, which usually consisted of burnt sausages and tea too strong to drink. "Oh, you could have run a diesel engine on it," Danny tells us of the tea. Being a good friend of Eddie's, Jim Falls made a habit of ceiiing with the McHugh brothers in Ballymongan, but he found that by ducking out before late night tea—"for health reasons"—he often missed out on some of the best stories. He soon learned, however, to bring his own powdered hot chocolate and take a cup of boiled water. That way he could stay on for the full night's craic without being subjected to the bachelors' rough fare.

Having Eddie do all the cooking was only one of the ways John took advantage of him. Toward the end of John's life his cars were no better maintained than he was. One in particular caught fire in the chapel parking lot. In another anecdote, John attempts the steep drive up Aghalunny Glen in the Sunday traffic after mass, cursing full blast at his old Cortina, "Go on, you whore you, don't let 'em all pass you!" One attempt to motor home up the glen seemed particularly doomed one icy day when Eddie was enlisted for help. As Danny recalls,

> *Cars were all passing him, you see. Everybody else was getting up only John. The temper would have went with John, and he just stamped the petal down and revved the life out of it, you know, but he couldn't get nowhere.*
>
> *So somebody who was passing said that if he got a big of weight in the boot [car trunk].*
>
> *So Eddie would have been a good weight, big heavy man.* ◊ *He thought he'd be the handiest weight he'd get.*
>
> *He says, "Eddie, would you get in there to the back and see would we get home?"*
>
> *So Eddie gets into the boot, and he reversed down in below Danny McHugh's and foot the board again and he nearly got up the glen but didn't make it.*
>
> *And down again to Danny McHugh's and there were people about complaining and scolding him. Somebody said, "John, if you tried Magherakeel you might make it." There'd be no traffic on Magherakeel. Wouldn't have been as slippy, you see.*
>
> *So John headed off to Magherakeel, and he did get up Magherakeel. On home and into the house and on later in the*

*evening somebody dropped in. Chatted John a while, then,
"Where's Eddie?"*

*"Oh good God!" he says, "Eddie's in the boot! I forgot all
about him!"*

And Eddie was that modest he wouldn't have made a noise.

Perhaps John's most marked trait was his temper. If anything annoyed him he was full of bluster, sometimes throwing his darts into the fire when he lost a game, sometimes barking out exasperated curses at whoever asked him too many stupid questions, which were more often than not intended to wind him up. As Mickey Joe Gallen remembers, "Generally he shot things he didn't like." Crows, cranes, kittens—if it annoyed him and the shotgun was handy, it was in danger, as were gateposts and chimneys in the surrounding area.

With such a reputation, John could be counted on for volatility, even to the point of being used as an unwitting confederate in one locally famous trick. One night I asked Danny about whether John McHugh and Johnny Owens, the well-known trickster, would have gotten along well together.

> DANNY: *No. Definitely wouldn't.*
>
> RAY: *Yeah?*
>
> DANNY: *No. Definitely wouldn't.*
>
> RAY: *Two big characters in the same place sometimes
> don't work too well together?*
>
> DANNY: *Yeah. For starters, Johnny, like myself, didn't
> take a drink. John McHugh hadn't much time for anybody who
> was Pioneer, you know. You were useless, you know. You weren't
> part of his company. No. Didn't get along. You heard the one
> about the hair clipping?*
>
> RAY: *No.*
>
> DANNY: *Johnny had been making drains, you see, and
> Willie McLaughlin with a digger, there making drains, and
> there was lorry [truck] loads of stones coming regular. So they
> just tipped the stones on the roadside, and after an hour or two
> they were away. It didn't really matter.*

But John McHugh and Eddie, here, was heading to the town on a Friday, and this load of stones had been tipped halfway across the road. And John mustn't have seen it because he went right up with the car. ◊

And Johnny and Willie McLaughlin were watching, and they said it was like "The Dukes of Hazzard." The car just went up on her side and she come back down again. ◊

And John stopped, and of course, when Johnny Owens seen John stopping he hid. And John give Willie McLaughlin a tongue-banging over this having a load of stone out on the road.

So they went on to town anyway, and there was no more word about it.

The next day, in Owens's, Willie McLaughlin and Johnny went in for their dinner, you see.

So Johnny picks up the phone, and he rang up to Maggie Byrne.

John McHugh hadn't a phone at the time, but John was sort of a traveling barber. He cut hair for anybody.

And he says to Maggie Byrne, he says, "Would you tell Charlie to slip over to John McHugh's and tell John that Willie McLaughlin is in Owens's, and he wants his hair cut now at dinnertime.

And ◊ *John McHugh was the last man in the world Willie wanted to see, you see, because of the day before.*

So as soon as Johnny put down the phone, Willie, he reached for the phone, he says, "I'm not getting into trouble with this bloke again." And he rings up to Maggie. He says, "Don't be sending Charlie over for John McHugh, for I don't want to see him."

"Oh," Maggie says, "too late, Charlie's already gone." ◊

So Johnny, he disappears, and John McHugh lands. Willie said he come into the house carrying a lady's shopping bag, or a . . . handbag. You know, the wee handbag, that's what he kept

*the clippers in. And he had a bad leg at the time, before he got
in the hip joint.*

> *And he put Willie on a chair in the middle of the floor,* ◊
> *and Willie said, "He got a hold of a lump of hair in one hand
> and he'd just limp round," he says* ◊, *"and clip wee bits." And he
> says, "What he didn't clip, he nearly pulled out anyway.* ◊

Throughout the year at any given social gathering at my house, hearing
a story or two about John was a happy inevitability for me. Sitting in the
man's former home ceiliers and guests could not help but remember him.
At the singing session mentioned before with Danny, Sally Kelly McHugh,
Patrick McElhill, Mickey Hegarty, Danny Gormley, Billy McGrath, and
James Hugh O'Neill, John's "short fuse" sustained conversation for a little
over half an hour. After some talk of John's love/hate relationship with his
dog, James Hugh asked, "What was the one about the fly?" Danny took
up the story.

> DANNY: *He was on the Forestry, you see. And it seems
> they all used to get together for their tea, you see, at dinnertime.*
>
> *But John had got the cup of tea ready and was getting out
> the sandwiches, and he looked at this big fly that had lit in his
> cup of tea, one of them Daddy Longlegs.*
>
> *And he says, "That's terror," he says, "that that wee black
> bastard had to light on my cup and there's twelve thousand
> acres of bushes around here!"* ◊
>
> SALLY: *John was a character, now.*
>
> DANNY: *Oh, there were some great yarns. The night he was
> waked here, they heared more yarns. It went on all night, you
> know. They made them, you know, when they ran out of them.
> But a lot of them there'd be something about 'em, you know.*

John's temper was story-worthy in itself, and more often than not it
was exactly when he was at the height of one of his rants that he blurted out
some of his most memorable lines. More than simply an irritable person,
John was and is also appreciated for a certain verbal gift. Several enjoyed
braving his temper to wind him up and see if his exasperation would lead

to something quotable. Billy McGrath continues the riff of John McHugh stories:

> *The time that this man here worked in the Forestry, you mind? James Patrick Collins, he still works in the Forestry. He went to the bog, I think it was a Saturday, and he asked John to come to the bog.*
>
> *"Aye, no problem," John says. "I'll be in the bog surely, James Patrick."*
>
> *So they landed at the banks about half eight. John was the wheeler. James Patrick was cutting. Must be some of the Fallses I think was filling.*
>
> *John McHugh, he says, "How far out is these to be wheeled, James Patrick?"*
>
> *"Oh," James Patrick says, "out to that wee height there, you know."*
>
> *John went out with a barrow full of turf, and he says, "Is it this wee height, James Patrick?*
>
> *"No, no, no. Go on ahead, that next wee height."*
>
> *John wheeled on, anyway. "This wee height, James Patrick?"*
>
> *"No, no. That next wee height."*
>
> *John left down the barrow and he says to him, "Are we fucking cutting or dragging?!"* ◊
>
> *He wasn't going to have it.*

Always surrounded at home or in the pub by contemporaries and younger men in search of craic, John could also be counted on for a yarn when he was in a better mood. Several of John's favorite stories are told not only for their entertainment value but also as remembrances of his gift for storytelling. After listening with Danny to a tape PJ and Mickey Joe Gallen made of John in 1987, PJ remembered several of John's "party pieces," favorites in his repertoire he was often called upon to perform.

> *Mind about the time that Tommy Keenan moved to Castlederg? Tommy went down to the town, got drunk, and he come back up to the park, you know, the housing estate. And all*

the houses look the same, and he couldn't mind what house he lived in.

So he asked some of these young boys about the street, "Could you tell me where Tommy Keenan lives?"

And, sure, the cub says, "Aren't you Tommy Keenan?"

He says, "I know I am, but I can't know where I live."

Used to be a good one of John's.

PJ continued with his account of one of John's more public triumphs.

PJ: *Oh now. But you could have put him any road, hey. We put him on the stage one night. Did you ever hear tell of Conal Gallen, the comedian?*

RAY: *Yeah.*

PJ: *He was in Pettigo one night. Your Paul was there [to Danny]. I mind coming around to lift John to go to Pettigo. Pat Logue was going and Leo Keegan. And your Paul must have been in it.*

Conal Gallen, he was only new out at this time, and he was telling away at jokes on the stage, and nobody was laughing at 'em.

I went to the toilet one time—the toilet is just, you know, in Potter's, you go in by the stage, the toilets was in behind the stage.

RAY: *Yeah.*

PJ: *And I was chatting to Gallen, and I says "Call up John McHugh. He's down there." Jeez, Gallen called him up, sir, and John went up on to the stage, no problem at all.*

RAY: *Is that right?*

DANNY: *Mmm.*

PJ: *Aye. Up on to the stage and he told the—mind the joke, you'd hear it on radio, mind the one about, mind the boy started to grow the big ears, mind, like the horse, or the donkey?*

RAY: *Yeah?*

PJ: *He went to the doctor anyway. And the doctor looked
at him and tested him and sounded him, and he wrote out a
prescription.*

He says, "There's your prescription. Go and lift it now."

And he says, "What is it?"

*Says, "It's tablets," he says, "take one or two of them
everyday."*

*The boy says, "Will that cure me?"—his ears had started to
grow big, see.*

*"Ah, it'll not cure you," he says, "but it'll keep you from
dunging on the street." ◊*

*And John, he just smiled. But jeez, the whole place
went mad, hey. Started to laugh and Gallen put him down.
Wouldn't let him tell a second one.*

Taken as whole, this cycle of anecdotes portrays John McHugh warts
and all: rancorous, merry, unlucky, carefree, stingy, generous, foolish, ingenious, useless to have around, useful to have around, always wild craic. As
Mary Alice Mongan put it, "Oh now, you could write a book on John. He
was very funny, you know, but at the same time, he was very thick."

More complicated than some, John may stand in for the complexity
of us all. As a character type, he is difficult to pin down, but his status
as a character is never in question. The John McHugh of local character
anecdotes shares traits with several of the types we have seen before—the
hapless farmer, the coarse talker, the rough bachelor, the man of words,
and in some cases even the fool. Though never a trickster or codder, John
is nonetheless fair game as a target, for he may be counted on for a satisfying reaction and a quick recovery. On occasion he may be "beat" by his
neighbors and friends, but when faced with an outsider and thrust upon the
stage, he outshines even the professional comedian. The general agreement
that there will never be another like John reminds us again of the general
opinion in Aghyaran that ours may be an age of refinement and prosperity,
but these come at a price and the transaction is final.

Local character anecdotes provide a conceptual stage upon which people may consider human nature and the range of possibilities for how one may act in response to the persons, events, and conditions that constitute one's environment. On such a stage, the value of transgression and the attractiveness of vice must be entertained, and thus John finds his place in collective memory. John is no model for proper behavior, but he is celebrated for living an untamed life that most of us will only enjoy through stories. Like Falstaff, John is eventually rejected as a model for behavior, but he is nonetheless indulged as an embodiment of local and perhaps more universal recalcitrance towards conformity and official culture in its many forms. In the process of hearing and telling these stories about John, one cannot help but better discern usually unstated societal rules for behavior while at the same time questioning their ultimate authority.

Concerning methodology, John in all his complexity presents a challenge to the usefulness of the character type as a meaningful construct when trying to come to a better understanding of characters who feature in more than one story. When dealing with someone who cannot be fully characterized in one anecdote or contained by one character type, perhaps we should consider personality traits as more appropriate narrative elements for investigation. A given combination of evident personality traits—self-centeredness, wit, insubordination, etc.—locates a character's individuality. At the same time, personality traits allow for generalization and comparison, for they may be shared by other characters, though in different combinations and proportions. Personality traits and the patterns of conduct they give rise to may be seen as possible responses to shared contexts and predicaments. Their range is limited but telling. They are recognizable stances eloquent of values and ideological orientations to the world from which people may choose or evaluate their own stances. Personality traits are, in the end, generalizations about actual individuals rendered in a tighter scale than are character types. Establishing a narrative persona as an amalgamation of several personality traits allows for the appearance of greater complexity and psychological realism than would representing an individual more simply and briefly as a type.

Consider a parallel dynamic in literature. In an insightful essay, William Dodd explores how Shakespeare gives psychological depth to his characters through the representation of verbal and social interaction (1998). Coinciding with an emerging market economy and newfound social mobility, Shakespeare's strategies for characterization mark a shift away from using ready-made dramatis personae drawn from collective religious culture. Shakespeare, Dodd argues, mastered the portrayal of characters as amalgamations of "emotional stances" and "affective preferences" actively engaged in the dialogic construction of self and society. The stage provided people in early modern England a site for the exploration of human behavior at a time when traditional, essentialist values and notions of selfhood came into conflict with newer, more pragmatic and competitive modes of self-definition and evaluation. Dodd observes:

> The public theater was uniquely equipped to represent this emerging mode of identity construction in its fictional interactions, holding up a mirror in which spectators could contemplate and evaluate the very processes of their own social and individual becoming. (1998:149)

Part of my ongoing argument is that local character anecdotes in Aghyaran allow for similar conceptual work to be achieved in the midst of socioeconomic change. As did patrons of the Globe Theatre, Aghyaran ceiliers and wake-goers may evaluate themselves through evaluating celebrated characters' affective preferences in the midst of competing discourses.

My main interest here in Dodd's thinking centers on a parallel between his conception of Shakespeare's dramatic characters and my understanding of Aghyaran anecdote characters. Whether we're investigating Shakespeare's plays or local character anecdotes in Aghyaran, the very project of focusing attention on individuals, through characterization, may also provide us a glimpse into collective concerns. Inspired by Pierre Bourdieu, Dodd's thinking about a given character's individual uniqueness, relative to his or her collective significance, is instructive:

> We need of course to allow for the fact that in many cases a character's set of emotional stances may not be a unique individual combination but a manifestation, rather, of what Pierre Bourdieu calls *habitus*. This term is used by Bourdieu to refer to 'systems of durable, transposable *dispositions*' produced in a group or community by a particular environment. . . . *Habitus* is a concept which has more explanatory power than, say, social type, since it embraces a wider range of features that might otherwise be mistaken for an individual conformation. (1998:153–154)

Understood as manifestations of *habitus,* local characters do more than recall individuals as singular instances of humanity for reasons of sentiment, grief, or entertainment. Understood as manifestations of *habitus*, local characters do more than cluster into neat, broad categories of type that make mental associations convenient. The notion of *habitus* invites us to recognize in the character the reflection not only of an individual but also the social, temporal, and cultural environment to which he or she is inevitably portrayed as a respondent.

The local character is derived from both personal elements, the raw materials of anecdotes, and "abstract typical traits" (Fishelov 1990:74) that command extra-personal associations, perpetuate notions of collective identities, and establish a sense of continuity from one person to another and one time to another. Local character anecdotes are uniquely suited to people's efforts to, in Durkheim's formulation, represent themselves to themselves.

Exercising memory during grief, people participating in conversational storytelling at the wake may benefit from the act of recall. Marshaling verbal talent as entertainment, people seeking the diversion of the ceili may simply enjoy the display of oratorical skill and the artful manipulation of language. Yet on some level, the characters that organize people's narratives at wakes and ceilis also provide a vehicle through which to conceive the group by contemplating the individual. Understood as manifestations of *habitus*, local characters may be appreciated as narrative constructions that answer to collective concerns while making these concerns all the more apparent.

Any given narrative persona is not a transparent representation of the individual who lends it a name. If an anecdote is about John McHugh, it is simultaneously about the interests of those who shape his memory through storytelling. An individual's portrayal is a product of and for the individuals who constitute the speech community that prizes such portrayals. Although ostensibly about individuals, local character anecdotes serve with other genres of storytelling to shape an idea of collectivity based not simply on one identity but on several potential ones comprising varying combinations of notable traits and behaviors.

Community does not exist apart from narratives, such as anecdotes, and practices, such as wakes, that assert community. Individuals, however, do independently exist. One way to imagine the group is to consider the individuals who constitute it. To speak of everyone is too large a task, so only certain individuals are regularly selected. Among them are characters: those who embody traits of extra-personal significance and collective interest, traits that are simultaneously entertaining. Eventually, everyone will be treated as if a character in narratives performed at his or her wake. But until then characters attract the most attention, and the anecdotes about them bring narrators and listeners together in circles of participation that create community while simultaneously representing those who comprise and may symbolize it.

10

Patterns and Implications

Franz Boas—pioneer of anthropology and folklore studies in the United States—declared that studying the creations of a group of people, particularly folklore, is paramount because this practice "has the merit of bringing out those points which are of interest to the people themselves" (1970 [1916]:393). If we are concerned with culture, with the dynamic interaction between the individual and the collective, paying attention to what concerns people everyday and to their own articulations of mind affords the most ethnographic insight. Embracing Boas's priorities, I began research in Aghyaran with the goal of understanding and telling others about this community by attending to the expressive forms people there find most meaningful.

Brought into the circle of Aghyaran wakes and ceilis, I began to appreciate the centrality of these events as opportunities for the enactment of community life. Finding people at wakes and ceilis enthusiastically engaged in storytelling, I began to investigate the social work accomplished through specific stories molded to specific situational contexts. As it happens, the most popular genre of storytelling at wakes and ceilis—the local character anecdote—is one in which the portrayal of individuals allows for, among other things, meditation on contrasts between past and present ways of life. Swapping local character anecdotes during social interaction, people in Aghyaran simultaneously entertain themselves and contemplate the range of possibilities for being an individual within a group in the midst of change.

As we have seen, portrayals of known local individuals in these anecdotes take shape in patterned ways through generic conventions shared by Aghyaran storytellers and audiences. Represented as characters in narrative, these individuals become rhetorical constructs of collective value and significance. Given the long-recognized role of the audience as co-author in face-to-face oral performance (Lord 1960, Duranti and Brenneis 1986), characters and the anecdotes told about them may also be seen as products of collective authorship. The audience as understood by the storyteller has a substantial influence in the myriad choices the storyteller makes in an effort to construct narrative that resonates with his or her audience. In general terms, the storyteller's genius may be understood as the ability to use language in creating and sustaining human communities (cf. Briggs 1988:xv).

Whether an individual characterized in a given anecdote appears as a familiar type or appears through a cycle of anecdotes as a more singular combination of traits, character types and traits continually reasserted in Aghyaran anecdotes emanate from a remembered amalgamation of storytelling over time. Stories that feature such characters responding to a shared social and cultural environment inevitably exhibit collective concerns, ethics, and aesthetics. While specifically personal identities are proposed, fixed, and commemorated in local character anecdotes, tellers of anecdotes give voice to both the individual and the group in the same breath.

I chose to focus on the local character anecdote as a genre because it is clearly a form of folklore in which my Aghyaran friends and neighbors have invested their intellectual, emotional, and artistic energies. Here is a body of popular narrative, a vernacular oral literature, that serves in part as a community study established by the very members of that community. My hope is that I have allowed the people of Aghyaran to represent themselves in their own terms. My hope is that in coaxing the explicit from the implicit—in drawing generalities from a wealth of specifics—I have distilled the insight of others rather than imposed my preconceptions on their words and actions.

～❧

To further extend and link other people's ideas, we must review certain materials to answer lingering questions in a more declarative fashion. What concerns preoccupy Aghyaran storytellers and audiences? What issues are at stake in this body of narrative ideally suited for both celebrating local individuals and proposing a community self-portrait? What conclusions can safely be drawn from local character anecdotes about culture, collective memory, and local identity in Aghyaran?

Taken as a whole, the types of humanity most often commemorated in both celebratory and critical character sketches establish a range of potential ideological stances and ways of living through which storytellers and audiences may evaluate their own ideological stances and ways of living. In order to elucidate statements made through local character anecdotes we should review the limited but telling range of the reoccurring character types in comic anecdotes, the most popular variety of local character anecdotes within the larger genre. True, a particularly celebrated character such as John McHugh cannot be contained by any one character type when an entire cycle of anecdotes about him is taken into consideration. Yet such cycles continually fix individuality in any given story through one character type or another from the available range to be reviewed.

The first group of character types illustrated in chapter 8 included the old-fashioned hapless farmer, the newer and more aggressive farmer-capitalist, and three unrefined character types associated with the past—the rough-living bachelor, the unmannerly but direct talker, and the uneducated rustic. Though relatively distinct from one another, these types share certain things in common. These types in particular depend on the contrast between past and present for their rhetorical impact. None are fully acceptable as exemplars for contemporary behavior, but their reception gives rise to sufficient ambivalence for storytellers and audiences to contemplate both the gains and losses that accompany change locally understood as modernization. In general these character types elicit ambivalence, but the extremity of their behavior ensures that they are eventually more rejected than celebrated. Implicit criticism, even rejection, will be all the more apparent when we compare this first group of character types to the second group discussed in chapter 8—those types appreciated as embodiments of community genius and wit.

Remaining for the moment with this first group, let us consider the underlying issues that motivate telling anecdotes about these types. The laid-back farmer of the past and the more entrepreneurial one of the present offer themselves as a clear antithesis. Both evoke ambivalence. The old-fashioned farmer is at turns lazy, hapless, and never "too fussed" about work. Through this type locals acknowledge and perhaps affirm outsiders' stereotypes of country bumpkins leading a slower pace of life, but this type is also consigned to the past as an emblem of outmoded ways. When compared to the contemporary farmer-capitalist, however, the hapless farmer of the past may be appreciated for his understanding that there is more to life than labor and economic gain. One issue at stake in stories about both types is the proper place of work in daily life. Presumably the ideal balance of priorities concerning the balance of work and leisure is suspended between these two extremes. Ideal convictions and behavior must be inferred because stories about those who embody the ideal middle ground do not conform to shared notions of what makes story-worthy material. One who works neither too much nor too little, who is neither overly invested in nor hopelessly indifferent to economic gain, simply is not the sort of character who inspires artful, entertaining narrative.

For his part, the capitalist farmer evokes ambivalence over both what may be considered success and to what extent change and outside influence should be embraced. The farmer-capitalist has perfected more efficient means for amassing the capital that begets profit. This would seem to be the dream of generations of Aghyaran people yearning to break out of an endemic cycle of poverty, but the laughter and head-shaking in response to anecdotes about farmer-capitalists indicate that many view some changes in attitude and behavior too great a price to pay. The farmer-capitalist is seen to have rejected a more communal and cooperative past way of living in favor of a newer, more individualistic and competitive one. Moreover, he is seen to have done so in response to outside influences emanating from the United States, the European Union, or in general a new culture driven by a market economy spanning the globe. This type represents an implicit threat to both local autonomy and traditional worldview and to the perceived legacy of a past that is not entirely negative. One family having more resources than another has always been a reality. Yet in the past, practices of cooperative labor and equipment sharing and an overarching ethic of equalitarianism—the impulse to mask or disregard differentiation in socioeconomic status—moderated possible tensions. Moving beyond ambivalence, many Aghyaran storytellers and audiences snub the farmer-capitalist as a threat to the civility and neighborliness associated with the past and still considered an elusive but worthy ideal in the present.

Turning to the three unrefined character types, we see again criticism of certain local ways of being. On some level, this criticism reiterates that of urban outsiders in particular, who are thought to consider themselves sophisticated and modern in comparison to those in rural backwaters. Contemporary Aghyaran storytellers and audiences distance themselves from the rough and unlearned of their own community by making fun of them, and in the process storytellers and audiences define themselves as more sophisticated and modern. Distancing is also effected through temporal associations. Like the old-fashioned hapless farmer, the types of the rough bachelor, coarse talker, and uneducated rustic are characterized as emblematic of a safely passed local past.

Emerging within the local community this self-imposed criticism also serves to preempt the negative stereotypes locals feel are imposed on them by outsiders. Especially in anecdotes in which less-refined local types confront outsiders and authority figures, these less-refined types become pointedly local heroes. They are *our* misfits and eccentrics who can be used to prove that people in Aghyaran "aren't so slack after all," quite often by turning outsiders' stereotypes of rural dwellers on their head. Like Goffman's in-group deviant (1963), local unrefined types are treated as strictly community property. Judged within the local community they may be found lacking or out of fashion. Nevertheless, if outsiders are content to judge all locals by the sort of people internally considered misfits or unfashionable eccentrics, then characters usually known for their marginality will be granted in narrative the ability to beat outsiders at their own game. So tapping into the dynamic of joke cycles about Paddy and the Yank and about the Irishman, the Scotsman, and the Englishman, Aghyaran anecdotes commemorate David Logue playing the rube to outwit the Crown's prosecutor, Willie Hunter shouting down the objections of dainty Belfast urbanites to rural living, Harry McDonnagh exposing the pomposity of the "bumming and blowing" returned Yanks, and John McHugh upstaging the professional comedian who has made a television and recording career of lampooning the thickness of country people.

Recasting such normally rejected characters as local heroes is not the only expression of ambivalence about them. True, unrefined types are mocked. At the same time the rough bachelor may be appreciated for his thrift and practicality, the coarse talker for his or her directness and refusal to kowtow to authority or to entertain others' affectations, and the unlearned rustic for using sound enough reasoning to make the most of what he or she knows. As seen in the implicit contrast between the old-fashioned laid-back farmer and the contemporary farmer-capitalist, ambivalence over these three unrefined types allows for a better appreciation of both what is worth preserving and what is now untenable in ways of life associated with the past.

So far, a number of reoccurring preoccupations in local character anecdotes have emerged. What has been lost and what has been gained in the midst of change? What constitutes success and quality of life? What is the proper balance of work and leisure and of cooperation and competition in a new socioeconomic environment in which basic needs can more reasonably be expected to be met? Which ostensibly local behaviors and ideological orientations should be celebrated and sustained and which should be happily laid to rest? The answers to these questions are not always clear and certainly vary by individual, but the fact that these questions continually reemerge grants us some insight into shared contemporary concerns.

More defined in Aghyaran anecdotes are a general appreciation of nonconformity within limits, and a willingness to entertain the proposition that some things were simply better in the past. We have also seen in anecdotes about farmer-capitalists and coarse talkers indications of a guarded tendency to exalt that which is local when faced with presumptive encroachments of outside authority or with the perceived disdain or patronization of outsiders. This guarded tendency becomes more defined in other anecdotes, to be discussed, about different character types.

At this point, only a few conclusions may be drawn about locally shared values and culture in Aghyaran at the present. Claiming, for instance, that "people in Aghyaran value equalitarianism and neighborliness" may be too overarching a generalization. Nevertheless, we can conclude that the critical backward glance is one shared strategy for coming to terms with the fact that the socioeconomic conditions that gave rise to these values are today under threat. Likewise, claiming that "people in Aghyaran harbor a dissenting attitude toward outside influence and centralized authority" would be true for many but not all. Nevertheless, we can surmise from Aghyaran anecdotes that people there are convinced of their marginal reputation in the wider world and eager to entertain creative challenges to this reputation.

With this second observation about expressions of tension between the local community and the wider world in mind, we cross over into one potential function of anecdotes about the second group of popular character types, which includes the man of words, the codder, the trickster, and the fool. Through these anecdotes Aghyaran storytellers choose and celebrate the types of humanity who may represent "us," our genius, the best of what "we" as a community have to offer. Contrast between past and present ideological stances and ways of living is less pronounced than in anecdotes about the first group of character types. Continual claims that there were more witty local characters in the past, however, reiterate the notion that contemporary social life—full of the alienating effects of televisions and cars—suffers in comparison to the social life of a recent past remembered as full of camaraderie and communal, homespun entertainment.

Again, challenges to stereotypes of Aghyaran people as rustics are found mostly in anecdotes that portray men of words such as Willie Duffy and Paddy O'Donnell encountering outsiders such as checkpoint soldiers. Such anecdotes proclaim, in part, that "we may be relatively poor and isolated, but we are intelligent, undeserving of condescension, and perfectly capable of upholding order on our own terms without outside interference."

Still, the majority of anecdotes about this second group of character types portray locals interacting with other locals. Proclaiming the cleverness of locals, contradicting otherwise negative stereotypes, may be one issue at stake in many anecdotes about Aghyaran's witty characters. Yet the majority of these anecdotes establish a dialogue about the excellence that may characterize the community as a whole and about what criteria may be used to evaluate personal excellence within the community.

If many Aghyaran people do indeed value equalitarianism, then the status of any given community member cannot be based on that individual's wealth or power as conventionally understood. As it happens, Aghyaran anecdotes about witty characters portray them as mostly friendly competitors in a local economy of respect and individual reputation, an economy that ignores materialistic standards. Wealth and power have traditionally been limited. In the not-too-distant past, characterized by poverty despite constant labor, wealth and power were considered more the result of arbitrary happenstance—the situation one was born into—than the result and evidence of an individual's industry and superior character. We can safely assume that wealth and power were long considered unfair criteria for evaluating the worth of individuals. At least in the hospitable social circles assembled in appreciation of verbal skill, wit in its many manifestations has emerged as the currency of a local discursive economy of respect and individual status.

Proof of excellence despite poverty and impotence to control one's political and socioeconomic environment, wit is also the currency of respect and status in other genres. In legends, outlaws prove themselves heroic by escaping capture in the short term through bluff and trickery. In personal experience narratives, smugglers prove themselves heroic by outsmarting customs officials in contests of wit that are symbolically rich but, at the end of the day, relatively minor in the greater scheme of things.

In local character anecdotes, wit is most often manifested in verbal skills, the very skills that bring people together and enrich experience at wakes and ceilis. The men of words such as Jamie Hegarty, Joe Byrne, and Francie McHugh can turn any conversation into a show worthy of commemoration during later conversations. Some characters have the gift of quick thinking and the ability to compose a quick, disarming response whenever challenged. Others have the gift of apt or imaginative description and artful exaggeration. Clever use of language is also at the base of the codder's rhetorical skill in manipulating perception and spinning entertainment out of harmless deception. Using the same cerebral skills as the codder, the trickster takes on responsibility for sometimes more elaborate entertaining deception through manipulation of both words and entire situations.

Anecdotes about champions of the clever comeback, codders, and tricksters commemorate contests of words and deeds. Both the realities of social life and the generic conventions of what constitutes story-worthy material require implicit winners and losers. As we have seen, portraying any given individual as a loser is tricky business. One solution is easy: narrate events in which the outsider is the loser, events that both vicariously bolster and conceptually define the limits of the community as a whole. When all involved in a given reported event are community members, however, there must be another strategy for shaping narrative that avoids discord in the social world. In these cases, if an anecdote is to have any longevity both winners and especially losers must be characters in the local sense, people with status already established by collective appreciation of their extremity in some aspect of personality or another. So a known wit such as Mickey Byrne or a known trickster such as Tom McSorley may be "beat" because their reputations as winners are already assured by a wealth of other anecdotes about them. Stories about men of words being beat by other men of words, codders by other codders, and tricksters by other tricksters reflect in narrative a community bound in social reality by relationships between individuals. These relationships are founded in part on the urge to create narratable situations (cf. Harlow 1997) that in the end do no harm to these relationships.

Losers may also include community members whose status as characters is based on their always being losers. Through narrative, fools help define the sort of wit celebrated as distinctively local by embodying its opposite. There are understood rules in both narrative construction and social reality for how much fun may be had at the expense of a recognized fool, yet local celebrity status can never truly ameliorate a person's reputation as a fool, a recognized safe target. Choosing creative wit over material success as the standard for excellence in the local economy of reputation may avoid certain injustices but may also give rise to others.

Out of a sense of compassion for certain individuals cast as fools, and respecting the confidentiality of certain storytellers, I have not specified exactly who have become victims of storytelling and why. I will assert, however, that unfashionably eccentric but otherwise intelligent individuals can easily be made scapegoats. For all the important and often healing social work storytelling affords, it can also increase the misery of an unfortunate few. On the one hand, here is a strain of folklore that rewards talents of the creative mind regardless of material circumstance. On the other, the imperative to find grist for the narrative mill can trap some individuals in an endemic cycle of ridicule perhaps more difficult to escape than that of poverty. Here is an aspect of local culture that may not be praiseworthy but nevertheless cannot be ignored.

Taken as a whole, anecdotes about the range of popular reoccurring character types are eloquent of meditation on larger issues of immediate and shared concern in Aghyaran: the relative value of past and present ways of being, the relative authority of community insiders and outsiders, and the relative status assigned individual community members and types based on their relative intellectual and creative talents. Moreover, anecdotes about the range of most popular reoccurring character types constitute a body of local collective memory—transferable from the past and revisable in the present—that serves as a selective community self-portrait. Although largely comic and designed to entertain, these anecdotes use humor to attract attention long enough for storytellers and audiences to accomplish serious social work, much but not all of it laudable. Local character anecdotes matter because they are a vehicle through which people use the past in order to make sense of the present and guide each other into the future.

11

Storytelling, Commemoration, and Identity

Whether told at wakes, at ceilis, or in other contexts, local character anecdotes are narrative orderings of past events. Given that a primary performance context for telling local character anecdotes is occasioned by death, the memorial impulse of the wake begs stories that remember the dead, conjuring them back to life. At the nighttime communal debriefing of the ceili, daily confrontations with massive socioeconomic change spark conversation, and local character anecdotes provide both welcome distraction from and serious contemplation of the present through contrast with the remembered past. Local character anecdotes told in Aghyaran, then, join in a much larger project of commemoration, and a consideration of commemoration offers us a final perspective on what is at stake in telling anecdotes.

From annual Orange parades and urban gable end murals to the relatively recent explosion of local historical societies, commemoration is a shared drive of thousands of people across Northern Ireland. Whether they be marching in a parade or telling anecdotes at wakes and ceilis, acts of commemoration are often precisely where the community of the network and the community of the social imaginary come into dialogue, gesturing toward identity (Noyes 1995:471). In the same way that we considered the place and function of anecdotes within the broader generic system of Aghyaran oral traditions, we should consider the place and function of anecdotes within the broader range of Aghyaran commemorative practices.

Although etymologically the term *commemoration* only suggests some form of reminding, I use the term to suggest "remembering together," an activity invested in the creation and re-creation of collective memory (cf. Connerton 1989, Gillis 1994).[1] Put another way, commemoration, as I use the term, is community realizing itself through bids to represent a shared past. Having said this, however, I must clarify that different forms of commemoration evoke and seek to sustain a variety of coexisting and potentially overlapping communities in Aghyaran. The diversity of what is commemorated, how, by whom, and especially to what ends cannot be overlooked, but one commonality in this range of local commemoration is a preoccupation with collective identities.

Here we should pay close attention to the variety of groups and attendant collective identities to which different commemorative activities gesture. Although attention to detail reveals considerable complexity, a variety of coexisting communities, and overlap between these communities in Aghyaran, expressions of collective identity there tend to gesture either toward a sense of community based on sectarian affiliation or toward a sense of community based on shared experience within Aghyaran/Termonamongan/the Killeter area/the western Derg Valley as a recognized locality. Put in proper context, within the larger picture of commemoration in Aghyaran, swapping local character anecdotes at wakes and ceilis may be appreciated as a significant and potent vehicle for contemplating change and constructing a local identity that can moderate the rhetoric and effects of sectarian identity.

One type of community evoked through various commemorations is, on the whole, Christian and ecumenical. Many religious ceremonies with a commemorative aspect—such as observances at Easter and Christmas—continually reassert the collective identity of participants as followers of Christ. At Christmas, for example, leaders of the main churches gather in the centers of Killeter and Castlederg to lead crowds in singing carols common to Catholics and Protestants. The implicit and sometimes explicit message is that at least at this time of year all Christians have more in common than they have differences. In addition, we have already seen in chapter 4 how funerals in particular may commemorate individuals but also serve to incorporate the deceased into a more anonymous body of the dead, "the faithful departed," and reaffirm the shared faith of mourners in the coming resurrection. This applies equally to Roman Catholic, Presbyterian, Methodist, and Church of Ireland funerals. One dynamic common to both Christian calendar customs and funerals is the commemoration of certain individuals—whether a sacred figure such as Christ or a local deceased individual—as a means of evoking larger bodies of people connected by shared belief over time and across space. Despite the differences in communities evoked, this same dynamic of asserting collective identity by remembering the symbolically resonant individual is at work in several of the other commemorative forms to be discussed.

Bear in mind, however, that because ritual and symbol are always polysemic and because Aghyarn is home to several Christian churches, Christian community evoked through commemoration in Aghyaran may also take on specifically local, denominational, or potentially sectarian associations. Commemorations at Easter are the most obvious example of denominational and political communities being collapsed. After attending Easter Sunday mass, republicans convene in the cemetery behind St. Patrick's Church to commemorate the 1916 Rising. There republican dignitaries, usually Sinn Féin party officials, give speeches about past and present republican struggle, recite the 1916 Proclamation of the Irish Republic, and read the county's "Role of Honour," a list of Tyrone republican paramilitaries and activists who have lost their lives during the Troubles since the early twentieth century. At each grave of a local republican interred at St. Patrick's, an appropriate individual, usually one who knew the deceased, says a few words remembering the deceased as a republican. Following this a color guard slowly lowers a tricolor as the Harvey-McGlynn-Connolly Republican Memorial Flute Band—which draws membership from Aghyaran and Castlederg—play "The Soldier's Song," the national anthem of the Republic of Ireland. The commemoration at each grave is concluded with the gathered crowd reciting a decade of the rosary. These activities are neither officially condemned nor condoned by the local clergy, but taking place on holy ground after mass and including the rosary, these republican commemorations clearly borrow from Roman Catholic funerary ritual and appropriate for their own ends some of the Church's traditional, institutional authority. Indeed, the fact that the rebellion commemorated took place on Easter is no coincidence, for the 1916 rebels were well aware of the Christian resonance of offering a blood sacrifice in the fight for national self-determination at this time of year associated in religious terms with death and rebirth.

Saint's day celebrations also admit the elision of several communities of shared collective identity that remain more distinct at other times. These celebrations simultaneously remind the faithful of the biographies of holy men and women in Ireland and reiterate the shared identity of those who participate in a catholic tradition, maintained by both Roman Catholicism and Anglicanism, that includes the veneration of saints. Nevertheless, customs such as constructing crosses out of rushes on February 1st as a reminder of St. Brigit's early ministry reference a specifically Irish past and are associated particularly with Roman Catholics throughout Ireland. Similarly, celebration of Our Lady's Day or the Feast of the Ascension on August 15th is identified particularly with Northern Irish Roman Catholics and has accrued nationalist, though not strictly republican, associations. Traditionally this is one of two main days on which the Ancient Order of Hibernians display Irish Catholic nationalist identity, parading in a style that in some ways mirrors that of the Orange Order. The other day chosen for parading by the AOH is March 17th, St. Patrick's Day; although celebrated by the Church of Ireland, St. Patrick's Day is in Ireland and worldwide most often associated with the Roman Catholic Irish.

In addition to denominational and nationalist associations, St. Patrick's Day commemorations have a local significance. On this day, Aghyaran Roman Catholics make a pilgrimage to St. Patrick's Well in Magherakeel, where usually they are reminded by the parish priest that at this very location the patron saint of both Termonamongan Parish and Ireland as a whole began the spread of the true faith in Aghyaran. Here, St. Patrick's Day commemorations reiterate the collective identity shared by the community of the Roman Catholics of Aghyaran.

As elsewhere in Northern Ireland, political/ethnic collective identities conventionally labeled as sectarian—that is, Irish Catholic nationalist or republican, and British or Ulster Protestant unionist or loyalist—are asserted in Aghyaran through ritual, visual, musical, and poetic commemorative forms. In conceiving these two opposing communities—labeled for convenience as simply Catholics and Protestants—religious denomination serves as one of many markers of differential ethnic identity (see Buckley and Kenney 1995). In general, for republicans and loyalists, religion provides a source of ready-made symbolism and rhetoric from which to draw in their respective bids for legitimacy. Differences in religious doctrine between Roman Catholicism and the Protestant denominations are less relevant than the history of political conflict that the opposing communities commemorate as the origin of their opposing loyalties. In contrast, many nationalists and unionists—the more politically conservative elements in the Catholic and Protestant communities—are more willing to foreground denominational affiliation and doctrinal convictions in their efforts to define themselves through contrasts with "the other side of the house."

Already mentioned were republican commemorations in St. Patrick's graveyard at Easter. Like republicans throughout Ireland at Easter, Aghyaran republicans pin to their lapels small pieces of paper depicting green, white, and orange lilies—symbols of both Easter and the 1916 Rising. Irish tricolors and placards with republican slogans are attached to telephone poles, especially in the west of the parish where Catholics are in the majority. There are no republican commemorative parades in the parish, but some journey to take part in parades in Carrickmore, a republican stronghold in west central Tyrone, or in nearby Drumboe, Co. Donegal, the site of a 1923 execution of four anti-treaty IRA volunteers by the Free State Army during the Irish Civil War. Some years, the local GAA hall books a band that specializes in rebel songs, which commemorate the military victories but more often the mortal sacrifices of republicans throughout history in the local area and across Ireland. These songs are also sung at informal sessions either in certain Castlederg pubs or more often in the relative security of known republican pubs in surrounding Donegal towns. Also at Easter, there is often an increase in temporary republican graffiti, painted on local roads, bridges, and bus stops, that may remember, for instance, the words of 1916 rebel Patrick Pearse: "Ireland unfree shall never be at peace." In republican neighborhoods of Castlederg small murals commemorating local republican prisoners and martyrs are touched up, and curbstones are repainted green, white, and orange or gold. All these commemorative forms offer a chance for collective participation that reasserts shared identity of republicans in the local context while connecting with a wider imagined community of republicans throughout the North, the island of Ireland, and the Irish diaspora as a whole.

Local nationalists, those who have long believed in achieving a united Ireland through political means rather than military force, tend to focus their energy into expressions of what is considered indigenous Irish culture, including sports, music, and dance. Here the emphasis is on heritage more than history. Being understood to originate in the shared Irish past, however, grants these cultural forms authenticity, so their practice and celebration become a form of commemoration. Remember, though, that republicanism may be seen as a more militant subset of nationalism, and many republicans, too, are avid enthusiasts of Gaelic football, hornpipes, and step dancing, for example. Local branches of island-wide organizations such as the Gaelic Athletic Association and Comhaltas Céoltori Éireann serve as vehicles for the desire of both republicans and non-republican nationalists to preserve and promote native Irish culture.

Usually non-republican nationalists participate in the Ancient Order of Hibernians through its branch based in Carncorn, on the eastern peripheries of the parish. Claiming origins in the Penal Era as an association devoted to defending Roman Catholicism in Ireland, the AOH in Ireland continues to define itself primarily as a religious organization and secondarily as a nationalist one. AOH parade banners in western Ulster typically depict Sts. Patrick or Bridget, the Virgin Mary, proscribed masses in the wilderness during the Penal Era, or occasionally an historical figure such as Daniel O'Connell, the father of Irish constitutional nationalism.

The Carncorn AOH Accordion Band have often led pilgrims to St. Patrick's Well in Magherakeel on the saint's day. More recently, however, they have tended for a number of reasons to travel to larger St. Patrick's Day parades in England and the United States. One reason is that there is a large demand for such bands by Irish emigrant enclaves abroad, who tend to stage more elaborate St. Patrick's Day parades, and these days locals can afford to travel with the help of fundraising efforts. In addition, local support for the AOH is not what it used to be, so traveling elsewhere to perform is attractive. Over time AOH membership in Aghyaran has declined along with support of the old Nationalist Party and later the Social Democratic and Labor Party. The AOH Hall in Garvagh townland has been closed and reopened as a community center receptive to cross-community (mixed Catholic-Protestant) events. According to some, the SDLP has always been loath to waste campaign funds in Aghyaran, where Sinn Féin is much better organized though not universally supported among Catholics.

The Carncorn AOH leadership is also keen to avoid the charges of chauvinism and triumphalism leveled by many Catholics at the Orange Order. Moreover, not wanting to be dismissed by Catholics and Protestants alike as merely "Green Orangemen," mimicking the Orange style of display, the Carncorn AOH retired their aging parading banner and adopted a more American style of marching band uniform. Being based in a majority-Protestant area of the parish near Killen, they generally wish to avoid offending local Protestants by marching in territory recognized as Protestant or marching in other mixed areas. Therefore, they march only in areas, whether in Aghyaran and Castlederg or abroad, where they are clearly wanted. Although public expressions of shared identity by the non-republican nationalist community in Aghyaran have strong denominational associations and are inevitably political, people tend to be very careful about choosing forms of commemoration that will not aggravate sectarian conflict within the local community through potentially provocative display in contentious areas.

For their part, local unionists commemorate Remembrance Sunday, Armistice Day, and the Battle of the Somme as a way to honor the service of Ulster Protestants in the British armed forces. At the same time, the local community of unionists is reaffirmed and conceptually linked with the wider unionist community simultaneously conducting these commemorations in various locations across the province. In November artificial red poppies are worn on lapels, recalling the European battlefields of World War I where over twenty thousand Ulster Protestants lost their lives serving king and country. Poppy wreaths are also laid at the cenotaph in the center of Castlederg during commemorative prayer ceremonies on Armistice Day, at the eleventh hour of the eleventh day of the eleventh month. Especially on Remembrance Sunday in early November, the company of those commemorated is extended to members of the RUC, UDR, and RIR who have lost their lives during the Troubles, with poppy wreathes being laid on the graves of local members of the security forces slain in the line of duty. Through these commemorations, local unionists reaffirm their loyalty to the United Kingdom by recalling the ultimate sacrifices of their own community members. Privately, many bemoan the fact that, in their estimation, this loyalty is today poorly reciprocated by a British government seemingly intent on pulling out of Northern Ireland and ignoring her most faithful subjects. This cluster of commemorations of unionist service to Britain focuses more on the political aspects of shared unionist identity, whereas commemorations of seventeenth-century events such as the Siege of Londonderry include more attention to the shared unionist heritage of Protestantism and its defense in Ireland.

Parades organized by the Orange Order in observance of the Twelfth of July are the most celebrated commemorations that assert unionist community. On this day in 1690 at the Battle of the Boyne, the Protestant William of Orange—lauded as the guarantor of religious and civil liberties for Ulster Protestants—defeated the Catholic King James II—designated by unionists as the historical embodiment of despotism and "Popish error." The subsequent coronation of William of Orange as William III—or King Billy in popular parlance—is understood by unionists as having safeguarded Protestantism as the true faith of the British Empire and having secured their political legitimacy and dominance as a community in Ulster. More than other events commemorated, the Twelfth enfolds religion and politics in defining the province-wide unionist community as manifested in localities across Ulster.

In the weeks running up to the Twelfth both unionist and loyalist marching bands practice in the western Derg valley, but mostly in Killen and in Protestant sections of Castlederg. Meanwhile others decorate Protestant areas with red, white, and blue buntings, and with Ulster and Union flags. In addition, in nearby Castlederg and Omagh, arches erected over roadways incorporate Orange symbols linking the British Empire with Protestantism and metaphorically equating Ulster Protestants with the Jews of the Old Testament, God's Chosen People surrounded in the wilderness by hostile nonbelievers. Although there is no tradition of unionist or loyalist mural painting in Castlederg, red, white, and blue curbstones are touched up in anticipation of the Twelfth. In addition, Castlederg youths gather wood and other combustibles for Bonfire Night, on the eve of the Twelfth, when pyres topped with tricolors or sometimes effigies of the pope are set alight to cheers and the singing of unionist standards such as "The Sash My Father Wore" but also considerably more aggressive songs such as "The Billy Boys" ("We're up to our knees in Fenian blood/Surrender or you'll die"). In general during the Marching Season, as the late summer is called, loyalist paramilitary graffiti may appear overnight on buildings and roads in Aghyaran, but most public commemorations of the Twelfth are confined to areas outside the parish where Protestants are in a clear majority.

On the Twelfth in 2000, the 310th commemoration of the Battle of the Boyne, it was Castlederg's turn to host the north and west Tyrone regional parade. Sixty Orange lodges marched the nearly two-mile route around the mostly Protestant center and southern end of town to a demonstration field on the Enniskillen Road. Each lodge was led by their officers in dark suits, Orange collarettes, and bowler hats. They were followed by others supporting intricately painted banners usually displaying an equestrian portrait of William of Orange crossing the Boyne. Other banners included depictions of Old Testament scenes, crowns resting on Bibles, and martyrs for the Protestant faith such as Hugh Ridley and Nicholas Latimer, burned at the stake as heretics by Mary I. Behind the banners marched members of the lodge, dressed as were their officers, and behind the Orange men marched mostly bagpipe bands in kilts, or less often flute-and-drum or accordion bands in military-like uniforms.

On a platform in the demonstration field, Orange Order dignitaries received the various lodges and offered prayers remembering Orange brethren who had died in the previous year. They then passed resolutions in support of renewed loyalty to the "Protestant Reformed Evangelical Faith"; to "the Throne and Person of Her Most Gracious Majesty Queen Elizabeth II, Defender of the Faith"; to the Northern Ireland Assembly, provided that the union with Britain is maintained and that "IRA/Sinn Féin" not be allowed further recognition and authority without arms decommissioning; and to the "Orange Family worldwide." The main address by the guest speaker, Rev. Robert Creane, followed a fairly typical model that first thanked God for the "martyrs and heroes of the Faith" who have preserved Protestant heritage, then detailed external and internal threats to the Ulster Protestant community, and concluded with the proclamation that in the midst of great evil and moral decline the only way to defend "the Reformed Protestant religion and the power of the Gospel of Jesus Christ" is to return to and embody the Biblical principles for which "our forefathers suffered and died." Given that the prayers, resolutions, and addresses in the demonstration field are largely formulaic and quite familiar to yearly participants, the majority of people in the field either gathered into conversations or filtered back into the town to visit with others at the street stalls or in the pubs, Parish Hall, or Orange Hall.

On the whole, small-town Twelfth parades such as this one are usually sociable and peaceful affairs in contrast to parades in more contentious areas of bigger cities. Aghyaran Orangemen tend to share with local Hibernians the desire to avoid incitement within the local district and the strategy of removing their public activities to areas in which they are clearly wanted. Although there is an Orange Hall in Aghyaran townland, there is no depiction of William of Orange on the exterior, nor are there Ulster or Union flags flying from the roof, as there are on the Killen Orange Hall and Orange Halls throughout Ulster. This hall is mostly used for meetings and Aghyaran Accordion Band practices, but public marching practice is conducted usually in the majority-Protestant areas of Castlederg and in Killen.

Nevertheless, the tension between the aging face of conservative Orangeism and a younger, rowdier loyalist element found across the province was also seen at the Castlederg Twelfth with the inclusion of a few more aggressive, independent "blood and thunder" or "kick the Pope" bands. These bands include loyalist paramilitary initials and iconography in their banners and uniforms and are more willing to enter Catholic areas as a form of taunting or intimidation. In fact, other than these bands and the occasional spray-painting of graffiti, there are few avenues for publicly asserting loyalist convictions—chiefly, the willingness to use force to maintain the union with Britain—other than violence itself. Although the main Castlederg march in 2000 passed off without incident, during practice and smaller pre-Twelfth parades there were cases of vandalism of Catholic property, abusive behavior toward Catholics, and violations of the Parades Commission interdictions on entering Catholic housing estates. Some years have been even more confrontational, others less.

The majority of Orangemen with whom I spoke condemned such behavior, blaming alcohol and youthful disregard for authority. They lamented the fact that the younger loyalist element gives Orangeism a bad reputation in the media, which they maintained are predisposed to highlight negative aspects of the Twelfth celebrations. In addition, Aghyaran Orangemen identified loyalist bands from outside the local area as the worst offenders, and they criticized these outsiders for frustrating their efforts to celebrate their unionist heritage without damaging relations with Catholic neighbors. It's not that those Newtownstewart or Gillygooley boys are all that deep, the apologists tell me, but acting out is what you do when not at home.

Others are less willing to blame outsiders and see sectarian confrontation as the inevitable consequence of intrinsically belligerent custom justified as tradition and of the intransigence of the Orange Order to adapt to change. As novelist Glenn Patterson observes, the Twelfth is "the demonstration of nothing so much as the ability to march when and where the marchers please. The medium is the message and must remain inviolate" (2006:18). In a similar vein, I argue elsewhere that the formal features of the parade as a complex genre not only express but also implicate and encode a sectarian worldview (2007a).

Such arguments are debatable. Back on the ground and faced with conflicting loyalties to local vs. unionist community, some Aghyaran Orangemen attempt to avoid the dilemma altogether by attending perhaps the least contentious Twelfth celebrations in Ulster, held at Rossnowlagh, Co. Donegal—in the Republic. In Rossnowlagh, Orangemen enjoy both the solidarity of collective effervescence and some of the advantages of anonymity, but they do so as a clear minority group on stage in a less politically tense environment where the worse excesses of colonialism are considered safely in the past. The atmosphere is so relaxed that for decades many Donegal Catholics have gathered to enjoy the spectacle.

Despite the numerous foregoing examples, there also exists in Aghyaran a great deal of commemorative activity that has nothing to do with defining community in sectarian terms. Some commemorative forms such as horse plowing competitions and crafts fairs have less to do with asserting community than with preserving past ways, or at least reminders of past ways, understood to be threatened by modernization. Like many local character anecdotes, these events allow for evaluation of the present through contrast with the past, and this exercise potentially concerns everyone regardless of political, ethnic, or religious affiliations. If community is asserted it is that of a particular generational cohort, the community of those who have experienced sweeping change beyond their control and are uneasy with short-sighted, unthinking acquiescence.

I have asked several middle-aged to elderly men about what attracts them to anachronism. I have asked Barney McGrath why he continues to make creels and donkey carts, John Mongan why he hosts old farm machinery demonstrations, Danny Gallen why he collects old tools and household furnishings, and Jim Falls why he preserves a traditional thatched house previously abandoned to the elements. Some, such as Barney, try to explain their motivations on aesthetic grounds; they like to have certain stuff around for what it looks and feels like, for the pleasure it brings. Others such as John emphasize the importance of teaching younger generations about how their ancestors lived so that they will take less for granted. Others, such as Danny and Jim, explain that they appreciate what their tools and restoration projects remind them and others of: a world in which they were raised but one to which they can never return.

Material artifacts of the past are not automatically valued. They have different resonances for different people at different times. From the 1950s through the 1980s objects such as handheld scythes and horse-drawn grub-

Figure 11.1. Jim Falls

bers were discarded as soon as modern labor-saving replacements could be purchased. As Gerard Devine explained to me,

> *A lot of those things John [Mongan] and Danny [Gallen] gather up, well, we threw them out, just. It was all poverty to us, you know, the signs of poverty, and we couldn't get away from it fast enough. John was ahead of his time, getting all that started when people were still trying to get out of the past, maybe even ashamed of the past.*

Later he resumed this line of thought:

> *It's a sign of our wealth now, that we're taking an interest in the past. Now we have the time to look back at it. Couldn't have done it in the '50s or '60s. But there's something . . . now . . . something about loss, maybe. You see, we have the ability now to fly off to America on holiday instead, but there's some would rather think about what they already had. A lot of it's best left behind, but not all of it.*

Such as what, I asked. Gerard paused, then offered:

I just don't know really. Maybe we won't see that sort of cooperation again, when it all had to be done by hand. But there's more to it than that. Must be.

Evaluation of the contrast between past and present may not always be conclusive or easy to articulate to oneself and others in words. Yet the sort of commemoration in which Barney, John, Danny, Jim, and many others are engaged is eloquent of a determination not only to remember but also to reconsider, to leave a conceptual space between now and then, to resist if nothing else the finality and conclusiveness of the changes wrought over the last century. The widespread collection and replication of the past—a sort of voluntary museumification—seems to be motivated by a desire to temporarily interrupt modernization for the sake of meditation and appreciation, to take stock in the face of rapid and irreversible change.

Much of the energy expended on commemorating everyday life of the past combines with efforts to assert specifically local community. Here geography becomes an important factor in people's efforts to define themselves as a group through commemoration of a shared past and shared identity. The focus becomes Aghyaran community, identity, and history rather than Catholic or Protestant community, identity, and history. Local heritage is no more nor no less selective a construct than nationalist or unionist heritage, but privileging place as an organizing principle in commemoration allows for evaluation of the contrast between past and present in a potentially less divisive register.

Aghyaran magazine is a case in point. Founded in 1986 by Fr. Brendan McGinn, the annually published magazine consists mostly of contributions by locals that survey traditional culture and historical events, figures, and sites within the boundaries of Termonamongan Parish. Primary documents such as censuses, emigration statistics, and old photographs are often reproduced. Collectanea include ballads and recitations, tall tales, jokes, local character anecdotes, and historical and supernatural legends. As Fr. McGinn states in his foreword to the 2000 reprint of the first ten issues in a bound volume, the magazine committee adopted the goals of "committing to print traditions and history which could be lost and of fostering the sense of community and the sense of identity of the people." Moreover, the audience and sense of shared local community and identity the magazine is intended to foster extends beyond the physical boundaries of the parish to parts of the wider world where people from Aghyaran have settled. In fact, one of the reasons for reprinting the first ten issues was that so many of the original magazines were sent to friends and relatives who had emigrated to England, Australia, and North America. Although the magazine committee is entirely Catholic and the magazine has featured a number of Catholic topics, efforts have been made to include contributions by Protestants and to cover topics of interest to all regardless of their denomination.

Claiming all those who live in an identifiable locality as members of local community reorganizes collectivity and belonging in terms of shared experience within shared place. This strategy encourages a sense of literal and figurative common ground; it offers an implicit and at times explicit challenge to definitions of community posited in sectarian terms. Employment of this strategy and the assertion of explicitly anti-sectarian messages are a degree clearer in the commemorative work accomplished by the Killeter and District Historical Society, an organization that peaked in activity in the 1990s and then evolved into further community development projects.

The KDHS deserves special attention because it can be viewed as an institutionalization of the same motivations that lie behind the local character anecdote: coming to terms with change and mediating division. Essentially, the KDHS extended the spirit of the wake and ceili into the public realm, refusing to cede authority to the parades and murals in the larger, pervasive project of representing the past and establishing identity.

Consider first how the KDHS came into being. In 1988, graduates of the one-room schoolhouse in Gortnagross townland held a warm and well-attended reunion. The student body had always been denominationally mixed until the late 1950s, when the Derry Dioceses put increased pressure on Catholics to send their children to voluntary or maintained schools, whose curricula were supervised by the Catholic clergy. Many middle-aged and elderly Gortnagross graduates believe that going to school with members of other denominations instilled in them a sense of solidarity and common identity within the local community of Aghyaran, a sense that has been severely threatened by more recent events. At the reunion, Gortnagross School became emblematic of an ideal past way of life, and plans were floated to refurbish the school as a politically neutral community center. These plans failed for both political and economic reasons, yet a core group of nearly a dozen Gortnagross graduates and like-minded people began to discuss various potential projects designed to foster wider appreciation of local community.

This group included Catholic and Protestant teachers, civil servants, and farmers. Meeting in Castlederg, they discussed and abandoned several proposals for new organizations that would have in some way overlapped or competed with already existing initiatives such as cross-community dances and concerts in Killeter and the Ulster Project, which sends groups of Catholic and Protestant youths to socialize together in the United States. Finally, an historical society was suggested. Not everyone shared what might be considered an antiquarian interest in the past, yet what emerged from conversation was a vision of history as local rather than as sectarian—in other words, Derg Valley history rather than unionist or nationalist history. Hosting lectures on topics of shared interest could bring, it was hoped, Catholics and Protestants into the same room. Restoring historical sites of shared interest could redirect attention to shared local experience and culture.

The historical society idea became appealing once people began to think of exploring local history as a means to an end. As one of the founders told me, he was initially cautious because his first impression was that history in Northern Ireland only conjures images of division and grievance. He continued:

> *I knew I was no historian, but I am very interested in better relations so I joined in. Maybe I was a token Protestant. Maybe. But, I tell you, I hate the damned old elections. I hate when they rear their heads, remind people they're separated. This seemed like, the society looked like, a step in the right, or maybe a better direction.*

Those conditioned by certain images of the Marching Season may be surprised to know that these are the words of a loyal Orangeman.

In 1990 this group founded the Killeter and District Historical Society, choosing a name that avoided the primarily Catholic associations with "Aghyaran" and the primarily Anglican associations with "Termonamongan." As an historical society, its primary goal was distinctive: first and foremost, the group aimed to better local Catholic-Protestant relations. As the KDHS constitution states, the society's goal is "to promote and develop cross-community co-operation through the exploration and development of the history and culture of the district."

Lectures were organized on topics including townland histories, wakes and seasonal customs, local graveyards and archaeological sites, and the work of local poets. These lectures were held on winter evenings at the Derg Leisure Center in Castlederg, the nearest politically neutral public venue. Unfortunately, the early to mid-nineties saw setbacks in cross-community relations due to local, politically motivated violence and tensions relating to ongoing province-wide disputes over the routes of Orange Order parades. Attendance at the lectures varied. Some complained that weather and the travel distance to Castlederg made attending inconvenient, so attention shifted to securing funds for building a neutral venue in Killeter that could host future meetings and house the society's collection of historical domestic and farming implements. This new facility opened in the summer of 2002 and has been well used as a venue for a variety of local social events.

Although efforts to maintain the lecture series lost momentum, other efforts to direct attention to the local shared past flourished. This success was due, in part, to the value of sites on the landscape as physical reminders of ideological convictions. The society was particularly good at securing grants for historic preservation projects, and the sites chosen for restoration are telling. The first site restored—mentioned in chapter 1—was the pre-Reformation graveyard in Magherakeel townland, which both Catholic and Protestant families continue to use. By restoring the graveyard the society not only made it more accessible, but also marked it for display, inviting contemplation of the memories and ideas the site may evoke.

Magherakeel graveyard stands near the foundations of the original Catholic parish church, St. Caireall's, which was destroyed in the early 1600s during the Plantation. Given that the Church of Ireland reestablished St. Caireall's in 1693 and took over at least nominal control of Magherakeel graveyard, a strict nationalist interpretation of the site would characterize it as emblematic of Protestant encroachment on Catholic property. The KDHS, however, attempted to at least offer (if not fix) a different interpretation on the site. Theirs was a self-conscious attempt to render the graveyard as a place emblematic of coexistence, a place where Catholics and Protestants share common ground—sacred ground, no less. The KDHS's restoration turned the graveyard into a signifier of local community by evoking a critically more complicated past. In the present, several forms of commemoration can oversimplify the past in binary, Catholic vs. Protestant terms that can lead to fear, distrust, and justifications for violence. The KDHS's goal, however, was to offer resistance, to question whether public and assertive sectarian versions of the past can ever have the final word.

For these first preservation efforts and the potential messages conveyed, the society received a grant and an award from British Telecom. BT also hosted a reception at the site attended by politicians from across the political spectrum. It was good publicity for the society and provided considerable momentum for further preservation projects.

After the graveyard, the next site restored was a nearby lime kiln, a relic of rural industry used by Catholics and Protestants alike until just after World War II. Its significance lies not just in its being a vestige of the past, and its appropriateness lies not just in its being a politically neutral site. The kiln is emblematic of a time when farming and much of daily life had not yet become matters of more solitary and mechanized practice. Moreover, it evokes the idea that in a place where Catholics and Protestants lead the same way of life, they have more in common than they have differences. Without ever having read the works of E. Estyn Evans or his students and colleagues, the KDHS drew inspiration from the same principles underlying the Ulster Folk and Transport Museum and, arguably, folklife studies in Northern Ireland as a whole.[2]

The society continued with other preservation projects. If a nominally Catholic site was restored, a nominally Protestant site was also restored. More important than the equal balance struck was the choice of sites. The past is inscribed on the landscape, and by highlighting certain sites, the past is commemorated and messages are communicated: "There is common ground. Division is not preordained. To prove that the present need not be as it is, look to our past."

Danny McSorley, one of the society's founders, is Chief Executive of the Omagh District Council, a part-time farmer, and a Catholic. I asked him to evaluate the success of KDHS projects in promoting cross-community contact and a sense of shared local community. He felt that the society's revival of Killeter Fair in 1997, after a fifty-year hiatus, was ultimately more successful in having Catholics and Protestants mingle than the lecture series had been. Originally a monthly market for sheep and cattle, Killeter Fair in its revived form offers games, contests, crafts demonstrations, and musical and dramatic entertainment designed to highlight shared cultural heritage in the western Derg valley. What might be consid-

Figure 11.2. Killeter Fair, 2007

ered a merely nostalgic resurrection of a fair that had long outlived its economic usefulness—what might be dismissed as an insignificant provincial concern—was widely acclaimed as an exceptional opportunity for people from across the political spectrum to socialize and to imagine themselves as a community rooted in place. As a local Democratic Unionist Party politician told him: "You know, Killeter Fair *is* important."[3]

Furthermore, Danny McSorley was satisfied that by redirecting attention to shared place through the historic preservation projects, the society had found an avenue through which to reassert community as local and to emphasize less contentious elements of the past in the public realm. These efforts were admittedly selective in nature, but they served to balance the public sectarian representations of the past already so familiar from annual parades, gable end murals, and political ballads. As McSorley summed up his evaluation of the society's efforts to effect change:

> *Well, our efforts may not have made much of a difference,*
> *but it held things from slipping further. In any case, it gave*
> *Protestants signals that—after a long and vicious IRA border*

*campaign—that not all their Catholic neighbors, not even the
majority of them, wanted them gone, pushed out. Gortnagross
[School] may never be renovated, but community relations are
in some ways stabilized, and there was a very grim time when
this seemed impossible.*

Received wisdom about the division of the world into that which is Catholic and that which is Protestant is difficult to contest, but given the costs of such received wisdom, revision is urgent. To challenge a status quo bolstered by sectarian visions of the past and definitions of community requires an alternative vision of the past upon which the idea of local community may be based. By redirecting attention through commemoration to that which is local and shared, the KDHS challenges impulses toward segregation and difference. As Kevin Whelan reminds us, the appeal to "localism" can easily be construed as an appeal to conservatism in a world increasingly understood to be globalized (1993:13). Yet ordinary Catholics and Protestants in West Tyrone remind us that the appeal to the local need not be inherently provincial or reactionary. Local history can be of service in the present when marshaled as an appeal for a better future. Careful and quite self-conscious bids to define community in local terms can further social work of great moral weight and potential consequence.

Having reviewed a range of coexisting and even overlapping communities evoked through several forms of commemoration in Aghyaran, we recognize a basic contrast between appeals either to more or less sectarian definitions of community or to specifically local definitions of community. Commemorating certain individuals of collective resonance through anecdotes fits within the latter range of commemorative forms asserting local community. At the same time, a mourned individual depicted in narrative may come to symbolize that which is typical and often praiseworthy about not only those drawn together physically through commemoration, but also those in the wider world of the parish and region who are imagined to share similar attitudes and ways of living. Like wakes, ceilis are open to participation from all neighbors regardless of their denomination, and the similar forms of storytelling most popular at ceilis sustain much of the same social work accomplished at wakes. At stake in swapping local character anecdotes at wakes and ceilis are the same issues at stake in the KDHS's commemorative activities: coming to terms with change and mediating division by re-imagining and enacting local community and shared identity.

Concerning the effort to come to terms with change, swapping local character anecdotes at wakes and ceilis allows for contrast and evaluation of past and present ideological orientations and ways of being an individual within Aghyaran as a community. This commemorative activity in many ways parallels that of men such as John Mongan who use the traces of the past to take stock in the present. Recall the anecdotes about those unrefined character types associated with the past that evoke ambivalence. Recall the anecdotes about the old-fashioned hapless farmer and the contemporary competitive farmer-capitalist that establish an implicit evaluative contrast. Likewise, demonstration and documentation of obsolete ways of agrarian labor, reproduction or preservation of outmoded forms of transport, and efforts to rebuild less comfortable, less convenient thatched cottages all offer the opportunity to weigh the relative advantages and disadvantages of ways of living in the past against those in the present. Moreover, these old stories and these old tools are "ours," community property. Both establish a sort of community membership test. If you have the shared insights, attitudes, and expectations to laugh at an anecdote about John McHugh, then you are potentially "one of us." If you know that a certain strangely shaped piece of metal on the end of a wooden shaft is a turf spade—and especially if you can remember both the aching muscles and the uplifting sociability associated with using one on a work crew—then you are potentially "one of us." Both forms of commemoration advance the propositions of local community and local identity by putting on display locally shared knowledge as that which binds "us" and sets "us" apart.

Concerning the meditation on division, swapping local character anecdotes at wakes and ceilis, like reviving Killeter Fair, appeals to a local identity that has its uses in the midst of sectarian tension. To be clear, though, anecdotes in Aghyaran do not appeal to a local identity based on some dubious uniformity among community members. Anecdotes in Aghyaran appeal to a local identity based on several potential personal identities—the rough bachelor, the gossip, the trickster, the fool, the wily smuggler, the good mother, the quiet wee man, and so on. In other words, reoccurring character types found in anecdotes are eloquent of a range of personal identities considered specific to, or at least distinctive of, Aghyaran as a community. Local identity in Aghyaran—comprising a range of potential identities—is simply more complicated than sectarian collective identity, which allows for only Catholic or Protestant as meaningful categories. Therefore, the social work accomplished through anecdotes during Aghyaran wakes and ceilis potentially undermines the social work accomplished through other genres of folklore—the political ballad, parade, and mural—common in the public realm of, for instance, Castlederg's streets and Donegal's pubs. During wakes and ceilis Catholics and Protestants have the opportunity to come together in intimate social interaction, as part of one tradition, to remember. They commemorate and, in the process, imagine a shared local community in which faceless sectarian identity finds little relevance.

We have seen anecdotes in chapters 3 through 7 that would appear at first to call this seemingly optimistic conclusion into question by representing and perhaps countenancing sectarian division within Aghyaran. All is not good news: there is plenty of evidence of Catholic-Protestant tensions in Aghyaran, and certain stories and certain storytelling genres exacerbate these tensions (Cashman 2008b). On closer examination, however, ostensibly sectarian anecdotes reported here in fact support the claim that elevating the proposition of local community and identity over competing propositions of sectarian communities and identities is a critical function of swapping local character anecdotes at wakes and ceilis.

Recall anecdotes about Willie Duffy and Paddy O'Donnell verbally outwitting British soldiers at checkpoints. The larger political context of Northern Ireland causes these men as Catholics to come under suspicion. The fact that all those present during the times I heard these stories were Catholic allowed these stories to be told. Although they follow the same insider-beats-outsider pattern seen in anecdotes about Willie Hunter and the Belfast urbanites and about Harry McDonnagh and the returned Yanks, these anecdotes are not usually appropriate for mixed Catholic-Protestant company. Nevertheless, all these stories are essentially about a contest of wits between a local community member and a stranger, stories in which the insider is expected to emerge victorious despite his marginality or disrepute in the eyes of the outsider. The larger political context and implications cannot be ignored, yet fundamentally at stake is a vindication of local autonomy over outside interference.

Recall how Willie Duffy identifies the soldier's authority as entirely predicated on having a gun in his hand. He then figuratively disarms the soldier, as does Paddy O'Donnell in anecdotes about him at the Carrickmore checkpoint, through verbal wit—the same interactional virtuosity that brings storytellers and audiences together in appreciation of such narrated events. If the larger political context cannot be ignored, neither can the triumph of interactional virtuosity—that which distinguishes local community—over institutional authority imposed from without. Politics aside, this is the sort of triumph, a narrative trope, locally celebrated by Catholics and Protestants alike. It is expected as a convention of the genre, and it is in part what a sense of shared local identity is founded upon.

Recall anecdotes about the local priest and the B man. Here is a quintessentially Catholic character pitted against a quintessentially Protestant character in a story that concludes in most versions with the implication that the Catholic is instrumental in the Protestant's death. The clear sectarian implications cannot be ignored. But remember the ceili discussion reported in chapter 3 in which RUC officers, UDR and RIR soldiers, and especially B Specials were identified as more accountable for sectarian tension in the local community than the average British soldier sent to Ireland to do a job. From the perspective of ceili participants embracing a variety of political and apolitical stances, B men and later versions of B men (the UDR and RIR) represent the greatest threat to stable Catholic-Protestant relations in Aghyaran. B men are remembered as local Protestants who lived and worked alongside their Catholic neighbors, then violated neighborly conduct by asking them their names and searching their cars at nighttime checkpoints. Volunteering to police their own neighbors, to implement the will of the state, they privileged institutional authority, forsaking the vision of local community proposed by a range of communal sociability and commemoration. Moreover, in the eyes of Catholics and even some Protestants, they enforced an extra-local, province-wide source of inequity—Protestant entitlement and hegemony. By bringing home, to the local community, the larger political dilemma that cripples Northern Irish society as a whole, the B men soiled their own nests.

With this in mind, recall how in the anecdote mentioned the B man treats the priest poorly and concludes their exchange by asking him if he will be at Castlederg Fair, a local community event. The priest replies, perhaps cursing the B man, "I'll be there surely, but you won't." The subsequent death of the B man may be appreciated as symbolic of the extent to which the B man has removed himself from local community. Again, the political context cannot be ignored, for it makes the narrated events possible and their recall likely among Catholics. But in the face of sectarianism there can hardly be a more pointed assertion of the ultimate authority, perhaps even divine sanction, of local community as a rhetorical strategy and organizing principle for individual behavior.

Conditioned by images of conflict and violence from literature, film, and journalism, one may too easily suppose Northern Ireland to be an inhospitable, unlivable, or backward place. Such conditioning allows us to ignore what transpires in the more intimate, communal realms of wakes and ceilis. Without sustained observation and interaction in these more intimate realms, we may too easily overlook the artfulness of everyday verbal exchange and the critical power of local community as an idea.

Invested in ethnography, I have used folkloristic, anthropological, historiographic, and literary insights to explore stories in context as reflections of collective concerns in a certain place at a certain time. Understood in the context of a broad range of commemorative activity, swapping local character anecdotes at wakes and ceilis reiterates that the critical backward glance is at the heart of much cultural expression in Aghyaran today. People there are not gripped by sentimental or reactionary nostalgia as they collect obsolete tools or tell stories about dead people. As Alec Byrne encapsulated the local conventional wisdom about the past, "A lot of things were for the better and a lot of things were for the worse." By taking stock of the recent local past, people in Aghyaran are quite sanely engaged in a form of revision and resistance. They challenge both the presumption that modernization equals progress, and the impulse to romanticize the past. Likewise, they often challenge the dangerous reductiveness of sectarian identity politics, proposing instead a conceptual reorganization of community in local terms. By taking stock of themselves through storytelling—and particularly through anecdotes—they define who they have been, who they are, and who they can be.

Properly contextualized, the seemingly modest, commonplace genre of the local character anecdote can be seen to play a surprisingly central and powerful role in Aghyaran's local culture and social life. Imagining community while enacting it, anecdote tellers and audiences accomplish the crucial social work of reckoning personal and collective identity in the midst of socioeconomic change and sectarian division. At the wake and ceili, the local character anecdote facilitates the dialogue of the community as network and the community of the social imaginary—through the anecdote the two are mutually constitutive. The fragile but vital construction of community and local identity becomes possible through folklore.

Notes

Preface

1. Although "Catholic" and "Protestant" are religious categories, they serve as simplified labels for two populations in Northern Ireland who are also divided by ethnic identities—Irish vs. British—and political affiliations—nationalist vs. unionist. Although not everyone in Northern Ireland is religious, Northern Ireland has the highest church attendance in the British Isles. Although not everyone identifies him- or herself as either an Irish Catholic nationalist or British or Ulster Protestant unionist, most people do and are in fact encouraged to do so by contemporary government schemes to increase "parity of esteem" for "both sides" (Nic Craith 2002 and 2003). Most people in Northern Ireland simplify labels by speaking of Catholics and Protestants, regardless of whether all the people comprising these two populations are religious or politically involved.

Furthermore, nationalists and unionists as political groupings encompass, respectively, the smaller groupings of republicans and loyalists. For our purposes republicanism can be understood as the militant subset of Irish nationalism that involves paramilitary organizations such as the Irish Republican Army (IRA). In other words, nationalists are the people, mostly Catholics, who are invested in a unified Ireland, and republicans are nationalists who have historically resorted to or supported the use of armed force to press for a united Ireland. In a similar dynamic, we can understand loyalism to be the militant subset of Ulster unionism, involving paramilitary organizations such as the Ulster Volunteer Force (UVF). That is, unionists are those people, mostly Protestant, who are in favor of maintaining the union with Britain in the six counties of Northern Ireland, and loyalists are unionists willing to resist a unified Ireland through armed force.

2. Criticism of ethnographers' preoccupation with rural Irish communities and calls for the redirection of focus to Ireland's cities can be found in Wilson 1984, Peace 1989, and Curtin, Donnan, and Wilson 1993. Bridget Edwards shares my discontent with the efforts of those who in studying Ireland "link what is modern with what is urban, and what is urban with what is relevant" (1996:66) because they can lead to new narrow orthodoxies and reductionist approaches. Paying attention to forms of expressive culture in the rural west of Ireland, Edwards helps us reconsider the supposed dichotomies of the urban and the rural and of the modern and the traditional, while demonstrating the continued relevance of ethnography in rural settings.

3. Novelist Carlo Gébler's *The Glass Curtain* (1991) offers an in-depth humanistic exploration of Enniskillen in the aftermath of the IRA's 1987 Remembrance Sunday

bombing. Using Enniskillen as a microcosm, Gébler's account is a very accessible and discerning portrait of Northern Irish society as a whole in an interminable period of self-perpetuating violence prior to the mid-1990s ceasefires. Most palpable is a sense of hopelessness, punctuated occasionally by the humor and distraction of contradiction, irony, and absurdity. I see Gébler's Enniskillen as precisely the world the people of this study are reacting to and gradually putting behind them.

4. In November of 2001, the Police Service of Northern Ireland (PSNI) succeeded the RUC as part of the reforms endorsed by the 1998 Good Friday Agreement. Throughout, I will refer to the local police as the RUC rather than PSNI. This is a common practice among some Aghyaran nationalists, reflecting the position that the PSNI is different in name only, but my reason for continuing with "RUC" is that the late 1990s and the turn of the century will remain our ethnographic present.

5. A lime kiln is a large outdoor structure featuring a stone-lined inverted cone in which limestone is burned and rendered into powder. This powder was previously used in whitewash for houses or plowed into land reclaimed from bog in order to neutralize the acidic soil.

6. As a noun the term *ceili* is used both for neighborly social visits and, less often, for dances accompanied by live traditional music. Visiting in general is often referred to as ceiliing. Ceili can also be used as a verb, as in "We ceilied at the Gallaghers" or "I ceilied Jamie Barclay last Friday."

7. The notion of landscape as a vast mnemonic device for narratives treating the past is borne out in the works of, among others, Maurice Halbwachs (1941, 1992), Pierre Nora (1984, 1989), Tim Robinson (1986, 1995), Kent Ryden (1993), and Keith Basso (1996). History is the essence of the idea of place, contends Henry Glassie (1982, especially chapter 31). Location and the past are inextricably bound through narratives that impart, among other things, a sense of place. The materiality of location provides the catalyst for remembrance, draws the past into the present, and allows for the world of experience, memory, and ideas to be mapped onto landscape, rendering undifferentiated space as meaningful place.

8. My mumming experience as an initiation into community is the topic of "Mumming with the Neighbors in West Tyrone" (2000a). For an introduction to mumming in Northern Ireland today that includes the Ballymongan-Shanaghy rhymes, see Cashman 2000b. Cashman 2007b details the social and political implications of mumming in Aghyaran and across the border over time.

1. Goals and Orientations

1. The idea that the culture of a group may be illuminated through attention to their verbal art has a very long history, but here I take my cue from two seminal thinkers in the early days of modern anthropology. Inheriting a perspective on language and oral traditions heavily influenced by the work of Johann Gottfried von Herder, Franz Boas paid close attention to folklore out of a conviction that people's own creations and articulations of mind best offer the ethnographer an entry into their worldview (1970 [1916]). Bronislaw Malinowski also paid close attention to folklore, and eventually he became more concerned with contexts of folklore in use, rather than folklore texts alone. This led him to observe that speaking is doing, that language is a mode of social action (1959 [1923]). This perspective was different from but complementary to that of Boas, and it anticipated much work that eventually coalesced in the United States under the rubric

of the ethnography of communication. This perspective on language as social action also anticipated and at least indirectly inspired a shift in folklore studies from collecting texts for their antiquarian value to examining oral traditions in their performance contexts as a means of demonstrating the pragmatic, rhetorical, and social uses of folklore in face-to-face encounters.

2. Common in Irish English, *craic* is a loanword from Irish Gaelic meaning "fun" or "entertainment."

3. Ben-Amos's call (1969) for folklorists to eschew ethnocentrism by seeking out emic labels (native terminology) for genres and by attempting to understand genres in ethnic, local, or "inside" terms is a worthy ideological stance in line with the concerns in ethnoscience and the ethnography of communication for discovering emic points of view. It is possible, however, to discern emic generic categories even when no emic term is available. As E. 'Nolue Emenanjo notes, because there is no distinct word for "anecdote" in the Igbo language, folklorists were very late in recognizing the anecdote as a separate and significant genre in traditional Igbo oral narrative (1984:171). Lauri Honko suggests emic genre labels are usually the best starting point in the analytical task of genre recognition, but not the only or last consideration (1976:23–24). By extension Sandra Stahl argues convincingly in response to Ben-Amos that understanding genres is inherently an analytic effort and that in order to communicate with an academic audience, using etic terms should be permissible:

> [T]he question of etic versus emic genres can be very inhibiting if taken too seriously (i.e., if it seems to impose an ideology). Dan Ben-Amos (1969) ... does, I think, suggest that attention to ethnic (emic) genres represents both a more enlightened and an ethically superior concern than does attention to genres imposed as supposedly universal categories by the scholar. The point is well taken, at least insofar as it makes researchers aware of their own ethnocentrism. Beyond that, however, one must simply admit that genre recognition, and especially genre description, is an analytical activity. The scholar's audience is always the larger academic community, and the analyses offered by "natives" will have to be made meaningful in analytical terms the academic community will understand. (1989:13)

4. Alternatively labeled "popular memory," "social memory," or "cultural memory," the concept of collective memory is the subject of much debate among anthropologists, folklorists, and historians, so I should be clear about how the term has been used and how I use the term. According to Emile Durkheim's student Maurice Halbwachs, memory is a mutable and selective process—rather than a static system of storage and retrieval—and it is fundamentally socially constructed (1925, 1941, 1950, 1992). What individuals remember and how they do so is subject to collective concerns and shared modes of production for representation, particularly narrative. These collective concerns and modes of production are most apparent and assertive during commemorative events. Concerned with the past but responding to shared contemporary concerns, collective memory is, as Dan Ben-Amos characterizes the concept, "the creative imagining of the past in service of the present and an imagined future" (1999:299). Understanding that the individual and the group inevitably coexist in dynamic interrelationship, I use the term collective memory to name the mutable product of commemoration during social interaction. Preferring the term "social memory," Beiner offers a very helpful intellectual history of the concept (2006:23ff.), followed by a truly excellent Irish case study in the vernacular construction

of collective memory through folklore concerning the United Irishmen's Rebellion in 1798 (see Cashman 2008a).

5. A similar dynamic is at play among, for example, the Western Apache of Arizona (Basso 1979) and Mzeina Bedouins of the Sinai Peninsula (Lavie 1990), who establish a cast of typical local characters through brief conventionalized verbal performances. In both cases people use folklore to enact and evaluate various ideological orientations embodied by what Lavie calls "allegorical types" offering positive, negative, and debatable examples of behavior. Ultimately group identity is inscribed through metonymy, with character types serving as partial fragments standing in for different facets of the group as a whole.

6. See Morgan 2001 for an overview of the concept of the speech community and a succinct synthesis of how the concept developed over time. Irvine 1987 and Silverstein 1996 provide critiques of the concept that shift attention to shared linguistic knowledge as a resource rather than a determinant of conduct or worldview, and that caution against assuming ideological or behavioral homogeneity within a given speech community.

7. For the social construction of opposing Catholic and Protestant collective identities through commemoration in Northern Ireland's public realm, see Santino 2001 and Buckley and Kenney 1995. For commemorative parades in particular, see Bryan 2000a and 2000b; Jarman 1997; and Walker 1996. For urban murals and graffiti see Rolston 1991, 1992, 1995, 1999, and 2003; Jarman 1997 and 1998. For oral traditions, song, and narrative, see Glassie 1982a, 1982b, and 2006; Kelleher 2003; and Zimmermann 1967.

8. For comparison see Glassie 2005:381–385, where he challenges the usual assumed public/private dichotomy, a misleading legacy of property law, by discussing the importance of the intervening communal realm. In this realm in Northern Ireland, folklore forms, such as mumming (Cashman 2007b) or the local character anecdotes discussed here, serve to enact community and to balance the strident statements of political and religious identity made in public performances such as the Twelfth.

9. In coming to appreciate genre as an orienting framework for the production of discourse (paraphrasing Bauman 2004), folklorists have recognized that people accomplish different types of social work through different genres. Deserving further investigation is a related proposition that through genre the formal and the ideological are inextricably linked. Arguing that genre is not only a form-shaping ideology but also an ideology-shaping form, Cashman 2007a investigates public commemorative parades as a sectarian genre and the intimately performed local character anecdote as an anti-sectarian genre. Contrasting these two genres popular in the vernacular expressive repertoire of Northern Ireland illustrates how different genres may implicate, encode, and express different orientations toward the conception of community, belonging, and identity.

10. Directly influencing Glassie's and by extension my method of transcription is Dennis Tedlock's breakthrough ethnopoetic transcription of Zuñi storytelling in *Finding the Center* (1972). Tedlock's 1983 *The Spoken Word and the Work of Interpretation* further codifies his translation, transcription, and interpretation methods. These methods have been applied most often and most profitably to Native American materials, such as in Hymes 1981. However, the point of ethnopoetic transcription is to reflect on the page aspects of orality specific to a given speech community, so transcription conventions developed for Zuñi or Tlingit storytelling will not necessarily apply directly to Irish or African American storytelling. Conventions must be adapted while the conviction to create faithful, culturally relative transcriptions remains. Successful adaptations of ethnopoetic transcription to non-Indian materials include Briggs and Vigil 1990, Titon 1988, and Seitel

1980. Elizabeth Fine's 1984 *The Folklore Text* remains the folklorist's primary resource for deliberating the manifold considerations involved in translating performance style into print.

2. Aghyaran

1. Townlands are the smallest territorial units recognized in rural Ireland, nested within the larger units of the parish, district, county, province, and country. In this area of West Tyrone typical townlands comprise between ten and thirty farms, with individual farms ranging widely from as little as a couple to as much as a few hundred acres, with most in the range of twenty to sixty acres.

2. All quantitative demographics described here are drawn from the most recent Northern Ireland Census (2001), which is accessible on the Internet at http://www.nisra. gov.uk/census/start.html. Playing on the "East Asian Tiger" moniker given to the booming 1980s and '90s economies of Hong Kong, Singapore, South Korea, and Taiwan, the Republic of Ireland was dubbed the "Celtic Tiger" during the mid-1990s when a combination of large EU subsidies, low corporate taxation, increasing foreign investment, especially in information technology industries, and a well-educated English-speaking work force led to unprecedented economic growth with all the positive and negative consequences that entails. After an economic downturn in the wake of the attacks of September 11, 2001, a second surge in the Celtic Tiger began in 2003, spurred mostly by the construction industry striving to meet demands created during the original boom period. Along the Tyrone-Donegal border, the Celtic Tiger represents a dramatic reversal of the economic relationship between north and south. Within living memory, the poor of Donegal had traditionally sought economic opportunities across the border in Tyrone—whether through smuggling, legitimate employment, or, indeed, marriage—whereas now the flow has reversed in some respects.

3. See Kleinrichert 2001 for a synthesis of materials from public and private archives concerning republican internment on the *SS Argenta*.

4. Ged Martin's contribution to Malcolm Anderson and Eberhard Bort's *The Irish Border* (1999) offers a history of the ideological origins and political implementation of Partition. Accounting for the failure of the Boundary Commission, Martin explains in more detail how difficult, if not impossible, was the commission's task. He argues that the isolated Catholic and Protestant minorities on either side of the border and the inequities of both the Irish Free State and Northern Ireland demonstrate that "the Northern Ireland State as created in the early 1920s was a nineteenth-century answer that proved inadequate to tackle twentieth-century problems" (1999:57). Martin also points out the irony that the very people most vociferously opposed to Home Rule in Ireland—Ulster unionists—soon found themselves at the head of the only devolved government within the United Kingdom at that time.

5. See Bell 1978 for an analysis of labor- and equipment-swapping patterns based on questionnaires completed by people throughout Ulster and on recorded interviews with people from central Tyrone. Also referred to as neighboring, morrowing, and joining in other parts of Ulster, swapping regularly crossed the religious divide but not necessarily that of class. Big farmers tended to hire their labor and to be technologically self-sufficient and therefore tended to have little incentive to join in cooperative arrangements.

6. Memories of the incidents of political violence and individual deaths in the account that follows are widespread in Aghyaran. For corroboration and more detail about

individual deaths in Aghyaran and the Castlederg area, see *Lost Lives* (McKittrick, Kelters, Fenney, and Thornton 1999), an encyclopedia that offers brief biographical entries on all those who have died as a result of the Troubles.

7. Tyrone author Benedict Kiely briefly discusses the 1972 bombing in Killleter in his afterword to *Proxopera: A Tale of Modern Ireland* (1987:116). In this afterword, Kiely states that he renamed Killeter as Carmincross and reused the Killeter bride's death for the climax of his novel *Nothing Happens in Carmincross* (1985). He also mentions this tragic incident in *All the Way to Bantry Bay* (1978:34).

3. Ceilis as Storytelling Contexts

1. In addition to nighttime visiting at known ceili houses, people regularly visit during the day their elderly neighbors and relations who live alone. For example, Pat Den Gallagher visited with Mick Tom McSorley on a daily basis before Mick Tom moved to a nursing home. John Gallen stops in with his cousin and my next door neighbor Maggie Byrne after his last run busing children home from St. Caireall's Primary School. Neighbors and relatives visit each other's homes most often during Christmas, New Year's, and Easter. All of these social occasions revolve around conversation that potentially rises to storytelling.

2. In its noun form "cod" may also denote either a practical joke, one who instigates a practical joke, or a mess or botched job, as in "He made a real cod of the paint job." Playing the fool, practical joking, or other attempts at harmless deception may be referred to as "codology." "Cod" may also be used as a verb, meaning either to (attempt to) fool someone or to pull a practical joke.

3. As we will see in chapter 5 there is a great deal of overlap between the tall tale and the sort of improvisational artful lying known in Aghyaran as codding or codology. As Mody Boatright (1973:71) and Gerald Thomas (1977:8–9) observe, one of the primary functions of both tall tales and tall talk or artful lying is measuring the gullibility of one's audience and providing entertainment through contests of wit. Kay Cothran obviates debate over where tall talk ends and tall tales begin by paying attention to the context of social situation (cf. Bauman 1972) in which many forms of speech intermingle and constitute a form of sociability known as "talking trash" in the Okefenokee Swamp Rim (1974). Instead of attempting to delineate too rigidly between codology and tall tales in Aghyaran, it is more productive to acknowledge that ceilis and wakes are the social scenes wherein men with established friendships often avail of a range of expressive lying to challenge and entertain each other.

4. Wakes as Storytelling Contexts

1. From the early Christian to late medieval periods, erenach families were local caretakers of parish churches and Church lands, offered hospitality to visiting Church dignitaries, and frequently offered sons to the priesthood. John Mongan was aware of his family's historical role as erenachs of the parish of Termonamongan, and this likely informed his efforts to preserve local historical sites and heritage. In an article for *Aghyaran* magazine published the year after John's death, Michael McSorley offers a tribute to John that identifies him as "the erenach of our time" (1999). A seanachie, or *seanchaí* in Irish, is a traditional teller of a range of mostly historical lore, or *senchas,* that is valued more as

information from the past than as a form of aesthetically marked entertainment. This is in contrast to a *scéalaí*, who tells more stylized and often lengthier fictive stories that folklorists refer to as Märchen, hero tales, and romances, or *scéalta* in Irish. For more on this general distinction between types of traditional Irish storytellers and the genres in which they excel, see Zimmerman 2001:429–433, 447–450 and Delargy 1969 [1945]:6ff.

2. The Pioneer Total Abstinence Association of the Sacred Heart is a voluntary organization that was founded in 1898 by a Dublin Jesuit priest, Fr. James Cullen. Concerned about the worldwide stereotype of the Irish as alcoholics, the massive yearly expenditure on drink in Ireland, and the negative domestic, social, and ultimately moral consequences of alcohol consumption, Pioneers pledge to abstain from drink in order to better experience and embody Catholic spirituality. Like John Mongan, Danny Gallen, Alec Byrne, Sadie McSorley, Sally Kelly McHugh, Jim and Sarah Falls, and several others in Aghyaran are Pioneers. For a history of the Pioneer Association, see Ferriter 1999.

3. See Nolan 1990–1991:5, Ó Crualaoich 1990:148–149, and Taylor 1989b:181 for discussion of the notions of "good" or "timely" and "bad" or "untimely" deaths in Irish culture. Both Taylor (1989b:183–185) and Power (1993:25) note that for a "good death" among a people long familiar with endemic emigration, dying at home in Ireland—or "bas i nEirinn" as a familiar toast wishes—has great sentimental and symbolic importance.

4. Leaving mass cards is a relatively new Catholic custom that began after clergy in the early 1970s discouraged the long-held but potentially divisive custom of collecting offerings at the funeral mass and reading out the names of donors and the amounts offered. A mass card can be bought in local shops and some pubs for one pound. They are the same size as standard birthday and holiday greeting cards. On the front cover is a holy picture such as the Sacred Heart of Jesus, and the message inside states that a mass will be said by a particular monastic order for the person whose name the buyer inscribes on a blank line. There is another blank line for the one offering the card to write his or her name. Card vendors keep a list of how many cards were sold in memory of which persons and send these lists to the proper monasteries. Some families bury the cards with the deceased, and others read them for the names of offerers so that they can thank them later.

5. Described by Bauman as an "aesthetically marked and heightened mode of communication" (1992c:41), performance "sets up . . . a special interpretive frame within which . . . the act of communication is put on display, objectified, lifted out to a degree from its contextual surroundings, and opened up to scrutiny by an audience" (1992c:44). People at the wake later at night, then, have greater opportunity to push beyond chat and "break through" into performance, as Dell Hymes puts it (1975).

6. Crozier observes that although differentiations in status between mourners are ignored at wakes, precedence is afforded the next of kin. As such, the female next of kin who serve the mourners are not in as subservient a role as they would be in everyday hospitality (1989:86). Harris also supports Crozier's observation that women in general, whether the next of kin or not, enjoy attending wakes because they afford women the freedom to visit other households on their own, a freedom traditionally limited to men (1972:114).

7. There are, of course, exceptions to this generalization. Fr. Willie Sproule, for example, is widely appreciated as a character in his own right and known for attending wakes in order to hear anecdotes about the deceased's secular reputations, stories that occasionally find their way into his eulogies.

8. Although Arnold van Gennep never mentioned Irish wake and funeral customs in his foundational work *The Rites of Passage* (1960 [1908]), his perspective can be profit-

ably applied to Irish materials. Van Gennep noted that, across cultures, periods of major transition in the life cycles of individuals—such as birth, marriage, and death—are mediated by rituals that are regularly patterned. Rites of passage function as initiations, serving to remove an individual from one state, such as adolescence, and to symbolically reconstitute him or her in another, such as adulthood. According to van Gennep all rites of passage may be subdivided into rites of separation, transition, and incorporation, which also signal sequential phases in the symbolic transformation from one state to the next. See Cashman 2006b for an interpretation of John Mongan's wake, in van Gennep's terms, that offers a reconsideration of functionalism.

9. For accounts of the eighteenth- and nineteenth-century Irish wakes from which contemporary wakes derive, see Ó Súilleabháin 1967a and 1967b. Ó Crualaoich 1990 and 1998 offer interpretation of earlier wake customs as expressions of pre-Famine worldviews, while Ó Giolláin 1990 comments on the decline of wake customs under Church pressure and through general acculturation of bourgeois and modernizing impulses.

6. The Wider Range of Storytelling Genres

1. In this ballad a coachman falls in love with a rich farmer's daughter. The farmer accuses the coachman of theft and has him hanged, and the daughter commits suicide. Johnny Corry twice sang "The Little Pen Knife" for me and concluded one of his performances with a comparison of the ballad and the legend of Peggy Roe. He was struck by the parallel themes of the father's prohibition, the male lover's reputation tainted by accusations of being a thief, and the female lover's death. For liner notes and a version of Johnny singing this ballad, see James Foley's *Harvest Home: Songs and Crack from West Tyrone* (1991).

2. Jan Brunvand suggests a parallel evolutionary relationship between genres, with first-person memorates becoming over time and through transmission third-person supernatural legends (1986:161).

3. Although Proinsias Dubh's career as an outlaw led him to range across much of southwest Ulster, local tradition in Aghyaran maintains that he was born in Meencloghore, a townland in the southeast corner of the parish of Termonamongan. In current circulation are several legends of the outlaw's exploits, escapes, buried treasure, hanging, and burial not far from Aghyaran across the southern Donegal border in Carn graveyard. Johnny Corry's ballad "Bold Frank McHugh" recounts Proinsias Dubh's start as an outlaw, his being informed upon, and his capture near Irvinestown in Fermanagh. Like his "Little Penknife," Johnny's version of "Bold Frank McHugh" is recorded on James Foley's *Harvest Home* (1991). Proinsias Dubh is also a prominent figure in Ballymenone folklore (Glassie 1982, 2006). See Cashman 2000c for a consideration of the role outlaws such as Proinsias Dubh played and continue to play in Irish folklore as embodiments of folk morality and popular resistance to the inequities of centralized British authority.

4. American collections of tall tales include Randolph 1951 and Welsch 1972, and investigations of the social uses and formal aspects of tall tale telling in American settings include Bauman 1986 (chapter 5) and Mullen 1988 (chapter 8). For a more complete list of tall tale studies in the United States see Glassie 1982:737–738n9 and Mullen 1988:177n17. Although Boatright claims that the tall tale is a uniquely American genre that reflects early frontiersmen's response to the vastness of unsettled land (1949:85–95), several sources demonstrate that tall tales are equally familiar in Europe. These include

Henningsen 1965, Raspse et al. 1985 [1785], and Thomas 1977. See Glassie 1982:738–740n10 for a consideration of tall tales in Irish sources.

5. Mullen found this to be the case when talking to Texas raconteur of tall tales Ed Bell. Bell observed, "People don't have time to listen to stories much anymore. There's new ones coming on all the time that are, uh, keen little cutters and shorter, you know, and they like a short one with a heavy punch line" (1988:138).

6. Danny Gormley tells the same tall story, attributing it to Paddy McGoldrick, in *Ederney in Story and Song: Town Hall Reminiscences 1991–1993*, compiled and edited by Anita Gallagher and Patricia McGrath (1998).

7. Catherine Peck recalls feeling discouraged when she could not locate tellers of tall tales on the North Carolina coast, where people told her that she had arrived too late (1992). However, soon she realized that tall tales live on as stories embedded in local character anecdotes told about people remembered as tall tale raconteurs, such as Swain Lupton. This is analogous with the situation in Aghyaran.

8. As Elliott Oring reiterates in his investigation of the difference between jokes and humorous tales, "Humor depends upon the discernment of an appropriate incongruity" (1989:349), and the punch line is a principal device for revealing appropriate incongruity in jokes. While Oring is correct to assert that the punch line is the most important and conspicuous formal feature that separates jokes from tales, his observations about punch lines in jokes are equally valid for comic anecdotes in Aghyaran.

9. Despite the fact that many people claimed that accounts of supernatural phenomena and experiences are less commonly told today, I had little trouble eliciting these stories in one-on-one interviews and frequently heard them told by certain individuals at ceilis. Linda Ballard raises the interesting possibility that even when stories of the supernatural are no longer widely believed they may still be told not simply because they entertain but because "these stories express a sense of continuity and of empathy with the past" (1991:91). In this way, stories of mystery have a role, though an indirect one, in local historical discourse that compares past and present to reflect on the nature of change. In Aghyaran I recorded nearly 150 stories involving a supernatural element, some in multiple retellings and some in different versions from multiple narrators. The most common topics included ghosts, wraiths, death omens, the banshee, fairies, changelings, witchcraft, blinking (the evil eye), demonic possession, mysterious lights, miraculous cures, divine retribution for sins, and priests with special powers. Other, related stories included accounts of events that at first seemed supernatural but were later discovered to have rational explanations, and accounts of pranks played to highlight the gullibility of those who believe in fairies and ghosts.

11. Storytelling, Commemoration, and Identity

1. Detractors of the collective memory idea criticize the Durkheimian legacy of privileging the group and call for more attention to an individual's psychology and agency in social environments (Funkenstein 1989, Gedi and Elam 1996, Johnson 1998). Granted, collective memory exists in the same way society, culture, and tradition do—not as superorganic forces that transcend and control individuals, but as metaphors for human action, expression, and experience. It is not inconsistent, however, to assert that true agency rests with individuals while acknowledging that the cultural and temporal environment in which an individual is socialized provides the conceptual and expres-

sive tools through which that individual perceives and responds to his or her cultural and temporal environment. Although skeptical of truly individual consciousness, even Halbwachs observes that "While the collective memory endures and draws strength from its base in a coherent body of people, it is individuals as group members who remember" (in Coser 1992:22).

2. Referring to the establishment of the Ulster Folk Museum in Cultra, Co. Down, Evans wrote, "Here, at least, in the effort to record, preserve, and study traditional Ulster ways and values, a divided community appears to find common ground" (1965:355). See Cashman 1996 for a treatment of the politics informing the broader field of Ulster folklife studies as founded and still influenced by Evans.

3. The DUP politician's comment to Danny McSorley is remarkable in part because the DUP has served since its foundation in 1971 as the one of the most conservative voices of Ulster unionism. Led until recently by unionist hard-liner and Free Presbyterian minister Rev. Ian Paisley, the DUP has regularly been perceived by Catholics as an organization espousing fundamentally bigoted views.

Bibliography

Abrahams, Roger D. 1968. "A Rhetoric of Everyday Life: Traditional Conversation Genres." *Southern Folklore Quarterly* 32:44–59.

———. 1976 [1969]. "The Complex Relations of Simple Forms." In *Folklore Genres*, ed. Dan Ben-Amos, 193–214. Austin: University of Texas Press.

———. 1983. *The Man-of-Words in the West Indies: Performance and the Emergence of Creole Culture.* Baltimore: Johns Hopkins University Press.

———. 2005. *Everyday Life: A Poetics of Vernacular Practices.* Philadelphia: University of Pennsylvania Press.

Anderson, Benedict. 1991. *Imagined Communities: Reflections on the Origin and Spread of Nationalism.* New York: Verso.

Appadurai, Arjun. 1996. *Modernity at Large.* Minneapolis: University of Minnesota Press.

Austin, J. L. 1997 [1962]. *How to Do Things with Words.* Cambridge: Harvard University Press.

Baker, Ronald. 1982. *Hoosier Folk Legends.* Bloomington: Indiana University Press.

Bakhtin, Mikhail M. 1981. *The Dialogic Imagination,* trans. Caryl Emerson and Michael Holquist. Austin: University of Texas Press.

Ballard, Linda May. 1986. "The Concept of the 'Character.'" *Lore and Language* 5/1:69–77.

———. 1991. "Fairies and the Supernatural on Reachrai." In *The Good People: New Fairylore Essays,* ed. Peter Narváez, 47–93. New York: Garland.

Barrick, Mac E. 1976. "The Migratory Anecdote and the Folk Concept of Fame." *Mid-South Folklore* 4/2:39–47.

Barthes, Roland. 1970. *S/Z.* Paris: Seuil.

Basso, Keith. 1979. *Portraits of the Whiteman: Linguistic Play and Cultural Symbols among the Western Apache.* New York: Cambridge University Press.

———. 1996. *Wisdom Sits in Places: Landscape and Language among the Western Apache.* Albuquerque: University of New Mexico Press.

Baughman, Ernest W. 1966. *Type and Motif-Index of the Folktales of England and North America.* Bloomington: Indiana University Press.

Bauman, Richard. 1971. "Differential Identity and the Social Base of Folklore." In "Towards New Perspectives in Folklore," special issue of *Journal of American Folklore* 84:31–41.

———. 1986. *Story, Performance, and Event: Contextual Studies of Oral Narrative.* Cambridge: Cambridge University Press.

———. 1992a. "Contextualization, Tradition, and the Dialogue of Genres: Icelandic Legends of the *Kraftaskáld*." In *Rethinking Context: Language as an Interactive Phenomenon*, ed. Alessandro Duranti and Charles Goodwin, 125–145. Cambridge: Cambridge University Press.

———. 1992b. "Performance." In *Folklore, Cultural Performances, and Popular Entertainments*, ed. Richard Bauman, 41–49. New York: Oxford University Press.

———. 2004. *A World of Others' Words: Cross-Cultural Perspectives on Intertextuality*. Oxford: Blackwell.

Bauman, Richard, and Roger D. Abrahams. 1981. *"And Other Neighborly Names": Social Process and Cultural Image in Texas Folklore*. Austin: University of Texas Press.

Bauman, Richard, and Charles L. Briggs. 1990. "Poetics and Performance as Critical Perspectives on Language and Social Life." *Annual Review of Anthropology* 19:59–88.

Beiner, Guy. 2006. *Remembering the Year of the French: Irish Folk History and Social Memory*. Madison: University of Wisconsin Press.

Bell, Jonathan. 1978. "Relations of Mutual Help between Ulster Farmers." *Ulster Folklife* 24:48–58.

Ben-Amos, Dan. 1972. "Toward a Definition of Folklore in Context." In *Toward New Perspectives in Folklore*, ed. Américo Paredes and Richard Bauman, 3–15. Austin: University of Texas Press.

———. 1976 [1969]. "Analytical Categories and Ethnic Genres." In *Folklore Genres*, ed. Dan Ben-Amos, 215–242. Austin: University of Texas Press.

———. 1999. Afterword. In *Cultural Memory and the Construction of Identity*, ed. Dan Ben-Amos and Liliane Weissberg, 297–300. Detroit: Wayne State University Press.

Bendix, Regina. 1997. *In Search of Authenticity: The Formation of Folklore Studies*. Madison: University of Wisconsin Press.

Berger, Harris, and Giovanna Del Negro. 2004. *Identity and Everyday Life: Essays in the Study of Folklore, Music, and Popular Culture*. Middletown, Conn.: Wesleyan University Press.

Boas, Franz. 1970 [1916]. *Tsimshian Mythology*. New York: Johnson Reprint Corp.

Boatright, Mody. 1949. *Folk Laughter on the American Frontier*. New York: Macmillan.

———. 1973. *Mody Boatright, Folklorist: A Collection of Essays*, ed. Ernest Speck. Austin: University of Texas Press.

Bødker, Laurits. 1965. "Anecdote." In *International Dictionary of Regional European Ethnology and Folklore*, ed. Laurits Bødker, vol. 2, 26–27. Copenhagen: Rosenkilde and Bagger.

Botkin, Benjamin. 1949. "Anecdote." In *Standard Dictionary of Folklore, Mythology, and Legend*, ed. Maria Leach, vol. 1, 56. New York: Funk and Wagnalls.

Briggs, Charles L. 1988. *Competence in Performance: The Creativity of Tradition in Mexicano Verbal Art*. Philadelphia: University of Pennsylvania Press.

Briggs, Charles L., and Julián J. Vigil, eds. 1990. *The Lost Gold Mine of Juan Mondragón: A Legend from New Mexico Performed by Melaquías Romero*. Tuscon: University of Arizona Press.

Brunvand, Jan Harold. 1986. *The Study of American Folklore*. New York: W. W. Norton.

Bryan, Dominic. 2000a. "Drumcree and 'The Right to March': Orangeism, Ritual and Politics in Northern Ireland." In *We'll Follow the Drum: The Irish Parading Tradition*, ed. T. G. Fraser, 191–207. Basingstoke, Hants.: Macmillan.

———. 2000b. *Orange Parades: The Politics of Ritual, Tradition and Control*. London: Pluto.

Buckley, Anthony D. 1982. *A Gentle People.* Holywood, Co. Down: Ulster Folk and Transport Museum.

Buckley, Anthony D., and Mary Catherine Kenney. 1995. *Negotiating Identity: Rhetoric, Metaphor, and Social Drama in Northern Ireland.* Washington, D.C.: Smithsonian Institution Press.

Bufwack, Mary. 1982. *Village without Violence: An Examination of a Northern Irish Community.* Cambridge, Mass.: Schenkman.

Burke, Kenneth. 1973 [1941]. "Literature as Equipment for Living." In *The Philosophy of Literary Form: Studies in Symbolic Action,* 293–304. Berkeley: University of California Press.

Cashman, Ray. 1996. "E. Estyn Evans and His Lasting Importance to the Study of Folklore." *Folklore Forum* 27/1:3–19.

———. 1999. "A Letter from Ireland: The News from Ballymongan." *New Hibernia Review* 3/2:19–35.

———. 2000a. "Mumming with the Neighbors in West Tyrone." *Journal of Folklore Research* 37/1:73–84.

———. 2000b. "Christmas Mumming Today in Northern Ireland." *Midwestern Folklore* 26/1:27–47.

———. 2000c. "The Heroic Outlaw in Irish Folklore and Popular Literature." *Folklore* 111:191–215.

———. 2001. "Ethnohistorical Preservation and Persuasion in *Foras Feasa ar Éirinn.*" *New Hibernia Review* 5/4:147–152.

———. 2002. "Politics and the Sense of Place in Northern Ireland." *Folklore Forum,* 33/1–2:113–130.

———. 2006a. "Critical Nostalgia and Material Culture in Northern Ireland." *Journal of American Folklore* 119/472:137–160.

———. 2006b. "Dying the Good Death: Wake and Funeral Customs in County Tyrone." *New Hibernia Review* 10/2:1–17.

———. 2007a. "Genre and Ideology in Northern Ireland." *Midwestern Folklore* 33/1:13–28.

———. 2007b. "Mumming on the Northern Irish Border: Social and Political Implications." In *Border-Crossing: Mumming in Cross-Border and Cross-Community Contexts,* ed. Anthony Buckley, Críostóir Mac Cárthaigh, Séamas Mac Mathúna, and Séamas Ó Catháin, 39–56. Dundalk, Co. Louth: Dundalgan.

———. 2008a. Review of *Remembering the Year of the French: Irish Folk History and Social Memory* (Guy Beiner). *New Hibernia Review* [forthcoming].

———. 2008b. "Visions of Nationalism in Urban vs. Rural Northern Ireland." *Journal of Folklore Research* [forthcoming].

Cohen, Anthony P. 1982. "Belonging: The Experience of Culture." In *Belonging: Identity and Social Organisation in British Rural Cultures,* ed. Anthony Cohen, 1–17. Manchester: Manchester University Press.

Connerton, Paul. 1989. *How Societies Remember.* Cambridge: Cambridge University Press.

Coser, Lewis A. 1992. "Introduction: Maurice Halbwachs 1877–1945." In *On Collective Memory,* ed. and trans. Lewis A. Coser, 1–34. Chicago: University of Chicago Press.

Cothran, Kay L. 1974. "Talking Trash in the Okefenokee Swamp Rim, Georgia." *Journal of American Folklore* 87:340–356.

Crozier, Maurna. 1989. "'Powerful Wakes': Perfect Hospitality." In *Ireland from Below,* ed. Chris Curtin and Thomas M. Wilson, 70–91. Galway: Galway University Press.

Cunningham, Bernadette. 2001. "*Foras Feasa ar Éirinn* and the Historical Origins of Irish Catholic Identity." *New Hibernia Review* 5/4:144–147.

Curtin, Chris, Hastings Donnan, and Thomas Wilson. 1993. *Irish Urban Cultures*. Belfast: Institute of Irish Studies, Queen's University.

Dégh, Linda, and Andrew Vázsonyi. 1976. "Legend and Belief." In *Folklore Genres*, ed. Dan Ben-Amos, 93–123. Austin: University of Texas Press.

Delargy, James. 1969 [1945]. *The Gaelic Story-teller*. Chicago: University of Chicago Press.

Dodd, William. 1998. "Destined Livery? Character and Person in Shakespeare." *Shakespeare Survey: An Annual Survey of Shakespeare Studies and Production* 51:147–158.

Dorson, Richard M. 1972. "Legends and Tall Tales." In *Folklore: Selected Essays*, ed. Richard M. Dorson, 159–176. Bloomington: Indiana University Press.

Duranti, Alessandro, and Donald Brenneis, eds. 1986. "The Audience as Co-Author," special issue of *Text* 6/3:297–347.

Durkheim, Emile. 1960 [1915]. *The Elementary Forms of the Religious Life*. New York: Allen and Unwin.

Edwards, Bridget. 1996. "How the West Was Wondered: County Clare and Directions in Irish Ethnography." *Folklore Forum* 27/2:65–78.

Emenanjo, E. 'Nolue. 1984. "The Anecdote as an Oral Genre: The Case in Igbo." *Folklore* 95/2:171–176.

Fadiman, Clifton, and Andre Bernard, eds. 2000. *Bartlett's Book of Anecdotes*. New York: Little, Brown.

Ferriter, Diarmaid. 1999. *A Nation of Extremes: The Pioneers in Twentieth-Century Ireland*. Dublin: Irish Academic Press.

Fine, Elizabeth C. 1984. *The Folklore Text: From Performance to Print*. Bloomington: Indiana University Press.

Fishelov, David. 1990. "Types of Characters, Characteristics of Type." In *Literary Character*, ed. John V. Knapp, 422–439. New York: University Press of America.

Foley, James, et al. 1991. "Harvest Home: Songs and Crack from West Tyrone." Sound recording and notes by James Foley. Belfast: The Arts Council of Northern Ireland.

Forster, E. M. 1927. *Aspects of the Novel*. New York: Harcourt.

Funkenstein, Amos. 1989. "Collective Memory and Historical Consciousness." *History and Memory* 1/1:5–26.

Gallagher, Anita, and Patricia McGrath, eds. 1998. *Ederney in Story and Song: Town Hall Reminiscences 1991–1993*. Produced by the Border Counties History Collective. Ecclesville, Co. Fermanagh: Ecclesville Printing Services.

Gébler, Carlo. 1991. *The Glass Curtain: Inside an Ulster Community*. London: Abacus.

Gedi, Noa, and Yigal Elam. 1996. "Collective Memory—What Is It?" *History and Memory* 8/1:31–50.

Geertz, Clifford. 1973. "Deep Play: Notes on a Balinese Cock Fight." In *The Interpretation of Cultures: Selected Essays*, 412–453. New York: Basic.

Georges, Robert A. 1971. "The General Concept of Legend." In *American Folk Legend: A Symposium*, ed. Wayland D. Hand, 1–19. Berkeley: University of California Press.

Gillis, John R., ed. 1994. *Commemorations: The Politics of National Identity*. Princeton: Princeton University Press.

Glassie, Henry. 1982a. *Passing the Time in Ballymenone: Culture and History in an Ulster Community*. Philadelphia: University of Pennsylvania Press.

———. 1982b. *Irish Folk History: Texts from the North*. Philadelphia: University of Pennsylvania Press.

———. 1994. "On Identity." *The Journal of American Folklore* 107/424:238–241.

———. 2001. "Keating Hero." *New Hibernia Review* 5/4:152–154.

———. 2006. *The Stars of Ballymenone.* Bloomington: Indiana University Press.

Goffman, Erving. 1963. *Stigma: Notes on the Management of Spoiled Identity.* Englewood Cliffs, N.J.: Prentice-Hall.

———. 1971. *Relations in Public: Microstudies of the Public Order.* New York: Basic.

———. 1974. *Frame Analysis: An Essay on the Organization of Experience.* Boston: Northeastern University Press.

Goldstein, Kenneth S. 1964. *A Guide for Field Workers in Folklore.* Hatboro, Pa.: Folklore Associates.

Gumperz, John. 1968. "The Speech Community." In *International Encyclopedia of the Social Sciences,* vol. 9, ed. David L. Sills, 381–386. New York: Macmillan.

———. 1972. "Introduction." In *Directions in Sociolinguistics: The Ethnography of Communication,* ed. John Gumperz and Dell Hymes, 1–25. New York: Holt, Rinehart, and Wilson.

Halbwachs, Maurice. 1925. *Les Cadres sociaux de la mémoire.* Paris: F. Alcan.

———. 1941. *La Topographie légendaire des Evangiles en Terre Sainte: Etude de mémoire collective.* Paris: Presses universitaires de France.

———. 1950. *La Mémoire collective,* ed. Jeanne Alexander. Paris: Presses universitaires de France.

———. 1992. *On Collective Memory,* ed. and trans. Lewis A. Coser. Chicago: University of Chicago Press.

Harlow, Ilana. 1997. "Creating Situations: Practical Jokes and the Revival of the Dead in Irish Tradition." *Journal of American Folklore* 110:140–165.

Harris, Rosemary. 1972. *Prejudice and Tolerance in Ulster.* Manchester: Manchester University Press.

Henningsen, Gustav. 1965. "The Art of Perpendicular Lying," trans. Warren Roberts. *Journal of the Folklore Institute* 2:180–219.

Hobsbawm, Eric, and Terence Ranger, eds. 1983. *The Invention of Tradition.* Cambridge: Cambridge University Press.

Honko, Lauri. 1976. "Genre Theory Revisited." In *Folk Narrative Research: Some Papers Presented at the VI Congress of the International Society for Folk Narrative Research,* ed. Juha Pentikäinen and Tuula Juurikka, 20–25. Helsinki: Suomalaisen Kirjallisuuden Seura.

Hymes, Dell. 1968. "Linguistic Problems in Defining the Concept of 'Tribe.'" In *Essays on the Problem of Tribe: Proceedings of the 1967 Annual Spring Meeting of the American Ethnological Society,* ed. June Helm, 23–48. Seattle: University of Washington Press.

———. 1972. "Models of the Interaction of Language and Social Life." In *Directions in Sociolinguistics: The Ethnography of Communication,* ed. John J. Gumperz and Dell Hymes, 35–71. New York: Holt, Rinehart and Winston.

———. 1975. "Breakthrough into Performance." In *Folklore: Performance and Communication,* ed. Dan Ben-Amos and Kenneth S. Goldstein. The Hague: Mouton.

———. 1981. *"In Vain I Tried to Tell You": Essays in Native American Ethnopoetics.* Philadelphia: University of Philadelphia Press.

Irvine, Judith. 1987. "Domains of Description in the Ethnography of Speaking: A Retrospective on the 'Speech Community.'" In *Working Papers and Proceedings of the Center for Psychosocial Studies,* no. 11, ed. Richard Parmentier and Greg Urban, 13–24. Chicago: Center for Psychosocial Studies.

Jarman, Neil. 1997. *Material Conflicts: Parades and Visual Displays in Northern Ireland.* New York: Berg.

———. 1998. "Painting Landscapes: The Place of Murals in the Symbolic Construction of Urban Space." In *Symbols in Northern Ireland,* ed. Anthony D. Buckely, 81–98. Belfast: Institute of Irish Studies, Queen's University.

Johnson, John William. 1998. "Tradition." In *Encyclopedia of Folklore and Literature,* ed. Mary Ellen Brown and Bruce A. Rosenberg, 658–659. Santa Barbara, Calif.: ABC-CLIO.

Kelleher, William. 2003. *The Troubles in Ballybogoin: Memory and Identity in Northern Ireland.* Ann Arbor: University of Michigan Press.

Kennedy, Patrick, ed. 1872. *The Book of Modern Irish Anecdotes: Humour, Wit and Wisdom.* London: Routledge.

Kiely, Benedict. 1978. *All the Way to Bantry Bay.* London: Victor Gollancz.

———. 1985. *Nothing Happens in Carmincross.* Boston: David R. Godine.

———. 1987. *Proxopera: A Tale of Modern Ireland.* Boston: David R. Godine.

Kirshenblatt-Gimblett, Barbara. 1995. "Theorizing Heritage." *Ethnomusicology* 39/3:367–380.

———. 1998. *Destination Culture: Tourism, Museums, and Heritage.* Berkeley: University of California Press.

Kleinrichert, Denise. 2001. *Republican Internment and the Prison Ship Argenta 1922.* Dublin: Irish Academic Press.

Kuntz, Tom. 2001. "It's the Pith: Short Yarns that Are Long on Legend." *New York Times,* March 11, Week in Review, p. 7.

Labov, William. 1982. "Speech Actions and Reactions in Personal Narrative." In *Analyzing Discourse: Text and Talk,* ed. Deborah Tannen, 219–247. Washington, D.C.: Georgetown University Press.

Lavie, Smadar. 1990. *The Poetics of Military Occupation: Mzeina Allegories of Bedouin Identity under Israeli and Egyptian Rule.* Berkeley: University of California Press.

Leyton, Elliott. 1974. "Opposition and Integration in Ulster." *Man* 9:185–198.

———. 1975. *The One Blood.* St. John's: Institute of Social and Economic Research, Memorial University of Newfoundland.

Lord, Albert. 1960. *The Singer of Tales.* Cambridge, Mass.: Harvard University Press.

Malinowski, Bronislaw. 1959 [1923]. "The Problem of Meaning in Primitive Languages." In *The Meaning of Meaning,* ed. C. K. Ogden and I. A. Richards, 296–336. New York: Harcourt, Brace, and World.

Margolin, Uri. 1990. "The What, the When, and the How of Being a Character in Literary Narrative." In *Literary Character,* ed. John V. Knapp, 453–468. New York: University Press of America.

Martin, Ged. 1999. "The Origins of Partition." In *The Irish Border: History, Politics, Culture,* ed. Malcolm Anderson and Eberhard Bort, 57–111. Liverpool: Liverpool University Press.

McKay, Susan. 2000. *Northern Protestants: An Unsettled People.* Belfast: Blackstaff.

McKittrick, David, Seamus Kelters, Brian Feeney, and Chris Thornton. 1999. *Lost Lives: The Stories of the Men, Women, and Children Who Died as a Result of the Northern Ireland Troubles.* London: Mainstream.

McSorley, Michael. 1999. "John Mongan, the Erenach of Our Time." *Aghyaran* 14:41–44.

Metcalf, Peter, and Richard Huntington. 1991. *Celebrations of Death: The Anthropology of Mortuary Ritual.* Cambridge: Cambridge University Press.

Morgan, Marcyliena. 2001. "Community." In *Key Terms in Language and Culture,* ed. Alessandro Duranti, 31–33. Oxford: Blackwell.

Mullen, Patrick B. 1988. *I Heard the Old Fishermen Say: Folklore of the Texas Gulf Coast.* Austin: University of Texas Press.

Narváez, Peter. 1994. "'Tricks and Fun': Subversive Pleasures at Newfoundland Wakes." *Western Folklore* 53:263–293.

Nic Craith, Máiréad. 2002. *Plural Identities, Singular Narratives: The Case of Northern Ireland.* New York: Berghahn.

———. 2003. *Culture and Identity Politics in Northern Ireland.* New York: Palgrave.

Nolan, Peter. 1990–1991. "Death Is a Family Affair." *Folklife: Journal of Ethnological Studies* 29:65–68.

Nora, Pierre. 1984. *Les Lieux de Memoire.* Paris: Gallimard.

———. 1989. "Between Memory and History: *Les Lieux de Mémoire.*" *Representations* 26:7–25.

Noyes, Dorothy. 1995. "Group." *Journal of American Folklore* 108/430:449–478.

———. 2003. *Fire in the Plaça: Catalan Festival Politics after Franco.* Philadelphia: University of Pennsylvania Press.

Ó Crualaoich, Géaroid. 1990. "Contest in the Cosmology and the Ritual of the Irish 'Merry Wake.'" *Cosmos* 6:145–160.

———. 1998. "The Merry Wake." In *Irish Popular Culture 1650–1850,* ed. James Donnelly and Kerby Miller, 171–200. Dublin: Irish Academic Press.

Ó Giolláin, Diarmúid. 1990. "Perspectives in the Study of Folk-Religion." *Ulster Folklife* 36:66–73.

———. 2000. *Locating Irish Folklore: Tradition, Modernity, Identity.* Cork: Cork University Press.

Ó Laoire, Lillis. 2003. "Fieldwork in Common Places: An Ethnographer's Experiences in Tory Island." *British Journal of Ethnomusicology* 12/1:113–136.

Ó Súilleabháin, Seán (Sean O'Sullivan). 1967a. *Irish Folk Custom and Belief.* Dublin: Cultural Relations Committee of Ireland, Three Candles.

———. 1967b. *Irish Wake Amusements.* Cork: Mercier.

Oring, Elliott. 1986. "Folk Narratives." In *Folklore Groups and Genres: An Introduction,* ed. Elliott Oring, 121–146. Logan: Utah State University Press.

———. 1989. "Between Jokes and Tales: On the Nature of Punch Lines." *Humor* 2–4: 349–364.

———. 1992. *Jokes and Their Relations.* Lexington: University Press of Kentucky.

———. 1994. "Arts, Artifacts, and Artifices of Identity." *Journal of American Folklore* 107/424:211–233.

———. 2003. *Engaging Humor.* Chicago: University of Illinois Press.

Patterson, Glenn. 2006. *Lapsed Protestant.* Dublin: New Island Books.

Peace, Adrian. 1989. "From Arcadia to Anomie: Critical Notes on the Constitution of Irish Society as an Anthropological Subject." *Critique of Anthropology* 9/1:89–111.

Peck, Catherine. 1992. "Local Character Anecdotes Down East." *North Carolina Folklore Journal* 39/2:63–71.

Power, Rosemary. 1993. "Death in Ireland: Deaths, Wakes and Funerals in Contemporary Irish Society." In *Death, Dying, and Bereavement,* ed. Donna Dickenson and Malcom Johnson, 21–25. London: Sage.

Propp, Vladimir. 1968. *Morphology of the Folktale*. Trans. Laurence Scott. Austin: University of Texas Press.

Randolph, Vance. 1951. *We Always Lie to Strangers: Tall Tales from the Ozarks*. New York: Columbia University Press.

Raspe, Rudolph Eric, et al. 1985 [1785]. *The Adventures of Baron Munchausen*. London: Harrap.

Robinson, Tim. 1986. *Stones of Aran: Pilgrimage*. London: Penguin.

———. 1995. *Stones of Aran: Labyrinth*. London: Penguin.

Rolston, Bill. 1991. *Politics and Painting*. London: Associated University Presses.

———. 1992. *Drawing Support: The Murals of Murals in the North of Ireland*. Dublin: Colour.

———. 1995. *Drawing Support 2: Murals of War and Peace*. Dublin: Colour.

———. 1999. "From King Billy to Cúchullain: Loyalist and Republican Murals, Past, Present and Future." *Éire-Ireland* 33/2:6–28.

———. 2003. *Drawing Support III: Murals and Transition in the North of Ireland*. Belfast: Beyond the Pale.

Russell, Ian. 2006. "Working with Tradition: Towards a Partnership Model of Fieldwork." *Folklore* 117/1:15–32.

Ryden, Kent. 1993. *Mapping the Invisible Landscape: Folklore, Writing, and the Sense of Place*. Iowa City: University of Iowa Press.

Santino, Jack. 1988. "Occupational Ghostlore: Social Context and the Expression of Belief." *Journal of American Folklore* 101/400:207–218.

———. 2001. *Signs of War and Peace: Social Conflict and the Use of Public Symbols in Northern Ireland*. New York: Palgrave.

Seitel, Peter. 1980. *See So That We May See: Performances and Interpretations of Traditional Tales from Tanzania*. Bloomington: Indiana University Press.

———. 1999. *The Powers of Genre: Interpreting Haya Oral Literature*. New York: Oxford University Press.

Sherzer, Joel. 1985. "Puns and Jokes." In *Handbook of Discourse Analysis*, vol. 3, ed. Teun A. Van Dijk, 213–221. London: Academic.

Shuman, Amy. 1993. "Dismantling Local Culture." *Western Folklore* 52/2–4:345–364.

Silverstein, Michael. 1996. "Encountering Language and Languages of Encounter in North American Ethnohistory." *Journal of Linguistic Anthropology* 6/2:126–144.

Stahl (Dolby), Sandra K. D. 1975. "The Local Character Anecdote." *Genre* 8:283–302.

———. 1977a. "The Oral Personal Narrative in Its Generic Context." *Fabula* 18:18–39.

———. 1977b. "The Personal Narrative as Folklore." *Journal of the Folklore Institute* 14:9–30.

———. 1983. "The Personal Experience Story." In *Handbook of American Folklore*, ed. Richard M. Dorson and Inta Gale Carpenter, 268–276. Bloomington: Indiana University Press.

———. 1989. *Literary Folkloristics and the Personal Narrative*. Bloomington: Indiana University Press.

Tallman, Richard. 1974. "A Generic Approach to the Practical Joke." *Southern Folklore Quarterly* 38:259–274.

Taylor, Archer. 1970. "The Anecdote: A Neglected Genre." In *Medieval Literature and Folklore Studies*, ed. Jerome Mandel and Bruce Rosenburg, 223–228. New Brunswick, N.J.: Rutgers University Press.

Taylor, Lawrence J. 1989a. "Introduction: The Uses of Death in Europe." In "The Uses of Death in Europe," special issue of *Anthropological Quarterly* 62/4:149–153.

———. 1989b. "Bás InÉirinn: Cultural Constructions of Death in Ireland." In "The Uses of Death in Europe," special issue of *Anthropological Quarterly* 62/4:175–187.

———. 1995. *Occasions of Faith: An Anthropology of Irish Catholics.* Philadelphia: University of Pennsylvania Press.

Tedlock, Dennis. 1972. "On the Translation of Style in Oral Narrative." In *Toward New Perspectives in Folklore,* ed. Américo Paredes and Richard Bauman, 114–133. Austin: University of Texas Press.

———. 1983. *The Spoken Word and the Work of Interpretation.* Philadelphia: University of Pennsylvania Press.

Thomas, Gerald. 1977. *The Tall Tale and Phillippe D'Alcripe: An Analysis of the Tall Tale Genre with Particular Reference to Phillipe D'Alcripe's La Nouvelle Fabrique des Excellents Traits de Vérité together with an Annotated Translation of the Work.* St. John's: Department of Folklore, Memorial University of Newfoundland.

Thompson, Stith. 1961. *The Types of the Folktale.* 2nd rev. ed. Helsinki: Folklore Fellows Communication, no. 184.

Titon, Jeff Todd. 1988. *Powerhouse for God: Speech, Chant, and Song in an Appalachian Baptist Church.* Austin: University of Texas Press.

Tönnies, Ferdinand. 1998 [1887]. *Community and Society.* Trans. Charles Loomis. London: Transaction.

van Gennep, Arnold. 1960 [1908]. *The Rites of Passage.* Trans. Monika B. Vizedom and Gabrielle L. Caffee. Chicago: University of Chicago Press.

Walker, Brian. 1996. *Dancing to History's Tune.* Belfast: The Institute of Irish Studies, Queen's University.

Welsch, Roger. 1972. *Shingling the Fog and Other Plains Lies: Tall Tales of the Great Plains.* Chicago: Swallow.

Whelan, Kevin. 1993. "The Bases of Regionalism." In *Regions: Identity and Power,* ed. Proinsias Ó Drisceoil, 5–62. Belfast: Institute of Irish Studies, Queen's University.

Wilson, Thomas. 1984. "From Clare to the Common Market: Perspectives on Irish Ethnography." *Anthropological Quarterly* 57/1:1–15.

Wilson, Thomas, and Hastings Donnan. 2006. *The Anthropology of Ireland.* London: Berg.

Witoszek, Nina, and Pat Sheeran. 1998. *Talking to the Dead: A Study of Irish Funerary Traditions.* Atlanta: Rodopi.

Yerovich, Sally. 1983. "Conversational Genres." In *Handbook of American Folklore,* ed. Richard M. Dorson and Inta Gale Carpenter, 277–281. Bloomington: Indiana University Press.

Zimmerman, Georges Denis. 1967. *Songs of Irish Rebellion.* Dublin: Allen Figgis.

———. 2001. *The Irish Storyteller.* Dublin: Four Courts.

Index

Page numbers in *italics* indicate illustrations.
Proper names followed by an asterisk indicate pseudonyms.

RAY CASHMAN is Assistant Professor
of English and Folklore at The Ohio State University.